Lecture Notes in Computer S

Commenced Publication in 1973
Founding and Former Series Editors:
Gerhard Goos, Juris Hartmanis, and Jan van Lee

T0259898

Editorial Board

David Hutchison
Lancaster University, UK

Takeo Kanade
Carnegie Mellon University, Pittsburgh, PA, USA

Josef Kittler
University of Surrey, Guildford, UK

Jon M. Kleinberg
Cornell University, Ithaca, NY, USA

Alfred Kobsa
University of California, Irvine, CA, USA

Friedemann Mattern
ETH Zurich, Switzerland

John C. Mitchell
Stanford University, CA, USA

Moni Naor
Weizmann Institute of Science, Rehovot, Israel

Oscar Nierstrasz
University of Bern, Switzerland

C. Pandu Rangan
Indian Institute of Technology, Madras, India

Bernhard Steffen
TU Dortmund University, Germany

Madhu Sudan
Microsoft Research, Cambridge, MA, USA

Demetri Terzopoulos
University of California, Los Angeles, CA, USA

Doug Tygar
University of California, Berkeley, CA, USA

Gerhard Weikum
Max Planck Institute for Informatics, Saarbruecken, Germany

Audun Jøsang   Bengt Carlsson (Eds.)

Secure IT Systems

17th Nordic Conference, NordSec 2012
Karlskrona, Sweden, October 31 – November 2, 2012
Proceedings

 Springer

Volume Editors

Audun Jøsang
University of Oslo
Gaustadalléen 23b, 0373 Oslo, Norway
E-mail: josang@mn.uio.no

Bengt Carlsson
Blekinge Institute of Technology
Valhallavägen 1, 37179 Karlskrona, Sweden
E-mail: bengt.carlsson@bth.se

ISSN 0302-9743   e-ISSN 1611-3349
ISBN 978-3-642-34209-7   e-ISBN 978-3-642-34210-3
DOI 10.1007/978-3-642-34210-3
Springer Heidelberg Dordrecht London New York

Library of Congress Control Number: 2012949091

CR Subject Classification (1998): D.4.6, K.6.5, D.2, H.2.7, K.4.4, E.3, C.2

LNCS Sublibrary: SL 4 – Security and Cryptology

© Springer-Verlag Berlin Heidelberg 2012
This work is subject to copyright. All rights are reserved, whether the whole or part of the material is
concerned, specifically the rights of translation, reprinting, re-use of illustrations, recitation, broadcasting,
reproduction on microfilms or in any other way, and storage in data banks. Duplication of this publication
or parts thereof is permitted only under the provisions of the German Copyright Law of September 9, 1965,
in its current version, and permission for use must always be obtained from Springer. Violations are liable
to prosecution under the German Copyright Law.
The use of general descriptive names, registered names, trademarks, etc. in this publication does not imply,
even in the absence of a specific statement, that such names are exempt from the relevant protective laws
and regulations and therefore free for general use.

Typesetting: Camera-ready by author, data conversion by Scientific Publishing Services, Chennai, India

Printed on acid-free paper

Springer is part of Springer Science+Business Media (www.springer.com)

Preface

These proceedings contain the full papers presented at NordSec 2012, the 17th Nordic Conference on Secure IT Systems, held at Blekinge Institute of Technology in Karlskrona, Sweden, during 31 October – 2 November 2012.

NordSec was initially started in 1996 as a workshop series with the aim of bringing together researchers and practitioners working on computer security in the Nordic countries, thereby establishing a forum for discussions and cooperation between universities, industry, and computer societies. Since then, the workshop has developed into a fully fledged international information security conference, held in the Nordic countries on a round robin basis.

NordSec 2012 sollicited contributions in the form of full papers presenting mature work, short papers presenting ongoing work, and student posters. We received a total of 32 valid submissions of full papers, each of which was reviewed by at least three Program Committee members. Out of the submitted full papers, 16 were accepted for presentation at the conference. Also, some submitted full papers were accepted as short papers published in locally printed proceedings.

Since 2008, Nordsec has welcomed the participation of 2nd-year students of the international Erasmus Mundus Masters programme "NordSecMob", as well as other master's students in IT security, to present posters that show work done as part of their master's studies. The students' fresh and often radical ideas stimulate very interesting discussions among NordSec participants.

The combined effort of many people was needed for the organization of NordSec 2012, and we would like to give recognition to all who contributed to making the conference a success. We thank the Program Committee for reviewing the papers and discussing them, thereby creating the best possible program for the conference. We thank the subreviewers for the extra help they gave us with the reviews. We also thank the Poster Chair for helping the students to produce high-quality posters for the conference, and the invited speakers for agreeing to share their insights. Most importantly we are thankful to all the authors who submitted their papers to NordSec 2012, and to the conference attendees who took part in the discussions during the conference. Many other people also contributed in some way to the organization of NordSec 2012. We are also grateful to Blekinge Institute of Technology for allowing the conference to use its facilities, and to NetPort Karlshamn for sponsoring the welcome reception. As a result of your great efforts and contributions, NordSec continues to be a valuable meeting place for the information security community.

October 2012

Bengt Carlsson
Audun Jøsang

Organization

Conference Chair

Bengt Carlsson   Blekinge Institute of Technology, Sweden

Program Chair

Audun Jøsang   University of Oslo, Norway

Poster Chair

Stefan Axelsson   Blekinge Institute of Technology, Sweden

International Program Committee

Rose-Mharie Åhlfeldt	University of Skövde, Sweden
Magnus Almgren	Chalmers University of Technology, Sweden
Frederik Armknecht	University of Mannheim, Germany
Tuomas Aura	Aalto University, Finland
Stefan Axelsson	Blekinge Institute of Technology, Sweden
Martin Boldt	Blekinge Institute of Technology, Sweden
Patrick Bours	Gjøvik University College, Norway
Antanas Cenys	Vilnius Technical University, Lithuania
Lizzie Coles-Kemp	Royal Holloway College, UK
Mads Dam	KTH Royal Institute of Technology, Sweden
Geert Deconinck	KU Leuven - University, Belgium
Monika Desoi	University of Kassel, Germany
Sadek Ferdous	University of Glasgow, UK
Simone Fischer-Hübner	Karlstad University, Sweden
Anders Fongen	Norwegian Defence Research Establishment
Lothar Fritsch	Norwegian Computing Center
Dieter Gollmann	Hamburg University of Technology, Germany
Jonas Hallberg	Swedish Defence Research Agency
Carmit Hazay	Aarhus University, Denmark
Erik Hjelmås	Gjøvik University College, Norway
Christian Damsgaard Jensen	Technical University of Denmark
Henric Johnson	Blekinge Institution of Technology, Sweden
Kristjan Jonsson	Reykjavik University, Iceland
Hanno Langweg	Gjøvik University College, Norway
Peeter Laud	University of Tartu, Estonia
Helger Lipmaa	University of Tartu, Estonia

Radu Lupu	Politehnica University of Bucharest, Romania
Fabio Massacci	University of Trento, Italy
Sjouke Mauw	University of Luxembourg
Wojciech Mazurczyk	Warsaw University of Technology, Poland
Chris Mitchell	Royal Holloway College, UK
Simin Nadjm-Tehrani	Linköping University, Sweden
Kaisa Nyberg	Helsinki University of Technology, Finland
Lars Olaussen	Norwegian Security Authority
Jon Ølnes	Unibridge, Norway
Jakob Illeborg Pagter	The Alexandra Institute Ltd., Denmark
Marina Papatriantafilou	Chalmers University of Technology, Sweden
Christian W. Probst	Technical University of Denmark
Kai Rannenberg	Goethe University Frankfurt, Germany
Christian Rohner	Uppsala University, Sweden
Heiko Roßnagel	Fraunhofer IAO, Germany
Sini Ruohomaa	University of Helsinki, Finland
Andrei Sabelfeld	Chalmers University of Technology, Sweden
Anne-Karen Seip	The Financial Supervisory Authority of Norway
Bjørnar Solhaug	SINTEF, Norway
Teodor Sommestad	Swedish Defence Research Agency
Nils Kalstad Svendsen	Gjøvik University College, Norway
Jaak Tepandi	Tallinn University of Technology, Estonia
Dominique Unruh	Saarland University, Germany
Risto Vaarandi	NATO Coop. Cyber Defence Centre, Estonia
Bjørn Victor	Uppsala University, Sweden
Ymir Vigfusson	IBM Research Haifa, Israel
Benedikt Westermann	Norwegian University of Technology
Jan Willemson	Cybernetica Ltd., Estonia
Ender Yüksel	Technical University of Denmark

Subreviewers

Hugo Jonker	Andreas Leicher	Daniel Hedin
Tobias Pulls	Bart van Delft	Goekhan Bal
Vasily Mikhalev	Jun Pang	Fatbardh Veseli
Bingsheng Zhang	Hamid Ebadi	Jan Zibuschka
Sebastian Kurowski	Arnar Birgisson	
Sandeep Tamrakar	Musard Balliu	

Sponsoring Institutions

NetPort Karlshamn	http://www.netport.se/
Blekinge Institute of Technology	http://www.bth.se/

Table of Contents

Application Security

Designed to Fail: A USB-Connected Reader for Online Banking   1
*Arjan Blom, Gerhard de Koning Gans, Erik Poll,
Joeri de Ruiter, and Roel Verdult*

Security Add-Ons for Mobile Platforms   17
Benjamin Adolphi and Hanno Langweg

THAPS: Automated Vulnerability Scanning of PHP Applications   31
*Torben Jensen, Heine Pedersen, Mads Chr. Olesen, and
René Rydhof Hansen*

Security Management

Cyber Security Exercises and Competitions as a Platform for Cyber
Security Experiments   47
Teodor Sommestad and Jonas Hallberg

The Development of Cyber Security Warning, Advice and Report
Points   61
Tony Proctor

Towards an Empirical Examination of IT Security Infrastructures
in SME   73
Ramona Groner and Philipp Brune

How to Select a Security Requirements Method? A Comparative Study
with Students and Practitioners   89
Fabio Massacci and Federica Paci

System Security

There Is Safety in Numbers: Preventing Control-Flow Hijacking by
Duplication   105
Job Noorman, Nick Nikiforakis, and Frank Piessens

Coinductive Unwinding of Security-Relevant Hyperproperties   121
Dimiter Milushev and Dave Clarke

Retooling and Securing Systemic Debugging   137
Björn Ståhl and Per Mellstrand

Network Security

Cracking Associative Passwords.................................... 153
  *Kirsi Helkala, Nils Kalstad Svendsen, Per Thorsheim, and
  Anders Wiehe*

A Hybrid Approach for Highly Available and Secure Storage of
Pseudo-SSO Credentials 169
  Jan Zibuschka and Lothar Fritsch

Assessing the Quality of Packet-Level Traces Collected on Internet
Backbone Links.. 184
  *Behrooz Sangchoolie, Mazdak Rajabi Nasab, Tomas Olovsson, and
  Wolfgang John*

Trust Management

Everything But the Kitchen Sink: Determining the Effect of Multiple
Attacks on Privacy Preserving Technology Users 199
  Jason W. Clark

Can We Identify Manipulative Behavior and the Corresponding
Suspects on Review Websites Using Supervised Learning? 215
  Huiying Duan and Cäcilia Zirn

Privacy-Friendly Cloud Storage for the Data Track: An Educational
Transparency Tool 231
  Tobias Pulls

Author Index... 247

Designed to Fail:
A USB-Connected Reader for Online Banking

Arjan Blom[1], Gerhard de Koning Gans[2], Erik Poll[2],
Joeri de Ruiter[2], and Roel Verdult[2]

[1] Flatstones, The Netherlands
arjan@flatstones.nl
[2] Institute for Computing and Information Sciences, Digital Security Group,
Radboud University Nijmegen, The Netherlands
{gkoningg,erikpoll,joeri,rverdult}@cs.ru.nl

Abstract. We present a security analysis of an internet banking system used by one of the bigger banks in the Netherlands, in which customers use a USB-connected device – a smartcard reader with a display and numeric keyboard – to authorise transactions with their bank card and PIN code. Such a set-up could provide a very strong defence against online attackers, notably Man-in-the-Browser attacks, where an attacker controls the browser and host PC. However, we show that the system we studied is seriously flawed: an attacker who controls an infected host PC can get the smartcard to sign transactions that the user does *not* explicitly approve, which is precisely what the device is meant to prevent.

The flaw is not due to a simple implementation bug in one of the components (e.g. the device or the software components on the PC). It is a more fundamental design flaw, introduced in assigning responsibilities to the different components and designing the protocols between them.

The system we studied, used by the Dutch bank ABN-AMRO, was developed by the Swedish company Todos AB. This company has since been acquired by Gemalto. ABN-AMRO is one of the three biggest banks in the Netherlands, with 6.8 million customers. Given the popularity of internet banking in the Netherlands, this means that millions of these devices are in the field. The manufacturer claims this device is "the most secure sign-what-you-see end-user device ever seen"[1]; this paper demonstrates this claim to be false.

1 Introduction

For internet banking, many banks let their clients use a hand-held smartcard reader with a small display and keypad. In combination with a smartcard and PIN code, this reader then signs challenges reported on the bank's webpage, to log-on or to confirm bank transfers. Many of these systems use EMV-CAP (EMV-Chip Authentication Program), a proprietary standard of MasterCard

---

[1] http://www.gemalto.com/financial/ebanking/case_studies/ABN_AMRO.html

A. Jøsang and B. Carlsson (Eds.): NordSec 2012, LNCS 7617, pp. 1–16, 2012.
© Springer-Verlag Berlin Heidelberg 2012

built on top of the EMV (Europay-Mastercard-Visa) standard, as does the system discussed in this paper.

Such a two-factor authentication, which requires access to a smartcard and a PIN code, is of course much stronger than a traditional password. Still, a serious and fundamental limitation of these hand-held readers is that the very short challenges, of only eight digits, do not offer much scope for a message that is meaningful to the user. Often the eight digits are just a random number, in which case the user has no real idea what he is authorising. This means that a Man-in-the-Browser attack, where the attackers controls the browser on the client's PC, can still let someone unwittingly approve unwanted transactions.

This risk can be mitigated by letting the user sign additional challenges, for instance the amount or say the last eight digits of the bank account, which are meaningful to the user. Some online banking sites use such additional challenges for transfers with high amounts or transfers to bank accounts not used before by a customer. The downside of this is more hassle for the user, typing the extra challenges and responses. Also, a compromised browser could *still* trick users into signing these additional challenges, as a user cannot tell if an apparently random challenge is not in fact an amount or the last 8 digits of the attacker's bank account. Users could be asked to type in more than eight digits, possibly using devices with a bigger display, but clearly there will be a limit on how much hassle users are willing to accept.

Connecting the reader to the PC with a USB cable can solve the problem, or at least drastically reduce the risk and impact of Man-in-the-Browser attacks. The user no longer has to retype challenges and responses, making longer challenges acceptable. Moreover, the display can be alphanumeric (even if the keyboard is numeric only), allowing more meaningful challenges for the user. Not only security is improved, but also user-friendliness, as users do not have to retype challenges and responses.

The system we studied works in this way. Prior to confirming a bank transfer, the user sees details of the transfer he is about to approve on the display of the reader, as shown in Fig. 1. Gemalto calls this system SWYS, "Sign What You See". There is a patent application describing this solution [11].

Of course, connecting the reader to a PC introduces new risks: the PC could be infected and controlled by an online attacker. Such an attacker can then interfere with communication over the USB line, passively eavesdropping or actively changing communication. Still, the functionality exposed over the USB line can be very restricted, and given the simplicity of the device – and the obvious security requirements – controlling this risk seems easy. However, as this paper shows, the system we studied fails to properly ensure one of the core security objectives.

2   Background: EMV-CAP

The internet banking system we studied uses a variant of EMV-CAP, a proprietary standard of Mastercard that is widely used for internet banking.

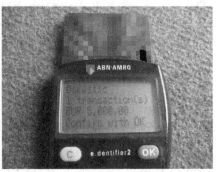

Fig. 1. The USB-connected reader, with the bank card sticking out the top, showing transaction details for the user to approve a login (left) or a bank transfer (right)

EMV-CAP is based on the EMV standard [9]. EMV, which stands for Europay-Mastercard-Visa, is used in most (if not all) banking smartcards.

In EMV-CAP, a regular EMV transaction is started but cancelled in the last step. In the course of an EMV-CAP transaction a smartcard generates two so-called *Application Cryptograms* (ACs) as proof of authorisation. The first cryptogram, an *ARQC* (Authorization Request Cryptogram), is used as authorisation of some online banking transaction. The second cryptogram, an *AAC* (Application Authentication Cryptogram), just serves to cleanly terminate the transaction.

These cryptograms are not digital signatures using asymmetric cryptography, but MACs (Message Authentication Codes) generated using a symmetric key shared between the bank and the smartcard (typically a 3DES key). We will still talk about the card 'signing' challenges, even though technically this terminology is incorrect. The reason for using symmetric crypto is historic: most modern bank cards are now capable of doing asymmetric crypto, but EMV was designed to be used with cheaper cards that did not.

EMV-CAP readers typically use an 8 digit numeric challenge, and respond with a 8 digit numeric response which is constructed from the first cryptogram, an ARQC, reported by the smartcard. In most modes of EMV-CAP the response is constructed by applying a bit filter to the ARQC, which selects some bits of the MAC and the least significant bits of the smartcard's transaction counter[2], which is reported by the smartcard together with the ARQC.

EMV-CAP has been largely reverse-engineered [8,15] and an informative description is leaked (apparently accidentally) in [5, Appendix 1]. This has revealed some potential for ambiguities [8] (e.g. between transactions to log-in and to transfer a zero amount) and, more worryingly, bad design decisions in some variants of EMV-CAP [15] (notably, *not* using unpredictable input, such as a nonce or transaction data, as input for the ARQC).

---

[2] Called the ATC, for Application Transaction Counter, in EMV terminology. The ATC is included in the computation of the ARQC, so the bank needs to know it to verify the authenticity of the response.

The system we studied also uses EMV-CAP, albeit with an additional twist, namely that there is an additional and unknown step to 'mangle' the challenge and the response, as explained in more detail later.

3   The e.dentifier2

The device we investigated is called the e.dentifier2. It is a smartcard reader with a display and keyboard, making it a class 3 device in the FinTS/HBCI classification[3]. The display can contain up to 68 characters. The keyboard provides numeric keys, an OK, and a Cancel button. The e.dentifier2 can be used for online banking with or without USB connection. Our attack only concerns the connected mode, but for sake of completeness we also describe the unconnected mode. As far as the interaction between the device with the smartcard is concerned, there is no difference, and the interaction is a regular EMV-CAP transaction.

3.1   Unconnected Mode

Without USB connection, the device behaves like a standard EMV-CAP reader: the user types in an 8 digit challenge and the reader returns a 8 digit response. However, the device does not quite conform to known variants of EMV-CAP, and the device performs some additional mangling of the data on top of EMV-CAP. The challenge sent to the smartcard for computing the ARQC is not identical to the challenge typed in by the user, but there is some additional hashing and/or encryption. This additional mangling means that there are unknown functions hard-coded in the device. The secrecy of these functions is not crucial for the security, but it does prevent interoperability with EMV-CAP readers issued by other banks, and it prevents the construction of a software emulation of the device, as is available for other EMV-CAP readers[4].

As already mentioned, the attack reported in this paper does not concern the system in unconnected mode.

3.2   Connected Mode

To use the connected mode, customers have to install a special driver (only available for Windows and MacOS). The web-browser then interacts with this driver via JavaScript and a browser plugin. The browser plugin checks whether it is connected to either the domain abnamro.nl or abnamro.com using SSL. If this is not the case, the plugin will not function. The Firefox plugin also allows local files to use the plugin. This might introduce security risks as, for example, this means that attachments in emails could also use the plugin.

In connected mode, an internet banking session starts with the reader reading the bank account number and the card number from the smartcard and supplying

---

[3] Available from http://www.hbci-zka.de
[4] Available from http://sites.uclouvain.be/EMV-CAP

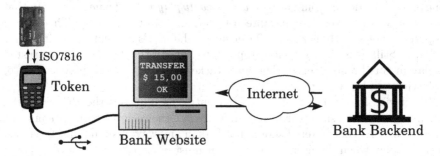

Fig. 2. Setup for internet banking with the e.dentifier; the web browser communicates over USB with the e.dentifier, into which the bank card is inserted

it to the web-browser. So the user does not have to type this in, making the system more user-friendly.

To log in, the reader first prompts the user for his PIN code. It then displays a message saying that the user is about to log in and asks the user to confirm this by pressing OK (see Fig. 1).

To confirm a bank transfer, or a set of bank transfers, the reader will again prompt the user for his PIN code. It then displays a message giving *the number of transfers* the user is about to approve and *the total amount of money* involved, and asks the user to approve this by pressing OK (see Fig. 1).

The additional security of the connected mode over the unconnected mode here is that *you see what you sign*, even if the browser or the PC it runs on is controlled by malware. Section 4 below discusses the security objectives to guarantee 'What-You-Sign-Is-What-You-See' in more detail.

Connecting the e.dentifier2 to a possibly infected PC by USB does introduce a new attack vector: malicious code on the PC could try to interfere with the device. Still, given the device is so simple and offers so little functionality, it should be possible to design and implement it so that it is secure against such attacks.

4   Security Objectives of WYSIWYS

The crucial security objectives to ensure *WYSIWYS* (What-You-Sign-Is-What-You-See) are that

- the text on the display is always included in the data that is signed,
- and that signing is only done after the user has given his consent.

Apart from the text on the display, the signature should also include some session-unique information, such as a nonce or transaction counter, to prevent replays.

The device has to be *a trusted display in the narrow sense*, by which we mean that what is displayed on the screen is (part of) what is signed by the smartcard. The device could also be *a trusted display in the broader sense* in that the messages displayed are guaranteed to originate from the bank. This second property is not strictly necessary for ensuring the user's consent in signing what is shown. Still, it is clearly a nice property to have; if the device is not a trusted display in this broader sense, then an attacker could use the display as part of sophisticated phishing attacks.

The device has to be trusted for PIN entry, as it passes the PIN code the user provides to the smartcard, so it should meet the security requirements this brings. The PIN code entered should not leak in any way: it should not be shown on the display when the user types it, and it must obviously not be revealed over the USB line. Only PIN codes entered on the keypad should be passed on to the smartcard as PIN guesses, and never data coming over the USB line. The latter would enable malware on the PC to perform a Denial-of-Service (DoS) attack, by blocking the card with three PIN guesses, or to guess the PIN code right in 0.03% of the cases (or more, if users can choose their own PIN [4]).

More generally, possibilities for interaction over the USB line have to be kept to a minimum: the device should not offer functionality for the PC to read data entered on the keypad over the USB line, or for the PC to send commands to the smartcard over the USB line (and then receive the card's responses). Clearly the device will have to send some commands to the smartcard on instruction from the PC, and then send back some of the responses, but such functionality should be limited to what is strictly necessary.

Note that it is the job of the smartcard to check whether the PIN code is correct. It is also natural that the smartcard only generates a signature after it has been supplied with a PIN code, and preferable does so only once[5].

Handheld readers for home use are typically not designed to be tamper-resistant or tamper-evident to any serious degree. This would make the devices far too expensive, while the online attackers that the reader is meant to protect against do not have physical access. (The FINREAD initiative [10] did aim at tamper-resistant readers, but was not successful because of the costs.) Still, although online attackers are the main threat, one should not overlook creative possibilities for attackers to get physical access. In the Netherlands criminals successfully tampered with readers that were available *inside* bank offices for customers to use, in order to obtain PIN codes and enough data to reconstruct valid mag-stripes. Of course, allowing the mag-stripe to be constructed from data supplied by the smartcard chip was a very bad design choice in EMV, and has since been remedied.

5   Analysis Tools

Reverse engineering the precise working of the system, and subsequently carrying out our attack, required eavesdropping and sometimes also actively altering traffic on the three channels shown in Fig. 2, i.e. communication (i) with the bank's website over HTTPS, (ii) between the PC and the reader over USB, and (iii) between the reader and the smartcard. For this we used various tools.

---

[5] Tests we have done with bank cards show that this indeed the case [1].

HTTP(S) Communication. To intercept and modify network traffic between the browser and the bank web application we used Fiddler2, a web debugging proxy[6].

ISO7816 Smartcard Communication. To eavesdrop on communication between the smartcard and the reader we initially used the APDU Scanner by Rebel-SIMcard[7]. This software and the associated hardware to physically intercept the traffic have been developed to study SIM cards (typically, to study how SIM locking works), but it works for any ISO7816 smartcard.

Later on, we also used a tool for smartcard communication analysis that we developed ourselves [6], which also allowed active Man-in-the-Middle attacks and replaying of earlier sessions to the smartcard reader. This tool consist of a USB-connected FPGA (Field Programmable Gate Array) and can be used for passive eavesdropping, relay attacks (where smartcard communication can be relayed for instance over IP), and active Man-in-the-Middle attacks. The design of this device is open and the software is available as under the GNU GPL.

Eavesdropping USB Communication. To eavesdrop on communication over the USB line we used USBTrace[8] and Wireshark[9]. USBTrace has the advantage that in addition to the raw traffic of individual packets it also shows the aggregated communication of larger messages that in fact take several packets. However, this also caused some confusion, as initially it was unclear what really went over the line.

Replaying USB Traffic. To replay USB communication we wrote our own software. The USB interface of the e.dentifier2 requires a vendor specific driver for communication. The workings of this driver is proprietary and not publicly available. We used the open-source libusb library[10] to build a simplified driver ourselves. Libusb takes care of all the low-level details of the communication between the computer and USB device. The driver we developed uses bulk data transfers, which are unspecified raw messages that allows a user to send and receive binary data with an arbitrary length. The eavesdropped communication showed that all communicated messages were a multiple of 8 bytes long. Although the details of the communication protocol were not available, it was rather simple to replay an earlier recorded transaction of USB messages. Since there is no authentication between the device and the bank, all features of the e.dentifier2 become available directly after plugging the device into a computer.

Man-in-the-Middle Attack on USB Traffic. Executing and validating the attack in a real online banking session required a Man-in-the-Middle attack on the USB traffic in which we actively altered some data. We could not find any existing software to carry out a Man-in-the-Middle attack on USB. We therefore did it

---

[6] http://fiddler2.com
[7] http://rebelsimcard.com/network-sim-apdu-scanner.html
[8] http://www.sysnucleus.com
[9] http://www.wireshark.org/
[10] http://www.libusb.org/

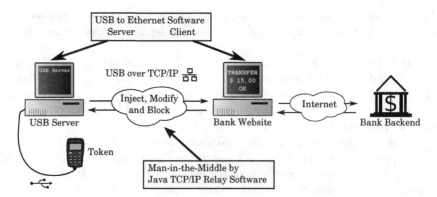

Fig. 3. Setup for Man-in-the-Middle attack on USB traffic; the communication between the browser and the e.dentifier2 is tunnelled over TCP/IP to another PC (labelled USB Server), which forwards it to the e.dentifier2

in a somewhat roundabout way, by tunnelling the USB traffic over TCP/IP, and then modifying this tunnelled traffic, as depicted in Fig. 3. We also considered reverse engineering and modifying the driver code, and tried to develop a custom device driver using the LibUsbDotNet library[11], but these alternatives seemed more work. Tunnelling the USB traffic over TCP/IP could be done with existing software, namely the *USB to Ethernet Connector*[12]. The advantage of this method is that there is no need to fully understand the USB protocol. Furthermore, the software of the banking application, notably the custom device driver, could be used without any modifications.

6   The SWYS Protocol

The tools described in the previous section allowed the reverse engineering of online banking with the e.dentifier2 in connected mode.

Fig. 4 outlines the abstract SWYS protocol for logging in or confirming a transaction (i.e. a bank transfer). In either case the web-browser sends so-called *signdata* to the reader. This signdata consists of two parts, namely some text (that is shown on the display) and some number (which is not):

- In the case of a login, the signdata text specifies the account number and bank card number; in case of a transaction, it specifies the number of transactions and the total amount (see Fig. 1).
- In the case of a login, the signdata number is a 4 byte value giving the current UNIX time; in case of a transaction, it is a 20 byte apparently random value.

In the protocol, the reader asks the smartcard to produce two cryptograms, using the GENERATE_AC command. Included in these commands is a 4 byte payload[13].

---

[11] http://sourceforge.net/projects/libusbdotnet
[12] http://www.eltima.com/products/usb-over-ethernet/
[13] Called the Unpredictable Number in EMV terminology.

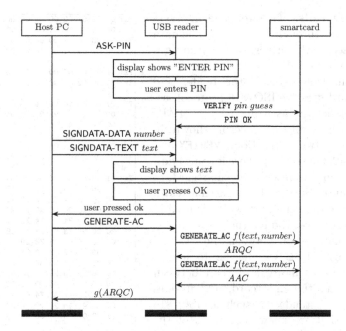

Fig. 4. SWYS protocol for log-in and for transactions

(As is usual in EMV-CAP transactions, the first cryptogram is an ARQC, the second an AAC, but these details do not matter here.)

By replaying earlier transactions, and varying the text and number parts of the signdata, we could confirm that this 4 byte payload does depend on both the text and the number. Hence this payload is written as $f(text, number)$ in Fig. 4. It has to depend on the text to make sure that 'we sign what we see'; including the number is useful to diversify the input and prevent replays, though the computation of the cryptograms will also involve the card's transaction counter. We do not know what the function f is.

To finish a transaction, the reader sends a response back to the web-browser, which is based on the cryptograms generated by the smartcard. Again, we do not precisely know how this response is computed, only that it depends on the ARQC reported by the smartcard. Hence it is written as $g(ARQC)$ in Fig. 4. So g, like f, is an unknown function that is implemented in the device.

ASK-PIN	01 03 04 00 00 00 00 00
SIGNDATA-DATA-LOGIN	01 03 05 06 00 00 00 00
SIGNDATA-DATA-TRANSACTION	01 03 05 16 00 00 00 00
SIGNDATA-TEXT	01 03 05 46 00 00 00 00
GENERATE-AC	01 03 06 00 00 00 00 00

Fig. 5. commands sent over the USB line

Protocol Details. The webpage interacts with the driver through JavaScript. The data that is passed to the driver, such as the sign-data, is TLV encoded.

Communication between the reader and the smartcard uses the ISO7816 protocol, using the instructions as defined in the EMV standard. The protocol excerpt shown in Fig. 4 involves two instructions, VERIFY and GENERATE_AC. On start-up there is some additional communication with the smartcard, to read out some of the data from the smartcard, such as the account number, which is used in communication over the internet.

The communication between the PC and the reader over USB was harder to understand. It involves more data than between the reader and the smartcard, and it does not follow any standards, such as ISO7816 and EMV, that we knew. For most of the traffic from the PC to the reader we could eventually determine the meaning, see Fig. 5. though we see some additional data for which the meaning is unclear. The reader responds with 01 03 02 00 00 00 00 00 to indicate OK. Fig. 6 contains a communication trace between computer and e.dentifier2. It shows the USB frames for a successful transaction of €123.00.

```
Tx: 01 03 01 02 00 00 00 00    ........
    00 02 65 6e 00 00 00 00    ..en....
Rx: 01 03 01 01 00 00 00 00    ........
    00 01 01 01 00 00 00 00    ........

Tx: 01 03 04 00 00 00 00 00    ........
Rx: 01 03 02 00 00 00 00 00    ........

Tx: 01 03 05 16 00 00 00 00    ........
    00 06 00 14 9a 2c 83 9a    .....,..
    00 06 4f 4f 3c 8e 3e b8    ..OO<.>.
    00 06 ef 39 0b 60 b9 46    ...9.'.F
    00 04 30 12 01 00 b9 46    ..0....F
Rx: 01 03 02 00 00 00 00 00    ........

Tx: 01 03 05 46 00 00 00 00    ...F....
    00 06 01 44 44 6f 6d 65    ...DDome
    00 06 73 74 69 63 20 20    ..stic
    00 06 20 20 20 20 20 20    ..
    00 06 20 31 20 74 72 61    .. 1 tra
    00 06 6e 73 61 63 74 69    ..nsacti
    00 06 6f 6e 28 73 29 20    ..on(s)
    00 06 45 55 52 20 31 32    ..EUR 12
    00 06 33 2c 30 30 20 20    ..3,00
    00 06 20 20 20 20 20 43    .. C
    00 06 6f 6e 66 69 72 6d    ..onfirm
    00 06 20 77 69 74 68 20    .. with
    00 04 4f 4b 20 20 68 20    ..OK h
Rx: 01 03 02 00 00 00 00 00    ........

Tx: 01 03 06 00 00 00 00 00    ........
Rx: 01 03 03 19 00 00 00 00    ........
    00 06 80 00 6d b8 c7 cc    ....m...
    00 06 ab 00 12 a5 00 03    ........
    00 06 02 00 00 00 00 00    ........
    00 06 00 00 00 00 00 00    ........
    00 01 ff 00 00 00 00 00    ........
```

Fig. 6. Communication between computer and e.dentifier2 over the USB line

7 The Attack

As can be seen in Figure 4, the reader sends a message to the host PC indicating the user pressed OK. After this the host PC sends a command to generate the cryptograms to the reader. This seems strange, as the reader would be expected to generate the cryptograms automatically after OK has been pressed. The driver on the host PC should not play a role in this.

This weakness can be exploited: by sending the request over the USB line to generate the cryptograms *without* waiting for the user to press OK, the cryptograms are generated and the reader returns the response over the USB line, without the user getting a chance to approve or cancel the transaction. To make matters worse, a side-effect of giving this command is that the display is cleared, so the transaction details only appear on the display for less than a second. We demonstrated this attack in an actual internet banking session.

This means that an attacker controlling an infected PC can let the user sign messages that the user did *not* approve, thus defeating one of the key objectives

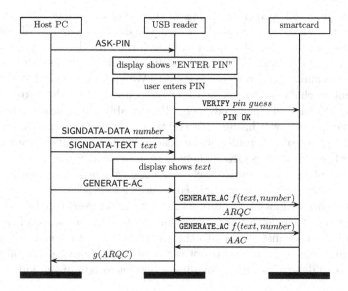

Fig. 7. Attack on SWYS protocol; the difference with Fig. 4 is that the driver directly gives the instruction to generate the ACs, without waiting for the user to press OK

of *WYSIWYS*. The user still has to enter his PIN, but this is entered at the start of a transaction, and after this no more interaction is needed from the user to sign malicious transactions.

8   Other Attack Scenarios

In a different approach we tried to manipulate the text displayed on the screen. For this we investigated whether the fact that not only the text on the display but also some random data is signed, introduced a flaw. If the text and random data would simply be concatenated, part of the text might be shifted to the random data. This would result in less text being displayed (for example only 'Press OK to continue'), while still producing the same signature. In our experiments this however did not work, suggesting that either some separator is used in the concatenation or a part of the USB packets is also included.

9   Extended Length Challenges

Initially it was mind-boggling to us how this vulnerability could ever have been introduced. Subsequently it became clear that the vulnerability may have been introduced as a side-effect of having additional functionality in the device, where the device shows *several* messages for the user to approve. Presumably this functionality is included for more complex transactions where more than 68 characters are needed to display transaction data.

We never observed such transactions in our use of the online banking system, but using our own driver we could see that the device is capable of doing this. Several messages can be sent to the reader in turn, with the next message being sent after the user presses OK, and then after the final message the driver can give the command to generate the response. We could observe that the 4 byte payload sent as challenge to the smartcard depended on all the texts that were sent to the reader and displayed there. Presumably the unknown function f implemented in the device hashes these texts together to compute this challenge.

For this variant of the protocol the reader needs to communicate with the driver after the user presses OK, namely to request the next part of the message. This might explain – but not excuse! – why the weakness has been introduced in the first place, and why it was missed in security reviews.

Note that this variant of the protocol results in an overloaded semantics for the OK button: it can mean an instruction (to the driver) to 'send more data to the display' or an instruction (to the smartcard) to 'go ahead and generate a cryptogram'. Since the reader is not aware of the meaning of the button, the host PC has to determine this, providing a possible origin of the vulnerability.

10   How Could – and Should – This Have Been Prevented?

The attack that we found is something that should have been detected, and – as we argue below – could have been detected. After all, the attack does not involve some detailed cryptanalysis, rely on a cleverly crafted man-in-the-middle attack, or exploit some subtle low level coding mistake. A patent application describing an e.dentifier2-like solution has been filed by the company that produces it [11]; the higher level description of the protocol given there does not include the vulnerability that we found.

We have no insight in the procedures followed in design, implementation, or testing, or indeed any of the associated documentation, so we can only speculate how the vulnerability could possibly have been missed. Still, we can consider how it could – and should – have been spotted, or, better still, prevented in the first place.

Firstly, the attack breaks one of the central security objectives of WYSIWYS. This security objective should be used as a basis for considering abuse cases. (If the EMV specs [9] are anything to go by, the security objectives may well be completely undocumented and implicit in the specs.) An obvious abuse case that could already have been identified in the early design phase is: (i) malicious code on the PC that tries to get the reader to sign without the user's approval.[14] It seems unlikely that the vulnerability could have gone unnoticed in design, implementation and testing if this abuse case was made explicit, as it would then have been considered by e.g. a reviewer of the specifications or tester of

---

[14] Other abuse case would be: (ii) malicious code on the PC tries to get the reader to sign something not shown to the user and (iii) malicious code on the PC tries to send a PIN code guess to the smartcard.

the implementation. In fact, one would then expect someone developing the spec or implementing it to notice the problem long before any post-hoc security evaluation.

As discussed in Section 9, it seems that the semantics of pressing the OK button is overloaded. This overloading could be spotted in a high level spec that only considers the interaction with the user, if in such a spec one tries to make the semantics of pressing OK explicit. Overloading the semantics of actions or cryptograms is also noted as a potential problem in EMV-CAP [8].

Formal techniques for protocol verification have been shown to be capable of handling complex real-life protocols. For example, it has been shown that the core of the EMV protocol can be fully formalised and that tools can then reveal known weaknesses [7]. Such techniques could also be used to look for weaknesses as the one discussed in this paper.

Finally, even if the problem went unnoticed in the design, the problem could still have been detected by more systematic testing. Exhaustive testing is of course impossible, even for a system as simple as this: the messages over the USB line are small but too long for exhaustively testing all possible contents. Still, the number of different *types* of messages over the USB line is very small. The number of internal states of the reader, which correspond to particular states of the simple protocol it implements, is very small too. So exhaustively testing every type of message in each protocol state is feasible, and this would have inevitably revealed the problem. Such testing can be done in a systematic and largely automated way using model-based testing [16].

11 Related Work and Related Online Banking Systems

We are not aware of any related work investigating USB-connected smartcard readers for internet banking. As discussed in Section 2, unconnected smartcard readers for internet banking has been thoroughly investigated [8, 15]. For contactless smartcard technology, such as Near Field Communication (NFC), there are several proposals [2, 13, 14] in the literature for secure internet banking.

There are other banks that use USB-connected readers that act as smartcard readers. The Gemalto website gives an overview of banks that use their products, but not all these systems work in the same way.

The Swedish Handelsbanken also uses a Gemalto reader, but here things work differently from the system described above. For internet banking with Handelsbanken, the reader is used to obtain bank account details from the smartcard so the user does not have to enter this manually. However, the display of the reader is not used at all, except to show a progress bar when entering PIN codes! To log in or confirm a transaction shown on the webpage, the user has to enter his PIN code on the reader, but all further interaction between the PC, reader and smartcard is invisible to the user. Effectively, this means that the class 3 smartcard reader (with display and keyboard) is only used as a class 2 smartcard reader (with keyboard but withour display). This suggests Handelsbanken does not consider Man-in-the-Browser attacks a serious threat, and only uses the USB connection to make internet banking more user friendly, as users do not have to type in their account numbers or re-type challenges and responses.

The only other USB-connected reader used for internet banking we are aware of is at another Swedish bank, SEB. SEB uses a reader from a different vendor, namely the DIGIPASS 920 by Vasco[15]. This reader is used similarly to the way Handelsbanken uses their reader, i.e. without using the display.

Unlike the systems above, which do not even try to achieve WYSIWYS, there are alternative systems for internet banking that do try to achieve this.

The German Volksbank uses the Sm@rtTAN optic where an optical signal (a flickering bar code) on the webpage is used to transmit information about the transfer to a handheld smartcard reader (which has an optical interface). The reader then shows transaction details and produces a confirmation code that the user has to type in. Advantage of this system is that communication is physically guaranteed to be one way – from the PC to the reader – unlike with a USB connection. The disadvantage is that it introduces a bit more hassle for the user, e.g. the user has to hold the reader in front of the bar code during the transmission of the data.

IBM's ZTIC (Zone Trusted Information Channel) is a USB-connected device with a small display [17, 18][16]. Unlike the devices mentioned above, the ZTIC has the capabilities to set up a secure channel to a remote site, meaning that it is a trusted display in the broad sense as discussed in Section 4. It can therefore provide stronger security guarantees than the devices above, at the expense of a more complex device, which now also is able to store key material (notably public keys to set up secure channels) and needs the cryptographic processing capabilities for this. The ZTIC does not have a keyboard, but does have a turn-wheel to allow user input, which can be used for entering a numeric PIN code.

12   Conclusions

The basic idea of having a simple USB connected device that provides a trusted display and keyboard for users to authorise transactions, by letting their smart-card provide digital signatures, is very sensible[17]. This makes it all the more disappointing that this particular implementation of the idea fails so miserably. It is ironic that a system that is marketed under the name SWYS, 'See What You Sign', should fail to meet the central security objective it is named after.

The weakness cannot be fixed by improvements in the device driver. The problem could be fixed in new versions of the card reader without requiring

---

[15] http://www.vasco.com/company/case_studies/seb.aspx

[16] http://www.zurich.ibm.com/ztic

[17] In fact, our initial motivation in reverse-engineering the system, in an MSc project by the first author, was to see if we could re-use the same reader, in combination with a different smartcard, for other applications where digital signatures are needed. Since the device itself does not need to contain any secrets, this should be possible; however, the unknown hashing mechanisms in the device, functions f and g in Fig. 4, currently still prevent this.

changes in the smartcard or the device driver. Of course, this leaves the practical problem that there are millions of card readers already deployed.

To make matters worse, the problem is not caused by a subtle flaw or low-level coding defect that is easily overlooked. The fundamental design decision of giving the PC such fine-grained control over the reader (in particular, letting the reader report to the PC that the user pressed OK, and then letting the PC instruct the reader to let the smartcard generate a cryptogram) goes against the whole idea of What-You-Sign-Is-What-You-See. This design decision does not inevitably lead to a security flaw, but it is clearly asking for trouble, and opens the door to a whole category of potential attacks.

We can only wonder what possessed the developers to design the system in this way, or indeed how banks deciding to use this system could have missed it in even a superficial security analysis.

The bank was informed about this vulnerability immediately after we discovered it. When informing them we supplied a video demonstrating the attack; by checking the logs of the bank's back-end they could confirm that this video showed an actual attack. The bank responded promptly and contacted their supplier. This resulted in swift action to develop an improved version of the reader, which will be rolled out in the course of 2012. The supplier confirmed to us that they have no other clients that use the system with this weakness; it seems that ABN-AMRO has been an early adopter of this particular product.

Our paper is not the first to signal problems with security protocols used in the banking industry. Several problems have been noticed in the past [3,12,15]. Banks are now wise enough to use standard cryptographic algorithms, such as 3DES, RSA, and SHA-1, and not to rely on proprietary ones. However, they do still choose to design their own security protocols and try to keep them secret. Given that security protocols can be so tricky to get right, we believe it would be better to adopt the same approach for security protocols as for cryptographic algorithms, and only use published protocols that have been subjected to a rigorous public review.

References

1. Aarts, F., Poll, E., de Ruiter, J.: Formal models of bank cards for free. Draft (2012)
2. Alpár, G., Batina, L., Verdult, R.: Using NFC Phones for Proving Credentials. In: Schmitt, J.B. (ed.) MMB & DFT 2012. LNCS, vol. 7201, pp. 317–330. Springer, Heidelberg (2012)
3. Barisani, A., Bianco, D., Laurie, A., Franken, Z.: Chip & PIN is definitely broken. Presentation at CanSecWest Applied Security Conference, Vancouver (2011), More info available at http://dev.inversepath.com/download/emv
4. Bonneau, J., Preibusch, S., Anderson, R.: A Birthday Present Every Eleven Wallets? The Security of Customer-Chosen Banking PINs. In: Keromytis, A.D. (ed.) FC 2012. LNCS, vol. 7397, pp. 25–40. Springer, Heidelberg (2012)
5. Check-In-Phone – Technology and Security, http://upload.rb.ru/upload/users/files/3374/check-in-phone-technologie_security-english-_2010-08-12_20.05.11.pdf

6. de Koning Gans, G., de Ruiter, J.: The smartlogic tool: Analysing and testing smart card protocols. In: IEEE Fifth International Conference on Software Testing, Verification, and Validation, pp. 864–871 (2012)
7. de Ruiter, J., Poll, E.: Formal Analysis of the EMV Protocol Suite. In: Mödersheim, S., Palamidessi, C. (eds.) TOSCA 2011. LNCS, vol. 6993, pp. 113–129. Springer, Heidelberg (2012)
8. Drimer, S., Murdoch, S.J., Anderson, R.: Optimised to Fail: Card Readers for Online Banking. In: Dingledine, R., Golle, P. (eds.) FC 2009. LNCS, vol. 5628, pp. 184–200. Springer, Heidelberg (2009)
9. EMVCo. EMV– Integrated Circuit Card Specifications for Payment Systems, Book 1-4 (2008), http://emvco.com
10. CEN Workshop Agreement (CWA) 14174: Financial transactional IC card reader (FINREAD) (2004)
11. Gullberg, P.: Method and device for creating a digital signature. European Patent Application EP 2 166 483 A1, filed September 17, 2008 (March 24, 2010)
12. Murdoch, S., Drimer, S., Anderson, R., Bond, M.: Chip and PIN is Broken. In: Symposium on Security and Privacy, pp. 433–446. IEEE (2010)
13. Ortiz-Yepes, D.A.: Nfc-cap security assessment. Technical report, IBM Zurich Research Laboratory (2009)
14. Saleh, Z., Alsmadi, I.: Using RFID to enhance mobile banking security. International Journal of Computer Science and Information Security (IJCSIS) 8(9), 176–182 (2010)
15. Szikora, J.-P., Teuwen, P.: Banques en ligne: à la découverte d'EMV-CAP. MISC (Multi-System & Internet Security Cookbook) 56, 50–62 (2011)
16. Tretmans, J.: Model Based Testing with Labelled Transition Systems. In: Hierons, R.M., Bowen, J.P., Harman, M. (eds.) FORTEST. LNCS, vol. 4949, pp. 1–38. Springer, Heidelberg (2008)
17. Weigold, T., Hiltgen, A.: Secure confirmation of sensitive transaction data in modern internet banking services. In: 2011 World Congress on Internet Security (World-CIS), pp. 125–132. IEEE (2011)
18. Weigold, T., Kramp, T., Hermann, R., Höring, F., Buhler, P., Baentsch, M.: The Zurich Trusted Information Channel–an efficient defence against man-in-the-middle and malicious software attacks. In: Trusted Computing-Challenges and Applications, pp. 75–91 (2008)

Security Add-Ons for Mobile Platforms

Benjamin Adolphi and Hanno Langweg

NISlab, Norwegian Information Security laboratory
Høgskolen i Gjøvik
2815 Gjøvik, Norway
`firstname.lastname@hig.no`

Abstract. We give an overview of existing security software on mobile platforms in form of firewalls and antivirus software. We investigate whether these solutions increase the security on mobile platforms, what limitations the platforms' security policies present and how current solutions work.

Keywords: Firewall, Antivirus Software, Android, iOS, Windows Phone.

1 Introduction

In this paper, we analyze the state of security software in form of firewalls and antivirus software on mobile platforms. We focus on the current state of the industry and not what would be possible under the assumption that the platform can be arbitrarily modified. Our goal is to give an overview how far the security software industry has come, which problems are encountered and whether it makes sense to offer security software on mobile platforms at all. As far as we know, this is the first attempt to present an overview of security software on mobile platforms.

Our investigations cover the Android, iOS and Windows Phone platforms. We chose Android and iOS because of their popularity. At the moment, both platforms have a combined market share of more than 80% [1]. We chose Windows Phone even though its market share currently is very low. The reason for that being that Microsoft has already had a lot of experience fighting malware on their desktop platforms and this might be reflected in their mobile platform. For the investigations, we chose the most current version of each of the platforms at the time of writing, which was Android 4.0.3, iOS 5.0.1 and Windows Phone 7.5. We limit our investigation to firewalls and antivirus software, because these are the add-ons recommended to average computer users, cf., e.g. the recommendations given by the Norwegian Centre for Information Security (NorSIS): Install operating system security updates, install application security updates, install antivirus/antispyware, use backups, activate firewall software [2].

The goal of the investigated security software is to increase the security of a system. On the investigated mobile platforms, the security model concerning application isolation is far more strict than on desktop platforms. We believe the reason for the stricter security model on mobile platforms is because the

A. Jøsang and B. Carlsson (Eds.): NordSec 2012, LNCS 7617, pp. 17–30, 2012.
© Springer-Verlag Berlin Heidelberg 2012

platforms are relatively new. While most desktop platforms try to be backwards compatible to support old applications, mobile platforms were created recently and could include new security technologies by design without having to support old applications. The main security mechanism of mobile platforms is that applications on these platforms are run in a sandbox, which decreases the capabilities of malware influencing system resources and other applications. While this security mechanism decreases the capabilities of malware, it also decreases the capabilities of security software that is not part of the operating system. The challenge is that malware can use any means trying to escape from the sandbox, while serious security solutions have to play by the rules of the platform.

On mobile platforms, the act of rooting (Android), jailbreaking (iOS) or unlocking (Windows Phone) exploits a vulnerability in order to break out of the sandbox and gain administrative privileges. This is usually performed by users who want to customize their mobile device beyond the possibilities that are offered by the platform. This widespread circumvention of security mechanisms is not present in desktop operating systems e.g. Linux, Mac OS X and Windows probably owing to the availability of administrative access of computer owners. However, since the exploits used to compromise the sandbox are publicly available, malware authors also have access to them and can use them in their malware to break out of the sandbox. At the moment, this has only been seen in the wild on the Android platform [3], but is a definitive possibility for future development. In contrast to that, it seems counterproductive that a user or even the security software itself has to circumvent the security mechanisms of the platform in order to work. As we will show, this is sometimes the case nevertheless.

2   Related Work

Much research has been done with respect to security solutions on mobile platforms in general. However, little has been published on the state of the industry of currently available firewalls and antivirus software on mobile platforms. One exception is a test report on anti-malware solutions on Android, which evaluates detection rates [4].

Concerning firewalls, the authors of [5] and [6] propose to use a firewall on Android to increase system security against malware, but give no further details on how this could be implemented. In [7], the authors state that firewalls on Android will only work with root permissions, but also do not offer an explanation.

Much more work has been done with respect to antivirus software. One problem that antivirus software faces on mobile devices in general is the fact that resources, especially when it comes to battery power, are limited. Multiple authors have addressed this problem by proposing to perform scanning in the cloud [8], [9], [10]. Other differences on mobile platforms compared to desktop platforms concerning malware detection can be found in [11].

Some work on malware detection on mobile platforms addresses the question which characteristics can be used to detect an infection by malware. These detection methods usually use unprivileged information that is not restricted by sandboxes. One example is to detect an infection by malware by observing the battery power usage of the device [12],[13],[14].

Other approaches for malware detection use the fact that on Android and Windows Phone, applications have to specify which permissions they require to run. The authors of [15] have analyzed almost 1,000 Android applications concerning the required permissions to see if this could be a feature that can be used to detect malware. The reasoning behind this can be seen from the following simplified example: An application that has the permission to access the Internet and read the user's address book is theoretically able to leak private information to arbitrary receivers and can therefore be seen as suspicious. Other applications that do not possess the combined permissions on the other hand can be classified as harmless.

A different approach is taken by the authors of [16], which propose a system that detects Android malware by performing static code analysis. The system is for example capable to detect applications that read the unique ID of the device. The authors also propose how the system could be used to remove the suspicious behavior from an application that otherwise contains useful functionality.

3   Firewalls

Firewalls are used to control the inbound and outbound network traffic of a system. On desktop platforms, this is used to restrict access to system services and to prevent applications on the system from leaking sensitive information to third parties. On mobile platforms, a third motivation can be identified: Network connections using mobile 3G networks are usually either expensive or volume restricted. Using a firewall, the network access of data-intensive applications can be restricted when not using a Wi-Fi network.

The permission system used in Android and Windows Phone offers the possibility to either completely allow or completely restrict network access on a per-application basis. A problem with this approach is that this can only be decided during install time and can not be changed during runtime. iOS on the other hand does not offer the possibility to restrict access to the network, giving every application full access even when this might not be required. The possibility to restrict applications in this way is a first step towards a per-application firewall provided by the operating system. However, this approach lacks flexibility. It would be desirable to restrict access more selectively, e.g. to only allow an application to communicate with a specific server or to only use a specific protocol. An overview of the possibilities that firewalls on desktop platforms offer can be found in [17]. Since these possibilities are currently not provided by any of the mobile platforms we investigated, firewalls can be considered a useful security improvement.

We will now present more details on existing firewall solutions on each of the investigated platforms.

3.1 Android

The Google Play Store, the official application distribution platform from Google, currently contains multiple firewall solutions for Android. All these do, however, require a rooted device. In the following investigation, we will explain the reasons behind this.

In order to acquire a representative sample of current firewall solutions for analysis, we searched the Google Play Store for the keyword *firewall* and chose the five currently most popular hits (in terms of user ratings):

- Avast Mobile Security 1.0.2129
- Droidwall 1.5.7
- Network Firewall 1.2.2
- Root Firewall 0.94
- Internet Firewall 1.10.27

We analyzed the applications by investigating their executable code. For this, we used the tools *dex2jar* and *jad* to transform Dalvik executables to Java bytecode and then to Java code. Our investigation shows that all of them are based on the packet filter *Netfilter*, which is part of the Linux kernel that is at the core of Android. It has to be noted that Netfilter is not necessarily included in the kernel of each Android device because the device manufacturers usually compile their own kernels with a custom configuration. From user-space, Netfilter is controlled by the commandline tool *iptables*, which requires root permissions to create new firewall rules and this is the reason why all firewalls require root privileges.

When analyzing the firewall rules used by the applications, we discovered that all of them except Network Firewall are based on an open source project called Droidwall [18]. This is probably one of the reasons that all of the firewall solutions offer the same functionality: They allow the user to make a decision for each installed application that possesses the permission to access the network. The user can choose whether the application is allowed to access the network when being connected to a Wi-Fi network or a 3G network. Netfilter in current Linux kernel versions does not provide the possibility to distinguish between single applications [19]. However, the sandbox model of Android is based on running each application as a separate user. This fact is used in all firewall scripts to allow or block network access to specific applications. The application Droidwall additionally offers the possibility to include custom iptables scripts to define additional firewall rules. This is a feature that only aims at advanced users with knowledge about iptables.

3.2 iOS

As far as our investigations have shown, the official application distribution platform for iOS, the AppStore, does not contain any firewall solution. To analyze the way firewalls could be implemented in iOS, we therefore turned to Cydia, an unofficial application distribution platform for jailbroken iOS devices.

Here, we found the application *Firewall iP 2.04-1*, which requires a jailbroken device. This firewall alarms the user when an application tries to open a TCP or UDP connection and offers the user control over the subsequent actions. It gives the user the choice to allow access once or to specify a permanent rule for subsequent requests of that application.

We then investigated the application more closely in order to understand how the firewall functionality was implemented. The description of the application contains a valuable hint: "It hooks into the applications and will warn you if the app wants to establish a connection [...]" [20]. Monitoring the network activity seems to be done by placing hooks in applications.

To determine how this is achieved, we investigated the application further. Apart from the actual application, Firewall iP also installs a *MobileSubstrate* library called *ZFirewall.dylib*. MobileSubstrate is a hooking framework for iOS devices that have been jailbroken [21]. It enables the creation of inline hooks for every function call and every Objective-C message invocation that an application can make. MobileSubstrate is a framework that allows developers to write extensions that hook specific functions/messages. ZFirewall.dylib is one of these extensions. The extensions are loaded by MobileSubstrate into running processes based on a filter that is specified in a *plist* file that accompanies the extension. In the case of Firewall iP, the extension is loaded in every application that links against the UIKit or ImageIO frameworks, meaning that the extension is loaded into every application that has a graphical user interface since they are all based on UIKit.

We took a closer look at the extension by disassembling it using the application *IDA*. We found that the library hooks multiple functions. Apart from hooking functions to get notified about user interface changes, it hooks the two system calls *connect* and *sendto* (see fig. 1), which are used to open socket connections and send data and can therefore effectively influence the network connectivity of an application.

```
__text:0000F6DC        LDR    R0, =(_connect_ptr - 0xF6E6)
__text:0000F6DE        LDR    R2, =(_orig__connect - 0xF6E8)
__text:0000F6E0        LDR    R1, =(__Z10my_connectiPK8sockaddrj+1 - 0xF6EC)
__text:0000F6E2        ADD    R0, PC
__text:0000F6E4        ADD    R2, PC
__text:0000F6E6        LDR    R0, [R0]
__text:0000F6E8        ADD    R1, PC
__text:0000F6EA        BLX    _MSHookFunction
__text:0000F6EE        LDR    R0, =(_sendto_ptr - 0xF6F8)
__text:0000F6F0        LDR    R2, =(_orig__sendto - 0xF6FA)
__text:0000F6F2        LDR    R1, =(__Z9my_sendtoiPKvmiPK8sockaddrj+1 - 0xF6FE)
__text:0000F6F4        ADD    R0, PC
__text:0000F6F6        ADD    R2, PC
__text:0000F6F8        LDR    R0, [R0]
__text:0000F6FA        ADD    R1, PC
__text:0000F6FC        BLX    _MSHookFunction
```

Fig. 1. Firewall iP hooking the connect and sendto system calls

Another way to implement a firewall on jailbroken iOS devices – that is currently not used by any application – would be to take a similar approach as the applications on Android do. The XNU kernel of Mac OS X contains a packet filter called *ipfw*, which it inherited from FreeBSD. From user-space, this packet filter can be controlled via a command-line tool with the same name. Porting this tool to iOS and creating a graphical user interface for it would result in a solution similar to the solutions on Android. Our investigations show that this approach can not easily be implemented since the iOS kernel currently does not include the *ipfw* functionality. As opposed to Android, compiling a new kernel is not possible since the source code for the XNU kernel used in iOS is not fully available.

3.3 Windows Phone

For Windows Phone, we were unable to find any relevant firewall solutions in the official application distribution platform Windows Phone Marketplace. As with iOS, we therefore turned to unofficial sources that require an unlocked device, the unofficial store called *Bazzar*. However, this store also did not offer any firewall solutions. As with Android and iOS, firewall solutions for unlocked devices should be possible since firewalls for the Windows Phone predecessor Windows Mobile do exist. For unlocked Windows Phone devices, no solutions seem to exist yet. We therefore could not investigate any firewall solutions for Windows Phone.

4 Antivirus Software

Antivirus software is used to detect malware. That this is a non-trivial problem, and was already described in 1985 [22]. Nonetheless, malware detection on desktop platforms has made significant progress since this initial finding.

On mobile platforms, the first malware called *Cabir* was discovered in 2004 on the Symbian OS platform [23]. Since then, malware on mobile platforms has developed from initial attempts, mostly created for fun, to a lucrative business for criminals. This development is analogous to the development of malware on desktop platforms [3], which can be seen from the malware's functionality. An analysis of all known mobile malware between 2004 and 2008 in [24] shows that a large percentage of malware was only manipulating the system for fun and did not include any harmful functionality apart from spreading. An analysis of all known mobile malware between 2009 and 2011 in [3] shows a completely different picture: A large part of malware either collects personal information about the device's user or brings their developers direct financial profit by sending text messages to premium rate phone numbers.

Before we start with the analysis of antivirus software on the different platforms, we will first take a look at how widespread malware on mobile platforms is today. Antivirus software is only useful if there actually is malware to protect against.

According to an analysis performed by the Finnish antivirus software manufacturer F-Secure, 64.8% of all mobile malware discovered in 2011 was targeting the Android platform [25]. For iOS, currently two malware variants, both from 2009, are known. Both target jailbroken phones and exploit a vulnerability when installing an SSH server on the phone after jailbreaking. Neither F-Secure nor we are aware of any malware that targets unmodified iOS devices and we are also not aware of any malware that targets Windows Phone. We suspect the main reason for this situations lies in the way applications are distributed to non modified devices. On iOS and Windows Phone, applications on unmodified devices can only be distributed using the official distribution platforms. These distribution platforms require an application to be reviewed before it can be distributed. On Android, this situation is different: Applications can be installed from untrusted third party sources and applications are not reviewed before they can be distributed through the Google Play Store.

Because of the malware distribution, it currently only makes sense to use antivirus software on the Android platform. This might of course change in the future, so we investigate the possibilities for antivirus software on the iOS and Windows Phone platforms as well.

4.1   Android

For Android, a wealth of antivirus software can be found in the Google Play Store. In order to get a representative sample of currently available antivirus software, we searched the Google Play Store for the keyword *antivirus* and chose the five most popular ones (in terms of user ratings):

- AVG Antivirus Free 2.11.1
- Antivirus Free 1.3.4
- Avast Mobile Security 1.0.2129
- Lookout Security & Antivirus 7.11.1-a7cf123
- Norton Antivirus & Security 2.5.0.398

To determine the functionality of the antivirus software on Android, we first installed them on a device. The first thing we checked was what they scan. We found that they either scan the installed applications or certain writable locations of the filesystem, first and foremost mount points of external media.

Compared to other platforms, the sandbox of Android is relatively liberal when it comes to accessing the filesystem. This and the fact that malware is relatively widespread on Android already can be seen as the reason for the extensive supply of antivirus software. On Android, applications are installed by copying an APK file (a ZIP archive that contains everything that the application requires like Java class files, native libraries and resources) to a certain folder in the filesystem. This folder is usually located under */data/app/*. The APK file is readable for every other application, which makes it possible to scan the APK file contents for malicious behavior. The same holds for reading files on the locations where external media are mounted, usually under */mnt/*.

We investigated the time when scans are performed. Android offers a lot of possibilities and all of these possibilities are used by the investigated scanners. An overview is given in table 1.

Table 1. Different scanning triggers of antivirus software on Android

Trigger	Description
On demand	The user requests the application to perform a scan.
New application is installed	The application is notified by the system when a new application is installed.
New medium is mounted	The application is notified by the system when a new external medium is mounted.
At predefined times	The user specifies a time at which scans are performed regularly.
On access	Applications on Android can register for being able to handle certain filetypes. The application will then be presented as a choice for opening the file when the user opens it. This can be used to scan files before they are opened somewhere else.
Continuously	Continuous scanning is the most battery power intensive method, but can e.g. detect the download of a malicious application and warn before it is installed.

Another interesting characteristic of antivirus software on mobile devices is where they scan for viruses. All the antivirus software that we investigated seem to perform the scanning on the device itself. Another possibility would be to perform scanning by a cloud based service to reduce battery consumption, as already explained in Section 2. We searched the Google Play Store for antivirus software that scan for malware in the cloud. At least two applications can be found that advertise with scanning in the cloud: *Bitdefender Mobile Security* and *SecureBrain Antivirus*.

The last thing we were interested in was what these scanners scan for. In order to find that out, we had to take a closer look at how these applications work. We first looked at the application *Antivirus Free* since it is by far the smallest application. The first step was to analyze which files this applications places in the filesystem. We found that the application installs a SQLite 3 database that contains entries for known viruses. At the time of analysis, this database contained 64 entries. We then took a closer look at how the application deals with this database by decompiling it to Java code as described in Section 3.1. We found that this database is periodically updated via the Internet. Each entry consists of a package name, a name and a description. The package name is enciphered with AES and then encoded using Base64 (see the decompiled code in fig. 2). When the application scans, it compares the package name of the application it currently scans with all the entries in the database. Obviously, this mechanism is not very strong. Only comparing package names makes it very easy for malware authors to evade detection. The only thing they need to do is change the package name of the application. All the application's functionality can remain the same.

```
public static String decrypt(String paramString1, String paramString2)
{
  try
  {
    Key localKey = generateKey(paramString1);
    Cipher localCipher = Cipher.getInstance("AES");
    localCipher.init(2, localKey);
    str = new String(localCipher.doFinal(Base64.decode(paramString2)));
    return str;
  }
  catch (Exception localException)
  {
    while (true)
      String str = null;
  }
}
```

Fig. 2. Package name decipherment method of Antivirus Free

The next application we investigated was *AVG Antivirus Free*. This application stores all detection settings in an XML file, which gives insight into how scanning is performed. Two interesting settings can be found that we suspect to be blacklists of malicious package names and filenames. However, these values are enciphered somehow. The decipherment algorithm was more complicated than for *Antivirus Free*, so we took another approach to decrypt these values. We used a tool called *apktool* to insert some code in the original application to print the deciphered values directly from memory. Our suspicion was correct. The settings contain a list of currently 316 package names that we can relate to known Android malware and a list of currently 42 filenames. Almost all of these filenames are *.exe* or *.bat* files, which are used on Windows, but not on Android. As opposed to Antivirus Free, this application performs the scanning not on the Java level, but using a native library called *libFileScanner.so*. In order to find out more about how this scanning process works, also had to decompile this library. We used the application *IDA* for this task. This investigation shows that the application uses these lists for a comparison when scanning the installed applications and external media. This application therefore only slightly more advanced than Antivirus Free. It not just compares package names. It also scans the filesystem for suspicious files, however, only for some Windows malware. During our investigation, we discovered settings for a so far not implemented feature that seems to indicate that AVG is planning to include heuristic malware detection in their application (see the decompiled code in fig. 3). That this feature is still in an early stage can already be seen from the creative ways, the word heuristic is spelled. Heuristic malware detection is a feature that is commonly found in desktop antivirus software, but we have not found it in any of the investigated scanners.

```
public static boolean getHuristicActiveKey()
{
    return a.getBoolean("hueristic_active", false);
}
```

Fig. 3. Hints of heuristic malware detection in AVG Antivirus Free

The next application that we investigated was *Avast Mobile Security*. The APK file of the application contains another APK file which seem to contain the Java part of the scanning engine and four files, which we suspect to be malware definition files for the ELF (the executable format used for native applications and libraries) and DEX format (the format used for Java class files on Android). The files are in a binary format that we do not understand, so we had to investigate further. The Java scanning engine passes the content of these files to an initialization function of a native library called *libavast-vps.so*, which also comes with the bundled APK file. When the application performs a scan, it can scan installed applications and the memory card. It enumerates the APK files of all non-system applications as well as all files from the memory card. It then reads the content of each file into a buffer and passes it separately from the Java scanning engine to the native library. The scanning function in the native library distinguishes between four filetypes: DEX files, ZIP files, ELF files and the EICAR file, which is a test file that is supposed to be detected by every antivirus software. In case the filetype is a ZIP file (APK files are basically ZIP files), it then extracts all DEX and ELF files and passes their content to the scanning function again. In case a scan of an application and not of a file is performed, the package name of the application is passed to the scan function, which then compares the package name against a black list of four package names that are hard coded in the library. If a scan of a file is performed, its content is scanned. In case of the EICAR file, this is a simple memory comparison with the content of the EICAR test file. If the file type is DEX or ELF, the file is scanned based on the definition files. The exact mechanism was not investigated further. From what we have seen, *Avast Mobile Security* is much more advanced than the previously investigated applications in that it compares actual file content and not just filenames or package names and also extracts archives. It also only scans for files that are relevant to the platform and not for example for Windows malware.

We did not fully investigate the detection mechanism of the other two applications *Norton Antivirus & Security* and *Lookout Security & Antivirus*. However, a quick look at the applications indicates that they use similar mechanisms as *Avast Mobile Security* since they both include files that we suspect to be malware definition files. Future work will be to find out if these applications include methods that we did not find in the investigated applications.

To summarize, we found the following criteria of how antivirus software on Android currently scan for viruses:

– Compare package names with a black list.

- Compare filenames with a black list.
- Compare the content of executable files with malware definition files.

While comparing package names is a detection method that is not found on desktop platforms since package names is a Android specific feature, comparing contents of executable files or simply comparing filenames can also be found on antivirus software on desktop platforms. A detection mechanism that is found on desktop antivirus software is heuristic detection, which does not detect malware by its signature, but by searching for suspicious behavior [26]. Our investigation shows that this is not implemented yet in any of the investigated applications, but at least AVG seems to be working on it.

4.2   iOS

When trying to find antivirus software for iOS, we searched the AppStore for the keyword *antivirus* and *malware* and only found one application that somewhat offers antivirus capabilities: *VirusBarrier 1.3*. We took a closer look at the application by installing it on an iOS device. We found that its functionality is limited. Unlike on Android, scans can not be performed on access or at regular intervals. The application also only supports scanning of files that are transferred between applications using so called file type handlers. This happens for example when the user receives a file via Email and wants to open it in another application. The user is presented with a list of possible applications to choose from that can open the filetype. In order to initiate a scan, the user has to manually select the VirusBarrier application. Since VirusBarrier is very limited in what it can scan on the device, it also offers the possibility to scan files stored on remote servers e.g. using Dropbox or FTP.

Apart from that, VirusBarrier does not scan for threats for iOS, but only for Mac, Windows and Unix malware. This is something that could be improved since there are actually weaknesses in iOS that have been exploited in the past like the *Malformed CFF Vulnerability (CVE-2010-1797)*, which was a vulnerability in the processing of fonts in PDF documents [27] and was used to jailbreak devices. Since there are vulnerabilities that could potentially threaten iOS users, e.g. by sending files via email or spreading them via Dropbox, it would be useful for the application to scan for files trying to exploit these vulnerabilities as well.

The reason for the limitation in scanning options lies in the iOS sandbox. As opposed to Android, access to the filesystem is very limited. To scan all installed applications, an antivirus software is required to be able to read the installation directories of the applications. This is not allowed by the iOS sandbox. It is also not possible to be informed about a new application being installed since iOS does not provide a notification mechanism for newly installed applications. One way to detect malicious applications running on the device would be to see which processes are running on the device. This is possible on iOS using the system call *sysctl*, which is not very well documented.

On a jailbroken device, the situation is different. Applications can access the filesystem with full administrative privileges and without restrictions from a sandbox. We therefore searched the unofficial Cydia store for antivirus software but could not find any application. This might be an indication that antivirus software on iOS is not seen as too relevant yet.

4.3   Windows Phone

When we were searching for antivirus software on the Windows Phone Marketplace and the unofficial Bazzar store, we were again unable to find any relevant solutions. On unmodified Windows Phone devices, access to the filesystem is restricted to an area called *Isolated Storage* and access to files outside this area or even to the installation directory of another application is not possible. There is also no way to get informed about other applications being installed or about running processes. On unlocked devices, where filesystem access beyond the Isolated Storage is possible, antivirus software can be implemented, but this has not been done yet.

That the manufacturers of antivirus software would like to sell antivirus software for Windows Phone, can be seen from the example of AVG. In 2011, the Windows Phone Marketplace briefly contained an application called *AVG Mobilation for Windows Phone 7*. The only way to scan for malware was to scan the media library of a device, which is accessible from a sandboxed application. But since there was no known malware for Windows Phone yet, the application was relatively useless and was therefore pulled from the Marketplace by Microsoft, partly also because of suspicions that the application was sending private information to AVG [28].

5   Conclusion

Compared to desktop platforms, firewalls on mobile platforms are not very sophisticated and widespread. All investigated applications need privileges for implementing firewall functionality that are not present on unmodified devices. Because of the stricter application isolation and security policies on mobile devices, which increase the security of the platform, but also restrict firewall solutions, this situation will not change unless the platform manufacturers are making fundamental changes to the security model of the platform. One such change could be to grant a small selection of trusted applications more extensive permissions than other applications. However, this would most likely make these applications a target for privilege escalation attacks.

The situation for antivirus software is similar. First attempts on iOS and Windows Phone show that the antivirus industry is interested in selling antivirus software for these platforms. However, they are prevented by the security model of the platform from creating a useful solution. Another reason for the absence of serious antivirus software is that there is no known malware on these platforms yet, which makes antivirus software rather useless. This might, however, change in the future. On Android, the situation is different. While there is already quite a lot of known malware, also quite a lot of possibilities to implement antivirus software exist. We see this as the reason for the large pool of antivirus software that is available today. Judging from our investigations, some of this antivirus software is rather trivial to evade, but more complex solutions and cloud scanning indicate that at least some of the antivirus software is approaching the sophistication of antivirus software on desktop platforms.

A summary of the available security add-ons for mobile platforms that have been identified in this paper can be found in table 2 (check marks in brackets mean that the security add-on is only available for jailbroken or rooted devices).

Table 2. Summary of available security add-ons on mobile platforms

	Android	**iOS**	**Windows Phone**
Firewall	(✓)	(✓)	-
Antivirus Software	✓	✓	-

References

1. IDC: Android- and iOS-Powered Smartphones Expand Their Share of the Market in the First Quarter, According to IDC,
   http://www.idc.com/getdoc.jsp?containerId=prUS23503312 (retrieved on: May 26, 2012)
2. NorSIS: Sikre PC-en din,
   http://www.norsis.no/veiledninger/sikre_PCen_din.html (retrieved on: August 07, 2012)
3. Felt, A., Finifter, M., Chin, E., Hanna, S., Wagner, D.: A survey of mobile malware in the wild. In: Proceedings of the 1st ACM Workshop on Security and Privacy in Smartphones and Mobile Devices, pp. 3–14. ACM (2011)
4. AV-TEST – The Independent IT-Security Institute: Test Report: Anti-Malware solutions for Android,
   http://www.av-test.org/fileadmin/pdf/avtest_2012-02_android_anti-malware_report_english.pdf (retrieved on: June 02, 2012)
5. Friedman, J., Hoffman, D.V.: Protecting data on mobile devices: A taxonomy of security threats to mobile computing and review of applicable defenses. Information-Knowledge-Systems Management 7(1,2), 159–180 (2008)
6. Shabtai, A., Fledel, Y., Kanonov, U., Elovici, Y., Dolev, S., Glezer, C.: Google Android: A comprehensive security assessment. IEEE Security & Privacy 8(2), 35–44 (2010)
7. Vidas, T., Votipka, D., Christin, N.: All your droid are belong to us: A survey of current android attacks. In: Proceedings of the 5th USENIX Conference on Offensive Technologies, p. 10. USENIX Association (2011)
8. Oberheide, J., Cooke, E., Jahanian, F.: Cloudav: N-version antivirus in the network cloud. In: Proceedings of the 17th Conference on Security Symposium, pp. 91–106. USENIX Association (2008)
9. Oberheide, J., Veeraraghavan, K., Cooke, E., Flinn, J., Jahanian, F.: Virtualized in-cloud security services for mobile devices. In: Proc. of MobiVirt 2008, pp. 31–35 (June 2008)

10. Portokalidis, G., Homburg, P., Anagnostakis, K., Bos, H.: Paranoid Android: versatile protection for smartphones. In: Proceedings of the 26th Annual Computer Security Applications Conference, pp. 347–356. ACM (2010)
11. Oberheide, J., Jahanian, F.: When mobile is harder than fixed (and vice versa): Demystifying security challenges in mobile environments. In: Proceedings of the Eleventh Workshop on Mobile Computing Systems & Applications, pp. 43–48. ACM (2010)
12. Jacoby, G., Davis, N.: Battery-based intrusion detection. In: IEEE Global Telecommunications Conference, GLOBECOM 2004, vol. 4, pp. 2250–2255. IEEE (2004)
13. Kim, H., Smith, J., Shin, K.: Detecting energy-greedy anomalies and mobile malware variants. In: Proceeding of the 6th International Conference on Mobile Systems, Applications, and Services, pp. 239–252 (2008)
14. Liu, L., Yan, G., Zhang, X., Chen, S.: Virusmeter: Preventing your cellphone from spies. In: Recent Advances in Intrusion Detection, pp. 244–264. Springer (2009)
15. Felt, A., Greenwood, K., Wagner, D.: The effectiveness of application permissions. In: Proceedings of the USENIX Conference on Web Application Development, p. 7 (2011)
16. Batyuk, L., Herpich, M., Camtepe, S., Raddatz, K., Schmidt, A., Albayrak, S.: Using static analysis for automatic assessment and mitigation of unwanted and malicious activities within Android applications. In: 6th International Conference on Malicious and Unwanted Software (MALWARE), pp. 66–72. IEEE (2011)
17. McDermott, P.: Personal firewalls..one more step towards comprehensive security. Network Security 11, 11–14 (2000)
18. Rodrigo: Droidwall homepage, http://code.google.com/p/droidwall/ (retrieved on: May 29, 2012)
19. iptables(8) - iptables man page, https://git.netfilter.org/cgi-bin/gitweb.cgi?p=iptables.git (retrieved on June 02, 2012)
20. Yllier: Firewall IP homepage, http://yllier.webs.com/firewall.html (retrieved on: May 27, 2012)
21. Freeman, J.: MobileSubstrate homepage, http://svn.saurik.com/repos/menes/trunk/mobilesubstrate/ (retrieved on: May 30, 2012)
22. Cohen, F.: Computer Viruses. PhD thesis, University of Southern California (1985)
23. Hypponen, M.: Malware goes mobile. Scientific American 295(5), 70–77 (2006)
24. Schmidt, A., Schmidt, H., Batyuk, L., Clausen, J., Camtepe, S., Albayrak, S., Yildizli, C.: Smartphone malware evolution revisited: Android next target? In: 4th International Conference on Malicious and Unwanted Software (MALWARE), pp. 1–7 (2009)
25. F-Secure Labs. 2012. Mobile Threat Report Q1 2012, http://www.f-secure.com/weblog/archives/MobileThreatReport_Q1_2012.pdf (retrieved on: May 23, 2012)
26. Szor, P.: The Art of Computer Virus Research and Defense. Addison-Wesley Professional (2005)
27. MITRE Corporation: CVE-2010-1797, http://cve.mitre.org/cgi-bin/cvename.cgi?name=CVE-2010-1797 (retrieved on: May 30, 2012)
28. AVG: AVG's response to community feedback regarding our Windows Phone 7 app, http://blogs.avg.com/product-news/avgs-response-community-feedback-windows-phone-7-app/ (retrieved on: May 10, 2012)

THAPS: Automated Vulnerability Scanning of PHP Applications

Torben Jensen, Heine Pedersen, Mads Chr. Olesen, and René Rydhof Hansen

Department of Computer Science, Aalborg University, Denmark
{tjens10,hpede06}@student.aau.dk, {mchro,rrh}@cs.aau.dk

Abstract. In this paper we describe the THAPS vulnerability scanner for PHP web applications. THAPS is based on symbolic execution of PHP with specialised support for scanning extensions and plug-ins of larger application frameworks. We further show how THAPS can integrate the results of dynamic analyses, generated by a customised web crawler, into the static analysis. This enables analysis of often used advanced dynamic features such as dynamic code load and reflection. To the best of our knowledge, THAPS is the first tool to apply this approach and the first tool with specific support for analysis of plug-ins.

In order to verify our approach, we have scanned 375 WordPress plug-ins and a commercial (monolithic) web application, resulting in 68 and 28 confirmed vulnerabilities respectively.

1 Introduction

In this paper we describe the THAPS vulnerability scanner for web applications written in PHP[1], a general-purpose scripting language specifically designed with web development in mind. The language is robust, quite "forgiving", and is available on a wide range of platforms, which makes it easy to get started with and well-suited for rapid prototyping and agile development. It is the language of choice for some of the most successful and well-known web-sites, with Facebook as the most obvious example, as well as for widely used web application frameworks such as Moodle, TYPO3, and WordPress.

Developing *secure* web applications is already notoriously difficult, as witnessed by the CWE top 25 list of vulnerabilities [5]. However, many of the features that make PHP a popular choice for web development, especially among novice programmers, also make it even harder to develop secure applications, e.g. the lack of variable declarations and strong typing. This is further exacerbated by the typical execution model of PHP, where scripts are essentially executed in the context of a web server, making even trivial programming bugs into potentially serious security vulnerabilities.

In the following we describe and discuss a newly developed vulnerability scanner, called THAPS, that automatically scans PHP source code for potential security vulnerabilities. The tool can be applied throughout the development of

---

[1] http://php.net

A. Jøsang and B. Carlsson (Eds.): NordSec 2012, LNCS 7617, pp. 31–46, 2012.
© Springer-Verlag Berlin Heidelberg 2012

an application and allows a developer to fix such bugs before the application is
widely deployed.

THAPS is based on symbolic execution of PHP code. This enables the scanner
to produce both precise and comprehensive vulnerability reports while retaining
a relatively low rate of false positives. We believe this is an important trait in
order to make the tool useful for a wide range of developers with particular
emphasis on novice PHP programmers.

As mentioned above, a number of very popular web application frameworks
are implemented in PHP, e.g., Moodle, TYPO3, and WordPress. Advanced
frameworks like these are often designed around a (relatively) simple core whose
functionality can be extended with plug-ins and/or extensions. Such an architecture can be quite problematic for a vulnerability scanner to handle since the
core in such a framework typically makes heavy use of dynamic code loading,
introspection, and reflection; all language features that are notoriosly hard to
analyse statically. Furthermore, the individual extensions and plug-ins are often
also hard to analyse statically, since they are likely to depend on functionality
provided by the core.

To overcome these problems, THAPS implements specialised support for scanning extensions and plug-ins of larger application frameworks, through so-called
framework models, as well as integration with dynamic analysis and a web crawler
in order to facilitate analysis of advanced dynamic features of PHP, such as dynamic code load and reflection. To the best of our knowledge, THAPS is the first
tool to implement this approach and to provide specific support for analysing
plug-ins.

The remainder of the paper is structured as follows: In Section 2 we first give
an overview of the general problem of writing secure PHP web applications and
scanning for vulnerabilities in such applications. Section 3 discusses the fundamental symbolic execution engine of our THAPS tool as well as the specialised
support for analysing plug-ins (Section 3.2). Integration with dynamic analysis
and a customised web crawler is discussed in Section 4 while our tool is applied
to real-world code and evaluated in Section 5. Sections 6 and 7 conclude with
related work, conclusions, and future work.

2   Scanning for Security Vulnerabilities in PHP Code

In this section we briefly describe two of the most common security vulnerabilities found in web applications, SQL injection and cross site scripting (XSS), and
further discuss some of the typical problems and challenges inherent in scanning
PHP code, e.g., the use of dynamic code inclusion, and plug-in based application frameworks. In Section 3 we discuss how THAPS can be used to find such
vulnerabilities.

We have chosen to focus on SQL injection and XSS vulnerabilities in this
paper for two reasons: they are very dangerous and commonly found in web
applications. That they are dangerous is evidenced by the fact that they are
ranked number one and four respectively on the CWE/SANS "Top 25 Most

Dangerous Software Errors" list [5]. Here "dangerous" is taken to mean that the error will "frequently allow attackers to completely take over the software, steal data, or prevent the software from working at all". Since 25.7% vulnerabilities in the Common Vulnerabilities and Exposures[2] (CVE) database were classified as either SQL injections or XSS (as of April 24th 2012), it is clear that these vulnerabilities are commonly found in web applications.

Briefly, an SQL injection makes it possible to rewrite a database query made from a web application to a database, which could give rise to unexpected behavior and result in either data loss or bypassing security restrictions, e.g., by leaking user names and concomitant passwords. In comparison, an XSS vulnerability allows attackers to inject malicious code into the client part of the application and thereby change the behaviour of the client-side, potentially leaking authorisation and/or private information.

As mentioned in the introduction, THAPS is a symbolic execution engine that finds (potential) bugs essentially by simulating the execution of an application along all possible code paths and tracking whether any data from an untrusted *source*, i.e., any input to the application (typically controlled by the user or environment), can flow into a *sink*, i.e., code that uses said data, e.g., for output or as arguments in API calls. This approach is inspired by two well-known techniques: *taint tracking* [9][7], based on run-time monitoring, and *taint analysis* [1,4], based on static analysis, that have both been applied successfully to protect web applications against attacks such as SQL injection and XSS.

2.1 Dynamic Code Inclusion and Reflection in PHP

The main challenge in developing a PHP scanner is that the PHP language contains features that are well-known to be difficult to analyse statically, e.g., dynamic code inclusion and introspection/reflection. Below we illustrate the issues with PHP code examples. The first example shows a common idiom for including another file, at run-time, into the currently executing file:

```
1  include "pages/". $_GET["page"] .".php";
```

The intention with the above code is to include a page located in the **pages/** subfolder, which is determined by the query string sent to the server which, in this case, is stored in the $_GET["page"] variable. This construction trivially leads to a vulnerable web application, since an attacker could easily include files other than the intended by (manually) manipulating the **page** part of the query. Including other files (both at run-time and at compile time) is a commonly used strategy for making the development of PHP applications more modular.

The following example illustrates the use of reflection to let user input directly determine what function is called:

```
1  $func = "ajax_" . $_GET["action"];
2  $func("argument"); // or call_user_func($func, "argument");
```

---

[2] http://cve.mitre.org

A similar technique is used in WordPress to implement an event system which WordPress plug-ins (used to extend the WordPress core functionality) can use to register call-back function and to handle various AJAX calls. The problem with these call-back function is that static analysis cannot determine which function is actually called and hence it cannot perform a safe and precise analysis.

The third and final example, shown below, is an implementation of the register_globals feature of PHP which is used to initialise the environment with variables containing user input:

```
1  foreach (array_merge($_POST,$_GET) as $key => $value) {
2      $$key = $value;
3  }
```

This feature has been deactivated by default in recent versions of PHP. However, an old version[3] of Moodle implements functionality that can emulate the register_globals feature. This functionality takes each POST and GET key-/value pair and makes a variable with the name of the key and assigns the corresponding value to it. An example would be a request with ?a=value&b=other added to the query string, which would assign "value" to the $a variable and "other" to the $b variable. If the register_globals feature is enabled, a sound analysis has to assume the value is tainted, i.e., potentially contains dangerous or unsanitised user input, if it has not been encountered before in the analysis. The difference between the register_globals feature and this Moodle functionality is that the latter can be placed anywhere in the file and from that point the analysis has to ignore all previous assumptions about the involved variables.

2.2   Application Framework Plug-Ins

In addition to the challenges presented by the dynamic language features of PHP, discussed in the previous section, there are also challenges specific to scanning large applications such as the generic application frameworks that are often used in web development. We will briefly discuss these in the following.

Large systems like WordPress, TYPO3, and Moodle allow third party developers and users to extend the functionality of the system through a plug-in architecture, often realised through deep and ubiquitous use of the (problematic) dynamic language features discussed in the previous section. Since core application functionality is often provided only through plug-ins, potentially developed by external (untrusted) third parties, it is important that a vulnerability scanner can reliably scan external extensions and plug-ins.

In previous work [8] we tested a number of existing vulnerability scanners to see if and how well they could be used to scan plug-ins and identify vulnerabilities. In summary, the results showed that the tested tools would either attempt to analyse not only the plug-in itself, but also the underlying core framework and then mostly fail due the the size of the combined system; or perform an analysis

---

[3] Moodle v. 1.6.2 (released in September 2006) in lib/setup.php

of only the plug-in but generate imprecise results, both missing real vulnerabilities (false negatives) and reporting non-vulnerabilities (false positives), since key functionality and assumptions/guarantees provided by the underlying core was missing in the scanner.

As an example the WordPress core code base is very large: In version 3.2.1, with no plug-ins activated, 13.918 built-in and six user defined functions[4] are called just for rendering the front page. Even with a dynamic analysis the results are likely to be overly imprecise. With the assumption that the core system is safe, the developers of plug-ins and extensions only have to check their own work. This, however, can be a difficult task as the extensions might use functionality provided by the platform and hence the analysis needs to know about this in order to identify vulnerabilities caused by the platform.

3   Symbolic Execution and Vulnerability Scanning

In the following we give an overview of the THAPS vulnerability scanner and discuss how it can be used to scan for vulnerabilities as well as some of the design and implementation issues encountered.

3.1   Symbolic Execution

THAPS is fundamentally a taint analysis based on symbolic execution of PHP. It is in the symbolic execution engine that vulnerabilities are detected and where reports are generated, containing details of each (potential) vulnerability. In essence, symbolic execution simulates all the possible execution paths in the application. To identify vulnerabilities, the taint analysis identifies where user input is able to enter the application, called a *source*, and how it is propagated through the application. If the *tainted data* reaches critical points of the application where it is able to alter the outcome of the application it has reached a *sink*. Every time tainted data reaches a sink without being properly sanitised first, a vulnerability is reported. Sanitisation is a process in the application where the data is secured in such way that it cannot change the outcome unexpectedly.

The symbolic execution is performed by traversing the abstract syntax tree (AST) of the target application and simulating the effect of executing the code contained in a tree node (see below). The AST is generated by the PHP-Parser[5] library which also provides functionality to traverse and manipulate the generated tree structure.

To simulate all the possible outcomes the analysis might need to store several (many) values for the same variable because of assignments inside different code branches. Whenever there are multiple values, the simulation has to be performed on each of these. We store the values in a *variable storage*, which also records what branch of the code the value belongs to. Figure 1 shows how the storage structure would look like after an analysis of the following code:

---

[4] Functions that allow users to configure and customise their WordPress installation.
[5] https://github.com/nikic/PHP-Parser

```
1   if ($a==0) {
2      if ($b==1) { .. }
3      else { .. }
4   }
5   elseif ($b==0) { .. }
6   else { .. }
7   if ($c) {
8      $ui = $_POST["a"];
9   } else {
10     $ui = "test";
11  }
12  echo $ui;
```

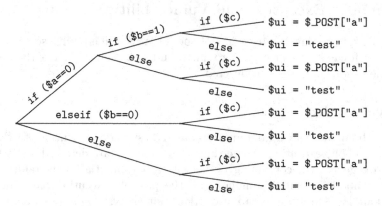

Fig. 1. Example of variable storage layout

The analysis has been divided into the following steps:

Body analysis where the global scope and the bodies of methods and functions are analysed. The statements in the program are divided into three groups: control structures, assignments, and the rest.

The control structures include statements where the control branches based on a condition. Whenever such a statement is reached, the corresponding branches are recorded in the variable storage (see above) and the conditions leading to a given branch are added to a dependency stack and removed again once the branch has been analysed in this new, extended context.

Assignment statements update the knowledge about variables in the variable storage by traversing the right hand side of the assignment and adding the result to the variable storage.

Pattern Detection where certain idioms, or programming patterns, that must be handled in a special way are recognised and processed. These patterns are an easy and useful way to configure and adapt THAPS to the programming style of a particular application or project.

This has proven particularly useful for recognising application specific methods for sanitising input and thereby reducing the false positive count. As an example, consider the following code snippet that shows an example of avoiding SQL injection by escaping all GET and POST values in the beginning of the application:

```
1  foreach ($_GET as $k => $v) {
2    $_GET[$k] = mysql_real_escape_string($v);
3  }
```

The above snippet could result in a (false positive) report if not handled specifically, because the number of user input variables is unknown and hence they would not be sanitised. When the pattern is recognised the analysis from this point on returns sanitised values if they are unknown in the variable storage.

The implementation is generalised so it is able to identify which variables that are sanitised and to which context the variables are sanitised, that is XSS or SQL injections.

A further use of pattern detection is to support *prepared statements*, another technique to prevent SQL injection, and thereby reduce false positives in applications using these.

Class processing where classes are analysed. The result of the analysis is a description of the class members and methods which is used when running the body analysis. The description tells if a method is potentially vulnerable.

The analysis of the methods is a body analysis (see above) with initial knowledge of tainted data in class members and parameters of the methods, and the **return** node will also create vulnerabilities as returned values has to be tracked as well.

When the analysis of a method is finished any potential vulnerabilities are further analysed in order to determine the source of the vulnerability. Here the source means the origin of the user input, so if the flow path of a vulnerability originates from a parameter, that vulnerability is grouped as a "parameter vulnerable" (see below). A vulnerability can be added to multiple groups:

Always vulnerable: vulnerabilities that are valid as soon as the method is called, the source is within the method.

Parameter vulnerable: vulnerabilities that are present if the source is a parameter.

Property vulnerable: vulnerabilities that are present if the source is a property (of a class).

Return always/parameter/property: is where the method could return tainted data which is considered a return vulnerability allowing for determining if the data is tainted.

Property vulnerable parameter/property: not really vulnerabilities, but needed to describe if tainted data is transferred to an object's properties by the method.

Global vulnerable: also not really vulnerabilities, but needed for the **global** keyword, simulating side effects of global variables.

Function processing where functions are analysed in the same way as methods are analysed in the class processing step (see above). It finds all functions (except built-in functions), makes an analysis of them, and stores a description of the functions similar to the one for methods from the class processing. The difference is that the descriptions only contain the *Always vulnerable, Parameter vulnerable, Return always/parameter,* and *Global vulnerable* information as functions do not relate to classes and hence do not have members to consider.

Inclusion resolving where the AST nodes representing file inclusion, i.e., an `include` statement, are replaced with the AST generated from the included file. This step will attempt to resolve which files are included at that exact point. It is however limited to simple inclusion, i.e., inclusion where the file is identified in the same line as the inclusion (see the code snippet below).

File inclusion based on run-time values, called dynamic inclusion (see code snippet below for an example), is not supported in the symbolic execution engine, since it is very imprecise at best and impossible at worst (as it may even depend on code not present during analysis). Instead, information about dynamic file inclusion may be collected during the dynamic analysis phase of THAPS and then used in the symbolic execution to resolve (some) of the dynamic file inclusions. The dynamic analysis is described in more detail in Section 4.

```
1  // Supported
2  include "file.php";
3  include CONSTANT_DIR."file.php";
4
5  // Unsupported
6  include $file;
7  include $file.".php";
```

We do not go into further details with the symbolic execution engine here, instead we refer to the full report [3].

3.2   Framework Models

As discussed in Section 2.2, in order for a vulnerability scanner to work well on extensions and plug-ins for application frameworks, it is necessary for the scanner to have at least some information about the structure and workings of the underlying framework. This includes APIs, protocols for plug-ins, functionality provided by the framework etc.

As an example of the latter, functionality provided by the application framework, we consider the database wrapper provided by WordPress, which allows the developers to access the database without knowing about the credentials and authorisation. The wrapper is instantiated by the core of WordPress and then used by extensions. To avoid analysing both the plug-in, the wrapper, and the core for each identified use of the wrapper functionality, we designed and

implemented the notion of *framework models* in THAPS. A framework model
can be seen as a template, or skeleton program, that superficially implements
core APIs and functionality from the application framework. THAPS can then
use these models as basis for analysing a plug-in in a more meaningful context.
This not only increases the precision of the analysis, but is essential for analysis
of plug-ins. Below we show a model of the database wrapper in WordPress:

```
1    class WPDB {
2        public function prepare($arg) { return $arg; }
3        public function get_results($arg) { mysql_query($arg); }
4        public function get_row($arg) { mysql_query($arg); }
5        public function get_col($arg) { mysql_query($arg); }
6        public function get_var($arg) { mysql_query($arg); }
7        public function escape($arg) { return
             mysql_real_escape_string($arg); }
8    }
9    $wpdb = new WPDB();
10   function esc_attr($a) { return htmlentities($a); }
11   foreach ($_POST as $key => $val) { $_POST[$key] =
          mysql_real_escape_string($val); }
12   foreach ($_GET as $key => $val) { $_GET[$key] =
          mysql_real_escape_string($val); }
13   foreach ($_REQUEST as $key => $val) { $_REQUEST[$key] =
          mysql_real_escape_string($val); }
```

When a plug-in is analysed the model is loaded and analysed before the actual
analysis and the gathered information is used during the analysis of the plug-in.

Knowing about the platform provided functionality is, however, not enough to
perform an analysis. Some platforms allow the extensions to have multiple entry
points and hence the analysis needs to analyse all of these. One way the plug-ins
are executed, besides being used as an entry point directly, is by registering its
own (call-back) functions to either events/actions (used by WordPress) or hooks
(used by TYPO3). This way a function will be called when this event is triggered
by the core system. The function call addAction("event","functionName")
from WordPress triggers the function functionName when event happens and
hence the model analysis has to emulate these events. This has been accomplished by allowing the model developer to specify function names that attaches
events and which argument that identifies the method.

It is, in general, hard to estimate the effort required to implement a model
from scratch, e.g., for a new system or framework, since the development time
depends on many factors such as the complexity of the system, how familiar the
developer is with the system, and how precise the model has to be. However, in
our experience a useful first version of a model can be developed within days if
not hours. As an example, the first version of the above model for WordPress
was developed in less than a day. Furthermore, models can be developed incre-
mentally, adding new API calls or events only as needed, e.g., when the false
positive rate for a particular system becomes too high.

4   Dynamic Analysis and Web Crawling

To overcome some of the uncertainties of the static analysis that reduce the
usefulness of the tool, especially dynamic file inclusion and the use of reflection,
we have integrated a dynamic analysis phase in THAPS that can be configured
to monitor specific dynamic elements. In this section we illustrate the kinds of
problems dynamic analysis can help solve and discuss how the dynamic analysis
works.

The first problem involves dynamic file inclusion. As discussed in a previous
section, file inclusion determined by user input is a typical pattern found in PHP
applications and, in particular, in application frameworks. Tutorials and forum
posts regarding the pattern are easily found on the Internet[6],[7]. An example of
this pattern is shown below, which illustrates how an input string from the user
is used to directly determine which file to include:

```
1  $page = $_GET["page"];
2  if (preg_match("#[a-z0-9]+#i", $page)) {
3      include "pages/" . $page . ".php";
4  }
```

The regular expression (line 2 above) ensures that input with special characters
is disallowed, preventing an attacker from navigating the file tree. Since the
user input is only available when the application is actually executing, the static
analysis cannot possibly determine which file is included and thus cannot perform
a sound analysis. In contrast, the dynamic analysis is able to determine (by
straightforward run-time monitoring) the exact set of files included during *one
particular* execution run of the target application.

A similar, but slightly different, problem is that some application architectures
make it difficult to analyse only a part of the application, e.g. where user input
is used to determine which files to include. This approach is shown below. Note
that the user input is only used to determine the branch of the switch and not
the file to include:

```
1  switch($_GET["page"]) {
2    case "products":
3      include "products.php";
4      break;
5    case "contact":
6      include "contact.php";
7      break;
8    case "about":
9      include "about.php";
10     break;
11 }
```

---

[6] http://www.digital-web.com/articles/easypeasy_php/
[7] http://www.codingforums.com/showthread.php?t=85482

This has the disadvantage for a pure static analysis that the number of execution paths in the symbolic execution can get very large, and thus take very long time to scan. Dynamic analysis can reduce the number of included files, as, in the case above, only one of the files will be included for each scan.

A somewhat different problem, albeit with some of the same fundamental characteristics as the above file inclusions, is the use of reflection to perform function calls. Again, where the static analysis cannot determine which function is called and hence fails to do a correct analysis (or results in massive over-approximation), the dynamic analysis can trivially extract such information at run-time. This is illustrated by the code snippet below that static analysis would fail to analyse correctly:

```
1  $func = "ajax_".$_GET["action"];
2  $func();
```

Static analysis would be able to determine that the function call is to a function whose name starts with "ajax_", but if the application has more than one function with that prefix it cannot tell which one. Again the dynamic analysis is able to determine which function is actually called and collect this data for use in the static analysis.

4.1   Implementation of Dynamic Analysis

To gather the required data during execution we have written an extension for the Zend[8] Engine. The Zend Engine is the run-time system underlying and executing PHP applications: after PHP source code is first parsed, it is converted into opcodes, that are then interpreted by the Zend Engine. The engine allows extension developers to hook into the execution of opcodes and, e.g., run a specified function when a given opcode is encountered.

Our extension works by first establishing a connection to a running MongoDB[9] database and generating a unique id to identify the current analysis run. We then add opcode hooks on function calls and "include/eval opcodes" for each request and record function calls and which files are included. This information is stored in the MongoDB database, under the unique id of the current analysis run.

When the analysed web application returns a response, through the web server that controls it, our Zend extension ensures that the unique analysis id is included in the response to indicate where the run-time information is stored in the database. This information is used by the static tool, so it initially can fetch the required information to make a complete scan on the basis of information found by the PHP extension.

Once the dynamic analysis is done, the static analysis is performed with this additional information, as shown in Figure 2. The collected information is used to analyse a specific branch of file inclusions and dynamic function invocations. However, the static analysis will still consider all branches in if and switches.

---

[8] www.zend.com
[9] www.mongodb.org

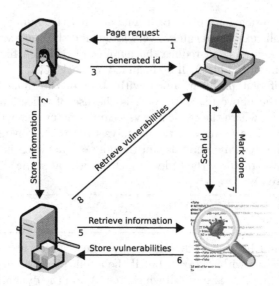

Fig. 2. Overview of the interaction between the dynamic analysis, and subsequent static analysis

In the next section we discuss how a *web crawler* can be used to automate the process of generating requests to, and responses from, the web application under analysis in order to generate enough information for the dynamic analysis to be useful.

4.2 Crawling a Site

The task of performing a request to a page, collecting the analysis id from the header information, and running the static analysis with the collected id easily becomes a tedious task if the site has many pages. We have automated this process by developing a *web crawler*.

To perform a crawl only a few inputs are required: the URL of the site on a web server with our Zend extension installed, the path to the source code, and an optional cookie that provides authentication on the site. During the crawl any vulnerabilities identified, will be displayed immediately.

Instead of developing a crawler from scratch, we have chosen to extend Crawler4j[10] as it is an open source, multi-threaded, cross platform crawler that is simple to use and extend. Crawler4j consists of two parts: a controller to setup how the crawler should behave, and the actual crawler which should be extended to add custom functionality, such as what should happen when the crawler successfully have visited a page. Although Crawler4j is a comprehensive and working crawler, it was necessary to modify it in order to support and provide access to the special cookies and analysis id's generated by THAPS.

---

[10] http://code.google.com/p/crawler4j/

With the provided information the crawler analyses the applications in two ways: from the web application where it extracts all the links from the pages and follows them as long they are not to an external site, and by accessing the files found in the application's file system directory directly.

The first approach tests the application the way the developer intended the site to be used, and the second reveals vulnerabilities in unintended accessible files, files that are secure when included, but not when accessed directly, and other unintended uses of the application. Combining these two approaches gives a more complete crawl of the entire web application.

5   Results

In order to examine and verify the effectiveness of THAPS, we have tested it against a number of WordPress plug-ins (to test the Framework Models discussed in Section 3.2) and against a commercial web-application, developed by a newly established company that wishes to remain anonymous (to test the integration of the dynamic analysis and to test how the tool handles a large real-world monolithic application). In the following we shall refer to this application as "System S".

WordPress. WordPress was chosen because it is one of the most popular and widely used CMSs[11]. Furthermore, the WordPress web site hosts almost 20.000 different plug-ins, with some of the most popular plug-ins having been downloaded more than 10 million times[12]. Hence, a vulnerability found in any one of these can have widespread consequences.

Our test was conducted by analysing the 300 most popular (according to the ranking on the WordPress web-site) plug-ins along with 75 arbitrarily chosen plug-ins. In total THAPS reported 273 vulnerabilities in 29 plug-ins. Of these, 68 were confirmed by manually making exploits for at least one vulnerability for each file in each plug-in, and acknowledged by the WordPress security team[13].

The results are summarised in Table 1. As shown, THAPS identified both XSS and SQL injection vulnerabilities, with a modest rate of false positives. The model approach allowed us to analyse the plug-ins separately, without having to re-analyse the entire core WordPress codebase — something which no tool we know of can currently do.

Most of the false positives are due to one of two things: The first cause of false positives is missing analysis of the behavior of built-in functions. Currently only a small subset has been implemented based on functions used in the scanned modules and functions used in known vulnerabilities. The second source of false positives is when a potential vulnerability is prevented by a "coincidence", i.e., when one SQL statement selects rows based on the input which cannot be exploited, and if this select returns rows there is a vulnerability based on the same input.

---

[11] http://w3techs.com/technologies/overview/content_management/all
[12] http://wordpress.org/extend/plugins/
[13] See http://packetstormsecurity.org/files/authors/9770 for a full list

Table 1. Scan results for WordPress extensions

Type	Found	Confirmed	Potential ①	FP	Unresolved ②
XSS	249	63	130	41	15
SQL injection	24	5	13	3	3
Total	**273**	**68**	**143**	**44**	**18**

① = The number of reported vulnerabilities that have not been examined.

② = Reported vulnerabilities that could be exploitable, but we were unable to confirm it with a reasonable exploit.

FP= False positives.

Table 2. Scan results for "System S"

Type	Found	Confirmed	False Positives
XSS	7	7	0
SQL injection	25	21	4
Total	**32**	**28**	**4**

Although the theoretical time-complexity of symbolic execution as implemented by THAPS is at least exponential in the size of the program, most of the plug-ins were analysed in a less than a minute, a few taking up to 20 minutes. In addition a few failed to complete within one hour at which point the analysis was cancelled.

"System S". For testing the dynamic analysis parts of THAPS, "System S" was chosen because it is a large, monolithic, real-world web application that has few entry points. Due to the size and structure of "System S", THAPS is unable to analyse it purely by symbolic execution. Instead dynamic analysis is performed (as described in Section 4) and the information gathered by the dynamic analysis is then used to guide the static analysis and avoid unused code paths.

The results of analysing "System S" are summarised in Table 2. As shown in the table, THAPS found 32 vulnerabilities in total, of which we confirmed 28 by generating exploits manually as well as confirming the vulnerabilities with the developers of "System S". Four of the reported vulnerabilities were unexploitable and thus marked as false positives. It follows from the results that the biggest problem in "System S" is to prevent attackers from performing SQL injection on the site. The system contains a lot of users but sign up is not open for public. Each user is a member of a group and some of the confirmed exploits only work when the user is a member of a certain group. Even though a valid user login is required to exploit some of the vulnerabilities, it was still possible to perform SQL injection on some of the publicly available pages.

6   Related Work

In this section we briefly survey related work, focusing on tools that are either static scanners or dynamic monitoring. In our previous work [8], we have performed a more comprehensive study and comparison of such tools. The results of this study have been used to guide the design and feature set of THAPS.

WebSSARI (now commercialised as CodeSecure) is able to perform a static analysis based on a tainting analysis [2]. The approach analyses a control flow graph generated from an abstract syntax tree and determines whether any path contains a source and a vulnerable sink without a proper sanitisation between. WebSSARI combines traditional secure information flow analysis with run-time monitoring into a sound analysis of web applications.

Xie and Aiken [10] presents an algorithm to improve the handling of dynamic features of PHP as well as large application during a static analysis. The algorithm uses symbolic execution on function bodies and keep descriptions of these parts for use when the functions are called. This technique is complementary to our approach and would likely enable THAPS to analyse bigger systems.

PHP Taint[14] is an implementation of dynamic taint analysis. It alters the Zend scripting engine to add additional information about all variables, and check this information when vulnerable functions are called. The current implementation lacks support for several language features and custom sanitisation like regular expressions, however, it allows for high precision detection of vulnerabilities.

RIPS[15] is one of the newest tools available. It analyses the code by performing taint analysis on a list of tokens generated by the built-in PHP tokeniser. RIPS is fast, but lacks precision in the analysis resulting in false positives, and support for object oriented code which limits the amount of applications it can analyse.

Fuzzing has proven to be an efficient technique to identify vulnerabilities in applications [6]. Wapiti[16] is a fuzzer targeted web applications combined with a database of known vulnerabilities. By combining these two methods Wapiti is able to find new vulnerabilities and ensure old ones have not been reproduced.

PHP Vulnerability Hunter[17] is another tool based on whitebox fuzzing and dynamic analysis that uses code instrumentation for better precision and coverage.

7   Conclusion

We have presented the THAPS vulnerability scanner for web applications implemented in PHP. We have shown how symbolic execution of PHP can be extended with two novel approaches: *framework models* and integration with *dynamic analysis*. The former allows tools to scan individual plug-ins or extensions, separately from the (large) underlying core framework, and the latter enabling analysis of advanced dynamic features, such as dynamic code load and reflection. To the best of our knowledge, THAPS is the first tool to implement and combine these techniques in one tool.

The general approach of THAPS was validated by analysing 375 WordPress plug-ins and a (monolithic) commercial web application, resulting in 96 confirmed vulnerabilities in total.

---

[14] https://wiki.php.net/rfc/taint
[15] http://sourceforge.net/projects/rips-scanner/
[16] http://www.ict-romulus.eu/web/wapiti/home
[17] http://www.autosectools.com/PHP-Vulnerability-Scanner

The main strands of future work currently pursued are: further experimentation/validation, improving the memory management of the symbolic execution, and automatically generating exploits.

References

1. Ashcraft, K., Engler, D.R.: Using programmer-written compiler extensions to catch security holes. In: Proc. IEEE Symposium on Security and Privacy (S&P 2002), pp. 143–159 (2002)
2. Huang, Y.-W., Yu, F., Hang, C., Tsai, C.-H., Lee, D.-T., Kuo, S.-Y.: Securing web application code by static analysis and runtime protection. In: Proceedings of the 13th International Conference on World Wide Web (WWW 2004), pp. 40–52 (2004)
3. Jensen, T., Pedersen, H.: THAPS—Analysis of PHP web applications. Master's thesis, Department of Computer Science, Aalborg University, Denmark (2012), http://plazm.dk/THAPS%20-%20detection%20of%20web%20application%20vulnerabilities.pdf
4. Benjamin Livshits, V., Lam, M.S.: Finding security vulnerabilities in Java applications with static analysis. In: Proceedings of the 14th USENIX Security Symposium. USENIX (2005)
5. Martin, B., Browne, M., Paller, A., Kirby, D.: 2011 CWE/SANS top 25 most dangerous software errors (September 2011), http://cwe.mitre.org/top25/index.html (last accessed June 10, 2012)
6. Miller, B.P., Fredrikson, L., So, B.: An empirical study of the reliability of unix utilities. Comm. of the ACM 33(12), 32 (1990)
7. Newsome, J., Song, D.X.: Dynamic taint analysis for automatic detection, analysis, and signature generation of exploits on commodity software. In: Proceedings of the Network and Distributed System Security Symposium, NDSS 2005 (2005)
8. Pedersen, H., Jensen, T.: A study of web application vulnerabilities and vulnerability detection tools. Project report (sw9), Department of Computer Science, Aalborg University (2011), http://plazm.dk/A%20study%20of%20web%20application%20vulnerabilities%20and%20vulnerability%20detection%20tools.pdf
9. Schwartz, E.J., Avgerinos, T., Brumley, D.: All you ever wanted to know about dynamic taint analysis and forward symbolic execution (but might have been afraid to ask). In: Proc. IEEE Symposium on Security and Privacy (S&P 2010), pp. 317–331 (2010)
10. Xie, Y., Aiken, A.: Static detection of security vulnerabilities in scripting languages. In: Proceedings of the 15th USENIX Security Symposium. USENIX (August 2006)

Cyber Security Exercises and Competitions as a Platform for Cyber Security Experiments

Teodor Sommestad and Jonas Hallberg

Swedish Defence Research Agency, Linköping, Sweden
{Teodor.Sommestad,Jonas.Hallberg}@foi.se

Abstract. This paper discusses the use of cyber security exercises and competitions to produce data valuable for security research. Cyber security exercises and competitions are primarily arranged to train participants and/or to offer competence contests for those with a profound interest in security. This paper discusses how exercises and competitions can be used as a basis for experimentation in the security field. The conjecture is that (1) they make it possible to control a number of variables of relevance to security and (2) the results can be used to study several topics in the security field in a meaningful way. Among other things, they can be used to validate security metrics and to assess the impact of different protective measures on the security of a system.

Keywords: research method, data collection, security competitions, security exercises.

1 Introduction

Cyber security is an important topic and a lively research area. A plethora of frameworks, methods, tools, and principles can be found in literature. However, few of these have been formally or empirically validated. Verenedel's [1] review of security metrics illustrates the lack of empirical basis underlying theories used in the security field. Of the 90 papers reviewed, a minority attempted to empirically validate the metrics or measurement method proposed, and these tests are often limited to a comparison to the beliefs of a group of experts. One reason for the scarcity of empirical testing is the difficulty to acquire relevant data.

There are several reasons for the lack of empirical data. Data related to security (e.g., incidents and security mechanisms used) are sensitive and often treated as confidential by organizations [2, 3]. This naturally limits the availability of relevant data for research in the field. Several analyses have been made of the information sharing issue [4, 5] and actors such as national Computer Emergency Response Teams have taken on a role as information mediators. However, information and data on security from operational environments is still unavailable to the public and the research community as a whole. Also, if actual incident data would become publicly available for a representative sample of organizations, it could be difficult to draw general conclusions from it. For example, if organizations would report their security

A. Jøsang and B. Carlsson (Eds.): NordSec 2012, LNCS 7617, pp. 47–60, 2012.
© Springer-Verlag Berlin Heidelberg 2012

solutions and the incidents they have experienced, this data would probably be biased because of the incidents they have failed to detect (e.g., cases when confidential data is read by unauthorized persons).

Although the lack of empirical data makes it difficult to study the security of operational systems, there are examples of studies that explore the strength of security measures using experiments or simulations. These include studies of protection against memory corruption exploits (e.g. [6, 7]), studies of denial-of-service attacks (e.g. [8]) and studies of the detection capabilities of intrusion detection systems (e.g. [9]). While these studies (and others not mentioned here) are able to quantify aspects related to security, the results lack properties necessary to make them a good support for decision makers in an operational scenario. In particular, they do not state how well different solutions work in practice when they are exposed to representative attackers. With few exceptions, quantitative security studies are made in settings with predefined attacks whose validity, considering operational scenarios, is unclear. For instance, the tests made in [6, 7] show how well different measures respond to a number of different attacks, but they do not show which of these attacks that will occur in practice when the system is attacked by intelligent adversaries.

This paper discusses the use of security competitions and security exercises (henceforth collectively referred to as security competitions) as a platform to obtain knowledge in the security field. Security competitions involve real attackers and, possibly, defenders drawn from a population chosen by the arranger of the competition and they are executed in an environment designed and implemented by the arranger. Additionally, competitions make it possible to specify goals for the attackers and the defenders. Their potential as a tool for education has been described in [10, 11] and lessons learned when using competitions as a tool in education can be found in [12]. This paper argues that competitions are usable as a tool for studying several attributes related to realistic attackers, realistic defenders, and realistic security processes.

The contribution of this paper is an analysis of the possibility to use security competitions as a platform for experimentation in the cyber security field. The paper describes typical arrangements in security competitions, suggests fields which could be further explored through competitions and presents examples of experiments that have been performed in similar arrangements. Its outline is as follows. Section 2 goes through the typical setup of security competitions and how this relates to experiments. Section 3 presents a non-exhaustive list of topics that would be possible to study through cyber security competitions, and relates previous work to these. In section 4, the overall idea is discussed. In section 5, the paper is concluded.

2   Security Competitions

Security competitions can take many forms. Examples include: iCTF [13], CSAW's Cyber Security Competition [14], Cyber Security Challenge [15], and the National Collegiate Cyber Defense Competition [16]. Variation exists between them when it comes to the actors involved, the environments used, and the incentives created for the actors. This section provides an overview of common components in competition design and how the design of a competition relates to the design of an experiment.

2.1   The Actors and Teams

Security competitions will involve a number of actors that participate in and manage the competition. The designer of a competition must determine to what extent the competition should be defense-oriented and to what extent it should be offense-oriented [17]. In a defense-oriented competition the focus is to practice methods that can be used to defend a system against cyber attacks; in an offense-oriented competition the aim is to carry out attacks. A defense-oriented setup will involve one or several teams that defend systems against attacks; an offence-oriented setup will involve one or several teams set out to carry out attacks. Defensive teams are often called blue teams and offensive teams are often called red teams. Mixed approaches involving both active blue teams and active red teams are also possible, i.e., where the red teams attack the blue teams' systems or all teams attack each other. The members of the teams involved in the competition are referred to as the *participants* of the competition.

When a competition is designed the orientation of the competition can be controlled and participants of a certain *competence* can be selected. To some extent, the arranger of a competition can also influence the *organization* of the teams involved, for example, by assigning roles and responsibilities to the participants.

The participants of the red and blue teams are the active actors of the competition. Two other types of actors are frequently involved in competitions: members of the green and white teams. The green team manages the environment and ensures that the systems used in the competition operate as intended, e.g., that all actors have proper access to the environment. The white team referees the competition and manages the incentives for the red and blue teams, e.g., creates the competition scenario.

2.2   The Competition Environment

The competition environment, i.e. the technical infrastructure, is managed by the green team. Among other things, it includes: network topology, operating systems, application software, configurations and user accounts. How these elements are composed will depend on the scenario and the purpose of the competition. The arranger will thus determine what the *targeted system* shall be, the *security mechanisms* included, and the known *vulnerabilities* it contains. Moreover, the arranger can determine what information is available to the participants concerning the competition environment. In other words, the arranger can control the *intelligence* the participants have.

The goal in most competitions is to represent some real-life situation or hypothetical security problem staged in a realistic manner, i.e., to make the competition environment realistic. However, creating a realistic environment can require a significant number of person-hours, hardware, software, and expertise. As a consequence, the realism is sometimes traded against costs and the competition environment is rarely a full-blown enterprise network, but rather a small and controlled environment. Another difference to typical enterprise networks is that computer networks used in competitions often are designed to include a large number of known *vulnerabilities*. A computer network with known *vulnerabilities* often fit the purpose of the competition better than well-hardened networks since a well-hardened network might require attackers to spend a significant amount of time searching for new novel software vulnerabilities (an aspect which few competitions focus on).

2.3   Goals and Rules for the Actors

Competitions may have several different goals, for example to offer a challenge, train, test the competence or increase the awareness of the participants. There are several articles describing setups with the goal to train the participants, e.g. [10, 18–22]. It is natural to dictate the rules and award systems for events where the competition-aspect is central, but it is also recommended for competitions that focus on the training and learning experience [23]. In general, some types of objectives are suitable for blue teams and some are suitable for red teams [23].

Rules and rewards are in place to make the competition develop as intended and would for example describe allowed (and disallowed) practices during the competition, how participants are scored in the competition, and non-disclosure clauses. A competition could for example disallow execution of distributed denial-of-service attacks since the infrastructure is not built for it, or forbid blue teams to change the software on certain machines because it is business critical in the stipulated scenario. The arranger could also limit the use of *tools* to a predefined set.

Scoring systems could for example reward a red team if they manage to read some file, gain certain privileges on a machine, or to cause denial-of-service on a machine, whereas blue teams could be rewarded for maintaining systems operational. As performance measurements are a natural part of a competition, they provide means to control the *goals of the participants*. It is also natural to record the *participants' time /success* when they work towards these goals.

2.4   Competitions versus Experiments

In an experiment, data collection and analysis follow a carefully worked-out plan. The basic requirement of an experiment is that different treatments are administered to different subject-groups or repeatedly to the same subject, and measurements are recorded after the treatment. A variable is either seen as a *dependent* variable, an *independent* variable, or a *nuisance* variable. A *dependent* variable is a measurement of the particular aspect one wish to observe; an *independent variable* is a treatment one wish to examine the effect of; *nuisance variables* are the factors which may have an effect on the *dependent variable*, but are outside of scope for the particular study. For the experiment to produce a reliable result, *nuisance variables* and *independent variables* needs to be controlled. Such control can be imposed by design or by randomization. [24]

As described above there are several variables that are possible to control and measure in a competition. The extent of this control is in some cases limited or costly (e.g., it is difficult to control the presence of software vulnerabilities which have not been made public yet). However, this paper argues that competitions can be designed so that the influence of independent variables on a dependent variable is measurable and the nuisance variables are handled in an acceptable manner. In this paper, the variables of concern to a security experimenter will be coarsely grouped into the following categories (introduced in italic in section 2.1-2.3): *Targeted system, Security mechanisms, Goals of participants, Vulnerabilities, Competence, Tools, Participants' time /success, Intelligence,* and *Organization*. These categories are referred to in the text of section 3.

3 Topics That Can Be Investigated in Security Competitions

The first five subsections below describe security-related topics that are possible to perform experiments on in conjunction to security competitions. The last subsection summarizes previous experimental studies similar to those proposed here. It should be noted that the enumeration below does not aim to be exhaustive. It should rather be seen as a set of suggestions made to inspire.

3.1 The Process Model of an Attack

There are several models over the steps an attacker takes during an attack. McQueen et al. [25] present a model over attacks with three "attacker subprocesses"; Olovsson and Jonsson [26] divided attacks into three phases; Schudel et al. [27] present another process model; Branlat and Morison [28] describe actions and interplay between attackers and defenders. However, there are few quantitative results showing that these qualitative models match the processes of actual attacks.

The student experiments performed at Chalmers [26, 29] and the experiments performed within DARPA's Information Assurance program [27, 30] are exceptions which offer some quantitative data on the different phases of an attack. In both these experiments observations are made of the time that attackers spend on different phases and if they succeed or not. More precisely, they investigate how *participants' time* is distributed over different phases in a process model and assess how different factors (e.g., *competence*) influence this.

A number of different factors influence how attackers spend their time and the activities they chose to perform. For example, the type of *intelligence* they have about the targeted system (e.g., network diagrams), the type of system that the *targeted system* is (e.g., web server or web browser) and the *security mechanism* used (e.g., dynamic defense [31]) can all be expected to influence the attack process in different ways. Experiments in conjunction to competitions could investigate how these factors influence the performance of the participants.

3.2 The Attributes of Successful Attackers and Defenders

There is no established theory concerning the *competences* an attacker or defender should have to be successful in its role. The *competence* of participants in a competitions (e.g. the factors enumerated in [32]) could be compared to the *participants' time/success* data in order to identify important determinants of success. Success for attackers could for example be measured as the time spent to achieve the goal; success for defenders could for example be measured as the portion of attacks that were prevented respectively detected by the defenders. In case the attackers or defenders operate as teams, the teams' mixes of *competence* can be assessed, perhaps in combination with the teams' *organization*.

Experimentation has been made on this topic as well. For example, the relationship between defensive success and the number of years at university (freshmen, sophomores etc.) has been assessed in [33]. The result suggests that seniors are tougher targets than freshmen. In [34] interviews of members in a red team are used to investigate what the key factors are for their effectiveness. The result of these interviews suggests, among other things, that it is difficult to identify attributes that reflect the effectiveness of a red team as well as the relationships between the effectiveness of individuals and teams. In other words, additional research is needed on this topic.

3.3 The Impact of Security Mechanisms on Success

Defenders can choose between a considerable number of *security mechanisms* to increase the security of their systems. By running competitions with and without a *security mechanism*, data on its practical effectiveness can be obtained. *Security mechanism* for a wide range of attacks can be tested in conjunction to a competition. This includes security mechanisms that protect against: buffer overflow attacks, denial-of-service attacks, SQL-injection, password-cracking, and network reconnaissance.

Two examples of tests involving security mechanisms are described in [35] and [36]. In [35], the impact of two *security mechanisms* against distributed denial-of-service attacks (and the combination of these two) is assessed during a competition. In [36] the targeted system is designed with four different sets of *security mechanisms* in order to assess the effectiveness of the defense-in-depth concept.

Moreover, in competitions that involve an active defense (i.e., a blue team) the impact of defender's management procedures and incident handling capabilities can be investigated. For instance, an experimenter can assess the effectiveness of administrators actively responding by different tactics. Effectiveness can for example be measured as the portion of attack goals that they prevented the attackers from accomplishing or the time it took the attackers to compromise the targeted system. In other words, *security mechanisms* that are active and adaptive so that they disturb the attack process can be evaluated in exercises involving live attackers. The "dynamic defense experiment" described in [31] is an example of this.

3.4   The Accuracy of Detection and Incident Analysis Methods

The targeted system can be equipped with systems that log events and states during the competition. Such logs are used together with other data in investigations that attempt to reconstruct the chain-of-events that occurred during an incident. This capability is relevant both in incident management [37, 38] and forensic investigations [39].

If the additional data collected during the competition includes detailed descriptions of the steps taken by the attackers, they offer a straightforward method to evaluate the accuracy of methods for reconstructing the chain of events from logs. For example, in the experiment described in [40], the capabilities of a system administrator to detect and analyze intrusions made during a competition is analyzed. The red team provided detailed logs on their actions and these were compared to the assessments made by the system administrator.

In general, a number of factors can be expected to influence the difficulty of identifying and analyzing incidents. For example, *tools* used by attackers, their *attackgoals* and their *success* can be compared to the assessment made by the incident analysis team and/or their incident analysis tools. An intuitive hypothesis is that attackers with *competence*, special *tools,* and good *intelligence* will be more difficult to analyze and detect than other attackers.

3.5   The Accuracy of Security Assessment Methods

Critique has been directed towards methods used in the security community to assess the security of systems. In particular, few methods that quantitatively predict or assess operational security has been validated empirically [1]. Security competitions can be used to test assessment methods that are classified as "system" or "vulnerability" in [1]. In other words, methods that aim to describe how components and their structure in the system relate to security and methods that aim to describe the existence or appearance of system vulnerabilities.

There are several possibilities to evaluate the usefulness of assessment methods in conjunction to offensive competitions. As long as the security competition can be constructed to represent scenarios that are covered by the model/metric, the "correct" value can be compared to the calculated value. In [41] assessments made by security experts on *participants' success* for remote code execution attacks made under certain conditions are compared to empirical observations. In [42] 16 security metrics based on vulnerability ratings are compared to the *participants' time* spent and *participants' success* when attacking a set of strategically designed servers. In [43] the relationship between two metrics is assessed.

3.6   Past Experimentation in Conjunction to Competitions and Exercises

To perform security experiments involving human actors is not a new proposal. Several lessons have been learned and documented from experimentation with real attackers: in [26, 29] issues in experiments involving live attackers are discussed, in [44, 45] experiences from several red team experiments performed at DARPA are summarized, and in [35] lessons learned from a long multi-team experiment are described.

Table 1 categorizes a number of experiments involving human attackers. It should be noted that all studies in Table 1 are not referred to as experiments in the original article, e.g., in [33] the data collection method is described as "observations of actual attacks carried out during the cyber defense exercise". However, they all hold all the features required (e.g., with respect to control) to be experiments. The table denotes if a variable within the type is treated as a dependent variable (D) or an independent variable (I) that is varied.

Table 1. Past experimental and observational studies performed with human attackers

Ref.	Topic investigated	Targeted system	Security mechanisms	Attack-goals	Vulnerabilities	Competence	Tools	Participants' time /success	Intelligence	Organization
[26, 29]	3.1							D [a]		
[27, 44]	3.1							D [a]		
[36]	3.1 & 3.3			I	I			D		
[31]	3.1 & 3.3			I	I			D		
[33]	3.2 & 3.3				I		I	D		
[46]	3.3	I		I	I			D		
[45]	3.3			I	I			D		
[35]	3.3			I	I			D		
[41]	3.5			I				D		
[42]	3.5					I		D		
[43]	3.5							D [b]		

[a] *Time spent on different attack-activities is assessed.*
[b] *Two metrics on success are compared.*

As can be seen from the table, not all setups include independent variables that are varied. In particular, [27, 44] explores the process of attacks and the behavior of a certain type of attacker and [43] assess the relationship between a theoretical metric for attack effectiveness and success in an offensive competition. In these cases a single experimental setup is repeated multiple times. It should also be noted that strict experimental control is not always imposed on all known nuisance variables before the observations are made in the studies in Table 1. For instance, the attackers in [33] and [43] are convenience samples rather than the result of a controlled selection process. Such limitations are a natural effect of the conditions for these experiments and do not necessarily affect the validity and relevance of the data for the problem at hand.

4   Potential Issues

This section comprises three subsections. The first subsection discusses the response variable(s) used in previous research. The second subsection discusses the cost of arranging competitions. The third subsection discusses some other issues with designing cyber security competitions as experiments and exploiting the produced data in research.

4.1   The Response Variable(s) – Participant's Performance

As can be seen from Table 1, the success of and/or time spent by participants is a popular response variable in experimental cyber security research based on competitions. Thus, the response variable is the success or failure of these actors when they attempt to perform well-defined tasks, or alternatively, the time it takes for them to complete the tasks. The time attackers need to accomplish a task is often referred to as the "time-to-compromise" [47–49] or the "adversary work factor" [44]. It is an established metric in the cyber security field to express the security level of a system. It is also commonly used when the security of physical systems is expressed. For instance, "net working time" is used to rate the security offered by safes [48]. Likewise, the probability that an adversary can succeed with an attack given specified conditions is commonly used in security assessments, e.g., in probabilistic risk analysis.

Time-to-compromise and success rate have an apparent value in decision making processes and research with this focus would certainly produce results with direct practical value. Few objections have been made against these metrics in literature. In fact, no direct arguments against them were found. The closest to an objection that has been found is given in [50], where it is argued that the process of discovering vulnerabilities in a software product is "believed to be chaotic" and that this would impede measurements of the time needed to complete a discovery. Still, even though the movement of a thrown dice is chaotic, a fair dice will on average yield six every sixth throw. If the chaoticness of the process of discovering vulnerabilities should be tested, competitions where the goal is to discovery new vulnerabilities seem to be a good place to make observations. For instance, it could be tested how variables related to *Competence* influence the process.

4.2   The Cost of Arranging a Competition

Arranging a competition is costly [22]. As discussed above it will be costly to simulate a full-scaled enterprise environment in a competition, however, even a more limited target system can introduce high costs. For example, realistic software environments will often involve licensed products imposing direct monetary costs. Moreover, competitions are often built around a fictive scenario to make them more intriguing. To build a target system that fits this scenario could require that changes are made to applications design, naming conventions used, etc. These costs will limit the freedom a researcher has to re-design a competition to produce a better experiment.

Furthermore, for some aspects of security it will be inherently costly to arrange competitions as a meaningful experiment. For instance, experimenters who wish to investigate the effort required to find new vulnerabilities in a software product can do so in a security competition. Different software products can be provided, and these may be developed according to different standards, red teams can be challenged to find previously unknown security vulnerabilities in the products, and their performance can be recorded. While such setups may be arranged, discovering vulnerabilities may in some cases require months or years of effort for a security professional [51]. Hence, attackers involved in this kind of competition must be prepared to spend a significant amount of time to generate useful data if relatively secure products should be studied.

4.3   Other Practical Issues

In addition to cost considerations and the competition setup there are matters that are difficult to study in a competition. For instance, it will be difficult to test attributes of social engineering attacks since the participants will be in a different context than during normal operations. For the same reason it will be difficult to test a blue team's active defense capability when attacks are sudden and unexpected (as they are for many organizations). Since the blue team will expect attacks, they will probably act in a different (more alert) manner. Other topics which appear difficult to assess via competitions include, but are not limited to, the monetary losses caused by adversarial activities, the incentives that real attackers or defenders act upon, and properties of the cyber security market.

Other practical considerations are of a more administrative nature. An experiment will produce data that is used to test or formulate hypotheses. The scientific process requires that the data is made available to other researchers and that experiments are possible to repeat by others. Some competitions might be impossible to perform under such circumstances. For instance, if a participating organization wishes to test their secret tools for their attacks, then the competition's data may be labeled as confidential and it will be difficult for others to repeat the experiment or even review the data produced. Moreover, researchers might need to change the competition in order to perform a well-designed experiment on the matter they are interested in. Such changes may conflict with other objectives of the competition, e.g., to offer an interesting, educating, and lively competition. The possible conflict between scientific research and other objectives of the competition is worth considering. It is the only important difference between an experiment made in conjunction to a competition and a traditional (standalone) experiment on the same topic.

The basic proposal of this paper is to perform experiments in conjunction to cyber security competitions. Either by formulating experiments as competitions to attract study-subjects or by getting involved in existing competitions in order to get access to an arrangement already paid for. We have been in contact with three established arrangers of competitions to gauge the possibility to use them for experimentation, given the issues discussed above. More precisely, they were asked if (1) it would be possible to collect data from the exercise and use it for research and (2) if it would be possible for researchers to influence the design of the exercise in order to produce a more interesting experiment. We believe that their answers points towards the potential of security competitions as a basis for experimentation.

Officials of Security Challenge [15] see no problem with the idea as such. However, it was also judged as likely that the privacy regulations in the Great Britain would make it difficult to use collected data for research purposes.

The director (Dwayne Williams) of the National Collegiate Cyber Defense Competition [16] replied that data recordings are unproblematic and have been made during past competitions, e.g. in the form of network packet recordings. When it comes to the design of the competition, it is likely that smaller changes to the targeted systems are acceptable; however, it is unlikely that alterations of the scoring mechanisms or putting requirements on the participants to perform additional tasks would be accepted.

The iCTF [13] is arranged by professor Giovanni Vigna at University of California Santa Barbara and already includes the collection of data for research. In fact, the last two competitions have been designed with this particular objective in mind. Data from the competition is published online [13] and empirical research results (see [43]) have been produced from the competition. Professor Vigna is also open for input on the design of the competition.

5   Conjecture

Cyber security competitions are popular. They are primarily held to offer the participants an interesting challenge and to educate and train the participants for real situations. The arranger of a competition controls a number of variables that are important in the cyber security field. This control makes it possible to design them as experiments where the subjects under investigation are the participants, their interaction with an external environment, and the actual system. To arrange competitions in order to conduct experiments can be costly. However, a large number of competitions are already carried out today. This includes high-profile events with hundreds of participants, national events involving multiple organizations, and small events executed by a couple of organizations or individuals. Experimenters who can influence the setup or take advantage of their existing setup can limit their experimentation cost significantly, while producing empirical data to test and formulate hypotheses.

References

1. Verendel, V.: Quantified security is a weak hypothesis: a critical survey of results and assumptions. In: New Security Paradigms Workshop, pp. 37–50 (2009)
2. Geer Jr., D., Hoo, K.S., Jaquith, A.: Information security: why the future belongs to the quants. IEEE Security & Privacy 1, 24–32 (2003)
3. Kotulic, A., Clark, J.G.: Why there aren't more information security research studies. Information & Management 41, 597–607 (2004)

4. Gal-Or, E., Ghose, A.: The Economic Incentives for Sharing Security Information. Information Systems Research 16, 186–208 (2005)
5. Gordon, L.: Sharing information on computer systems security: An economic analysis. Journal of Accounting and Public Policy 22, 461–485 (2003)
6. Wilander, J., Nikiforakis, N., Younan, Y., Kamkar, M., Joosen, W.: RIPE: Runtime Intrusion Prevention Evaluator. In: Proceedings of the 27th Annual Computer Security Applications Conference, ACSAC, pp. 41–50 (2011)
7. Shacham, H., Page, M., Pfaff, B., Goh, E.J., Modadugu, N., Boneh, D.: On the effectiveness of address-space randomization. In: Proceedings of the 11th ACM Conference on Computer and Communication Security, pp. 298–307 (2004)
8. Khattab, S.M., Sangpachatanaruk, C., Melhem, R., Znati, T.: Proactive server roaming for mitigating denial-of-service attacks. In: Proceedings of International Conference on Information Technology: Research and Education, ITRE 2003, pp. 286–290. IEEE (2003)
9. Ktata, F.B., Kadhi, N.E., Ghédira, K.: Agent IDS based on Misuse Approach. Journal of Software 4, 495–507 (2009)
10. Conti, G., Babbitt, T., Nelson, J.: Hacking Competitions and Their Untapped Potential for Security Education. IEEE Security & Privacy, 56–59 (2011)
11. Fanelli, R.L., O'Connor, T.J.: Experiences with practice-focused undergraduate security education. In: Proceedings of the 3rd Workshop on Cyber Security, Washington, DC, United states (2010)
12. Werther, J., Zhivich, M., Leek, T.: Experiences in cyber security education: The mit lincoln laboratory capture-the-flag exercise. In: The 4th Workshop on Cyber Secuirty Experimentation and Test, San Francisco, CA, United states (2011)
13. Vigna, G.: The UCSB iCTF, http://ictf.cs.ucsb.edu/
14. Polytechnic Institute of NYU: CSAW - CyberSecurity Competition, http://www.poly.edu/csaw2011
15. Cyber Security Challenge: Cyber Security Challange, https://cybersecuritychallenge.org.uk/
16. National Collegiate Cyber Defense Competition: Welcom to the National Collegiate Cyber Defense Competition, http://www.nationalccdc.org/
17. Patriciu, V.V., Furtuna, A.C.: Guide for designing cyber security exercises. In: Proceedings of the 8th WSEAS International Conference on E-Activities and Information Security and Privacy, pp. 172–177. World Scientific and Engineering Academy and Society, WSEAS (2009)
18. Wagner, P.J., Wudi, J.M.: Designing and implementing a cyberwar laboratory exercise for a computer security course. In: Proceedings of the 35th SIGCSE Technical Symposium on Computer Science Education - SIGCSE 2004, p. 402 (2004)
19. Schepens, W.J., Ragsdale, D.J., Surdu, J.R., Schafer, J.: The Cyber Defense Exercise: An evaluation of the effectiveness of information assurance education. The Journal of Information Security 1 (2002)
20. Conklin, A.: Cyber Defense Competitions and Information Security Education: An Active Learning Solution for a Capstone Course. In: Proceedings of the 39th Annual Hawaii International Conference on System Sciences (HICSS 2006), p. 220b. IEEE (2006)
21. Hoffman, L.J., Rosenberg, T., Dodge, R., Ragsdale, D.: Exploring a National Cybersecurity Exercise for Universities. IEEE Security and Privacy Magazine, 27–33 (2005)
22. Childers, N., Boe, B., Cavallaro, L., Cavedon, L., Cova, M., Egele, M., Vigna, G.: Organizing Large Scale Hacking Competitions. In: Kreibich, C., Jahnke, M. (eds.) DIMVA 2010. LNCS, vol. 6201, pp. 132–152. Springer, Heidelberg (2010)

23. Schepens, W.J., James, J.R.: Architecture of a cyber defense competition. In: IEEE International Conference on Systems, Man and Cybernetics, pp. 4300–4305. IEEE (2003)
24. Keppel, G., Wickens, T.D.: Design and analysis: a researcher's handbook. Pearson Education, Upper Saddle River (2004)
25. McQueen, M.A., Boyer, W.F., Flynn, M.A., Beitel, G.A.: Time-to-Compromise Model for Cyber Risk Reduction Estimation. In: Gollmann, D., Massacci, F., Yautsiukhin, A. (eds.) Quality of Protection, pp. 49–64. Springer US, Boston (2006)
26. Jonsson, E., Olovsson, T.: A quantitative model of the security intrusion process based on attacker behavior. IEEE Transactions on Software Engineering 23, 235–245 (1997)
27. Schudel, G., Wood, B., Parks, R.: Modeling behavior of the cyber-terrorist. In: Proceeding of Workshop on RAND National Security Research Division, pp. 45–59 (2000)
28. Branlat, M., Morison, A.: Challenges in managing uncertainty during cyber events: Lessons from the staged-world study of a large-scale adversarial cyber security exercise. In: Human Systems Integration Symposium (2011)
29. Olovsson, T., Jonsson, E., Brocklehurst, S., Littlewood, B.: Data collection for security fault forecasting: Pilot experiment, Dept. of Computer Eng., Chalmers Univ. of Technology, and ESPRIT/BRA Project no. 6362 (PDCS2), Toulouse (1993)
30. Levin, D.: Lessons learned in using live red teams in IA experiments. In: Proceedings of DARPA Information Survivability Conference and Exposition, pp. 110–119. IEEE (2003)
31. Kewley, D.L., Bouchard, J.F.: DARPA Information Assurance Program dynamic defense experiment summary. IEEE Transactions on Systems, Man, and Cybernetics - Part A: Systems and Humans 31, 331–336 (2001)
32. Guard, L., Crossland, M., Paprzycki, M., Thomas, J.: Developing an empirical study of how qualified subjects might be selected for IT system security penetration testing. Citeseer 2, 413–424 (2004)
33. Dodge, R.C., Carver, C., Ferguson, A.J.: Phishing for user security awareness. Computers & Security 26, 73–80 (2007)
34. Kraemer, S., Carayon, P., Duggan, R.: Red team performance for improved computer security. In: Human Factors and Ergonomics Society Annual Meeting Proceedings. Human Factors and Ergonomics Society, pp. 1605–1609 (2004)
35. Mirkovic, J., Reiher, P., Papadopoulos, C., Hussain, A., Shepard, M., Berg, M., Jung, R.: Testing a Collaborative DDoS Defense In a Red Team/Blue Team Exercise. IEEE Transactions on Computers 57, 1098–1112 (2008)
36. Kewley, D.L., Lowry, J.: Observations on the effects of defense in depth on adversary behavior in cyber warfare. In: Proceedings of the IEEE SMC Information Assurance Workshop, pp. 1–8 (2001)
37. Mitropoulos, S., Patsos, D., Douligeris, C.: On Incident Handling and Response: A state-of-the-art approach. Computers & Security 25, 351–370 (2006)
38. Werlinger, R., Muldner, K., Hawkey, K., Beznosov, K.: Preparation, detection, and analysis: the diagnostic work of IT security incident response. Information Management & Computer Security 18, 26–42 (2010)
39. Meyers, M.: Computer forensics: the need for standardization and certification. International Journal of Digital Evidence 3, 1–11 (2004)
40. Sommestad, T., Hunstad, A.: Intrusion detection and the role of the system administrator. In: Proceedings of International Symposium on Human Aspects of Information Security & Assurance, Crete, Greece (2012)
41. Holm, H., Sommestad, T., Franke, U., Ekstedt, M.: Success rate of remote code execution attacks – expert assessments and observations. Journal of Universal Computer Science 18, 732–749 (2012)

42. Holm, H., Ekstedt, M., Andersson, D.: Empirical analysis of system-level vulnerability metrics through actual attacks. IEEE Transactions on Dependable and Secure Computing (accepted, 2012)

43. Egele, M., Caillat, B., Stringhini, G.: Hit'em where it hurts: a live security exercise on cyber situational awareness. Computer Security (2011)

44. Schudel, G., Wood, B.: Adversary work factor as a metric for information assurance. In: Proceedings of the 2000 Workshop on New Security Paradigms, pp. 23–30. ACM (2001)

45. Levin, D.: Lessons learned in using live red teams in IA experiments. In: Proceedings DARPA Information Survivability Conference and Exposition, pp. 110–119 (2003)

46. Ryder, D., Levin, D., Lowry, J.: Defense in depth: A focus on protecting the endpoint clients from network attack. In: Proceedings of the IEEE SMC Information Assurance Workshop (2002)

47. Paulauskas, N., Garsva, E.: Attacker skill level distribution estimation in the system mean time-to-compromise. In: 1st International Conference on Information Technology, IT 2008, pp. 1–4. IEEE (2008)

48. Leversage, D., Byres, E.: Comparing Electronic Battlefields: Using Mean Time-To-Compromise as a Comparative Security Metric. Computer Network Security 1, 213–227 (2007)

49. McQueen, M., Boyer, W., Flynn, M., Beitel, G.: Time-to-compromise model for cyber risk reduction estimation. Quality of Protection (2006)

50. McHugh, J.: Quality of protection: Measuring the unmeasurable? In: Proceedings of the 2nd ACM Workshop on Quality of Protection, QoP 2006, Co-located with the 13th ACM Conference on Computer and Communications Security, CCS 2006, Alexandria, VA, pp. 1–2 (2006)

51. Sommestad, T., Holm, H., Ekstedt, M.: Effort estimates for vulnerability discovery projects. In: HICSS 2012: Proceedings of the 45th Hawaii International Conference on System Sciences, Maui, HI, USA (2012)

The Development of Cyber Security Warning, Advice and Report Points

Tony Proctor

School of Technology, University of Wolverhampton, Wulfruna Street,
Wolverhampton, WV1 1LY, UK
t.proctor@wlv.ac.uk

Abstract. The threat to electronic information systems increasingly has origins in organised crime or nation-state sponsored or supported activity. Any successful cyber security programme relies upon the sharing of information. How this is achieved is a question that does not currently have an answer. This paper defines and describes cyber security Warning, Advice and Reporting Points (WARPs) as a potential solution. WARPs are most commonly found in the UK and have their origin in UK Critical National Infrastructure. This paper identifies the origins of response to computer security incidents. It then discusses international and UK computer incident response before defining and describing WARP. In doing so it contributes the experience gained at the University of Wolverhampton (who began operating WARPs in 2007). This paper furthermore seeks to examine how the original aims for WARP have developed and progressed since the initiation of the WARP programme.

Keywords: security information, information sharing, Warning Advice and Reporting Points.

1   Introduction

WARPs have evolved from the Computer Emergency Response Team (CERT) concept. The first CERT was created in 1989 by the U.S. Department of Defense in response to the first major vulnerability exploit experienced on the internet in 1989, the Morris Worm.

The US Government through the Department of Defense deemed a response necessary in order to deal with future problems. In 1989 CERT was created in partnership with Carnegie Mellon University. Many nations have since followed this approach. Alternatively named response teams fulfilling a similar function e.g. Computer Security Incident Response Teams (CSIRTs) have also been created.

The UK Government created the Unified Incident Reporting and Alert Scheme (UNIRAS) to fulfil the function of a UK Government CERT. Now known as GovCertUK it is operated by the Communications Electronics Security Group (CESG) at Government Communications Headquarters (GCHQ), the UK national centre for signals intelligence. In addition CSIRTUK is operated by the Centre for the Protection

A. Jøsang and B. Carlsson (Eds.): NordSec 2012, LNCS 7617, pp. 61–72, 2012.
© Springer-Verlag Berlin Heidelberg 2012

of the National Infrastructure (CPNI). CPNI is the organisation responsible for the physical, personnel and electronic security of UK critical national infrastructure.

Many developed nations now operate CERTs and or CSIRTs. At the time of writing there are over 50 such operations [1]. They are defined as "*a service organization that is responsible for receiving, reviewing, and responding to computer security incident reports and activity. Their services are usually performed for a defined constituency that could be a parent entity such as a corporation, governmental, or educational organization; a region or country; a research network; or a paid client*", [2].

Based on the experiences of CERTs and CSIRTs, an opportunity was identified within the UK National Infrastructure Security Coordination Centre (NISCC, the previous incarnation of CPNI) for an alternative CERT, where advisories could be filtered to specific groups of users and experiences shared within these groups. Establishing trust was identified as essential in order that incidents could be reported from the ground level upwards (from the users), in addition to from the top downwards (from Government and the IT Industry). WARP continues to be part of the information sharing strategy for CPNI. To complete the introduction, in 1990 the Forum of Incident Response and Security Teams (FIRST) was established as the interaction between CERTs experienced difficulties due to differences in language, time zone, and international standards or conventions [3].

The remainder of this paper contributes the experiences of operating WARPs to the research community. This applied research is further supplemented by evidence from a structured interview conducted with the architect and originator of WARP. The University of Wolverhampton have functioned as a WARP operator since 2007.

2   WARP Definition

A WARP is a formal network defined by some common identifiers / requirements. It is a community where the commonality may be based on different factors. Indicatively these could be: the business sector, geographic region or other factors. The recommendation is that a WARP should consist of no more than 100 members. This is because WARPs seek to establish trust. This task becomes more difficult with higher numbers. In practice most operational WARPs consist of less than 50 members.

A WARP facilitates three main activities. These are warning, advising and acting as a reporting point for information security incidents. Each WARP requires a WARP Operator. The WARP Operator provides the system and service in order for the functions of a WARP to be available. It is a requirement by CPNI that WARPs are financially operated as a not for profit venture.

London Connects was established in 2003 for local government in London. It was used to facilitate a trial of the WARP concept. This WARP is now a major component of Information Security for London (ISFL). There are now a number of WARPs operating both nationally in the UK and internationally, supported by a number of different operators. WARPs exist in the public, private and voluntary sectors. Fig.1 shows the proportion of WARPs by sector type.

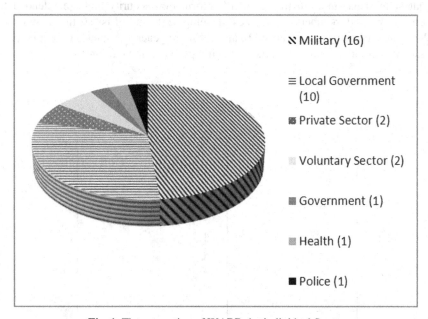

Fig. 1. The proportion of WARPs by individual Sector

2.1   WARP Warning Functionality

The majority of WARP alerts are distributed via email. However, alternative methods can be used. These include RSS, SMS or publication directly onto a website. WARP alerts are filtered so that the members can choose the categories of information for which they wish to receive alerts. This means that they do not have to receive everything that is issued by WARP. They only receive the information that is directly relevant to them. In this way it is envisaged that the WARP member is more likely to take the mitigating action required, on receipt of an alert.

Each WARP operator is responsible for identifying their information sources. This ensures that each WARP is focused specifically to the member community requirements. Some of these sources can be integrated via a web portal for easier viewing. These are analysed each day in order to construct alerts. A software system has been developed to facilitate WARPs. The Filtered Warnings Application (FWA) makes it easier for WARP members to select the alerts that they wish to receive and for operators to issue alerts to their members. Originally developed by Microsoft, the FWA is the property of CPNI. Whilst the use of the FWA is not a pre-requisite to WARP operation many WARPs have chosen to use this system. Fig. 2 shows how the software allows users to select from simple "tick-lists" in order to choose the information on which they wish to receive alerts.

Three types of alerts are issued by WARPs: Advisories, News and Warnings. Advisories are related to specific problems (e.g. a vulnerability in software) and usually require action (e.g. the application of a software update). News items contain the latest information from the world of information security and are intended to inform the WARP members of the latest developments and of issues that may occur in the future. Warnings are intended to alert of more general problems (e.g. a hoax or an issue that could develop into a more specific problem in the future).

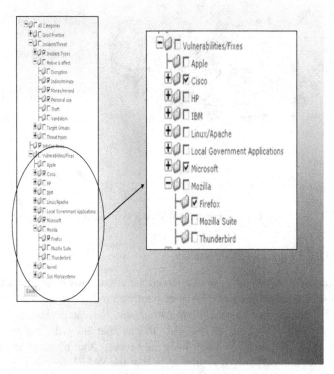

Fig. 2. The Filtered Warnings Application (FWA)

Each advisory shows the severity of any problem and is colour-coded to provide immediate identification. The other fields in an advisory include the source of the information, the software that is affected and the level of impact. A basic description of the problem provides for a prompt understanding of the issue. A more lengthy technical description is provided for members who have a greater technical understanding or those who require more information. The Common Vulnerability Exposure (CVE) code is included in the description. A CVE is the standard for information security vulnerability names [9]. Finally, a workaround describes the necessary mitigation steps. Fig. 3 shows a sample WARP Advisory and Fig. 4 shows a sample WARP News Item.

At the time of writing the WARPs operated by the University of Wolverhampton receive an average of 6 alerts (includes advisories and news items) each day. These are distributed to over 250 users in over 80 member organizations. WARP Warning functionality is well developed and widely used by all members.

High Rated Advisory
Source: Apple

10/09/2009 12:59:10
Categories: Apple
Software Affected: Apple iPhone, Apple iPod touch

Advisory: Apple iPhone / iPod touch Security Update

Impact: Security Bypass, Cross Site Scripting, Spoofing, Exposure of Senstive Information, Denial of Service

Description:

Some vulnerabilities, security issues, and weaknesses have been reported in Apple iPhone and iPod touch, which can be exploited by attackers in order to bypass certain security restrictions, disclose sensitive information, conduct cross-site scripting and spoofing attacks, cause a deprivation of resources, or to compromise a user's system.

Technical Description:

Some of the vulnerabilities are:

Vulnerability 1- An error in CoreAudio when processing sample size table entries of AAC and MP3 files can be exploited to cause a heap-based buffer overflow and potentially execute arbitrary code. (CVE-2009-2206)

Vulnerability 2- A vulnerability in WebKit can be exploited by attackers in order to conduct spoofing attacks. (CVE-2009-2199)

Please see the original advisory for more details.

Workaround:

Please Update to OS 3.1 or 3.1.1.

Further Information:

Original Advisory by Apple:
http://support.apple.com/kb/HT3860

Thank you for using the Filtered Warnings Application

Fig. 3. A Sample WARP Advisory

2.2   WARP Advice Functionality

Described by CPNI as "Advice Brokering" [5] this aims to establish both a dialogue amongst WARP members and the ability to link with experts in order to be able to address most information security issues. In a secure environment members are able to seek advice on security issues or share their own experiences and examples of best practice. Whilst there are occasional member requests for advice, this functionality is achieved primarily through regular WARP network meetings. Some WARPs also use a web-based forum. This is moderated by the WARP Operator who will encourage member participation. It can be used to identify topics of interest which may be developed into discussions or training sessions. Web-based forums are currently not widely used by WARPs.

Information disclosed may itself be used as material for alerts. Regular face to face meetings are facilitated by the WARP Operator. Advice is provided directly by the WARP Operator or indirectly through the numerous expert contacts that the operator develops. WARP Advice functionality is widely used by some members. This is most evident in the participation in WARP meetings. Outside of these meetings there is a low-level of requests for advice and information.

WARP News

Categories: Microsoft,Good Practice,InfoSec News,Incident/Threat
Date and Time issued: 23/10/2008 14:20:39

Important News: Microsoft Advance Notification for Critical Update

Microsoft have advised that an out of band update release is due to be made public at 1800 GMT on the 23rd October 2008.

Microsoft's standard practice is to bundle updates together and release these on a monthly basis. However, when critical vulnerabilities are discovered which require urgent patching, Microsoft can break the monthly routine and release out of sequence updates. It is therefore important that these patches are applied urgently as they are often associated with a high impact threat that is likely to be exploited.

GovCertUK recommend that departments test and apply this update across the enterprise as soon as possible. Further updates will be issued as soon as Microsoft releases more information.

Source: GovCertUK

References:
http://blogs.technet.com/msrc/archive/2008/10/22/advance-notification-for-out-of-bandrelease.aspx
http://www.microsoft.com/technet/security/bulletin/ms08-oct.mspx

Fig. 4. A sample WARP News item

2.3   WARP Reporting Point Functionality

CPNI [5] describe this as "Trusted Sharing". It aims to achieve a "trusted environment" that will encourage the sharing of sensitive information, specifically incidents and problems experienced by the members. WARP members need to know that their disclosure will not lead to any repercussion or embarrassment. It is necessary for the WARP Operator to become familiar with the members. It may also be necessary to anonymise information reported in order to develop trust. Sharing sensitive information can help members to take timely preventative action: the disclosure by one member alerts others to a potential problem.

WARP Reporting Point functionality is not widely used. It is achieved mainly via the reports from the member organizations at the network meetings. Some incidents are reported by WARP members because they either believe that a) it is useful for other WARP members to be aware of or b) because they believe that they have to report incidents to WARP or c) because the members need to report incidents to the UK CERT and reporting it to WARP will save them time as WARP will then report to the CERT. Overall, reports are limited in number and there is no obligation for members to report to WARP. UK Government places an obligation on public sector organizations to report incidents to the CERT and there is some evidence of a lack of clarity on what should be reported to whom (i.e. CERT or WARP?).

2.4   Information Sharing between WARPs

Information sharing takes place not only within WARPs but between WARPS. This occurs via several methods. Firstly, the FWA includes a function to create peer to peer links so that the news, alerts and advisories created by one WARP can be shared with another and vice-versa. Secondly, the WARP Operators Forum (WOF) facilitates information sharing between WARPs and strategic decision making in respect of the WARP programme. This is a closed forum for those involved in WARPs. Attendance is permitted only by invitation: the regular participants include WARP Operators, CPNI, GovCERTUK and the UK Ministry of Defence (MOD). This is extended by an on-line WARP Operators forum which facilitates information sharing outside of the physical meeting. As with individual WARPs, reports and incidents shared will be anonymised as appropriate.

3   Identifying the Benefits of WARPs

CPNI [4] describe the following as the reasons why WARPs are needed;

- There is a huge daily volume of security information generated to help protect IT systems. Staying informed is time consuming and often a luxury some cannot afford.
- Community members often lack the opportunity to share best practice and advice despite common needs.
- Lack of trust inhibits the sharing of sensitive information about problems with attacks on their IT systems.
- Solutions to some of these problems exist but can be costly.

Other work [10] describes the advantages of WARPs for nations who may not have the resources to implement full-scale computer security response teams. (This has been demonstrated in the creation of a WARP for the Republic of Ireland in lieu of a CERT). It highlights the attractiveness of WARPs to developing nations. Indeed, the paper proposes Community Oriented Security Advisory and Warning (C-SAW) teams that provide incremental growth from WARPs into CERTs. The main differentiator between WARPs and C-SAWs identified is the size of community supported and the dependency upon a relation with existing CERTs. Hence this represents one approach but there is no reason why WARPs cannot themselves be developed into CERTs.

The information provided by a WARP is customized in order to meet member requirements. The sources of information reflect this. They often include sector specific information and / or are recommended from within the member community. Multiple sources are used and they are verified for reliability and credibility. All alerts issued via WARP are subject to an authenticity check. WARP is adaptable to the on-going requirements of the membership. A WARP is interactive. It is not simply providing alerts. It includes the forums to share experiences and best practice. It facilitates expert advice and is a place to report incidents.

WARP membership helps to demonstrate that an organisation has a commitment to information security. Moreover, it can be an advantage for organisations seeking formal security certification. WARP membership has helped to satisfy some of the requirements of the information security management standard ISO 27001. It is also a recommendation of the code of connection to the secure Government network (govconnect) in the UK that those joining are members of a WARP. WARP can save a considerable amount of time, since the WARP Operator is researching vulnerabilities rather than the individual member organisations having to undertake this work.

Previous work [11] has defined the main security issues and trends that have been observed whilst operating WARPs. The majority of problems reported, related to accidental data loss rather than malicious behavior or attacks. Problems associated with portable media were highlighted. A number of personnel related issues were observed. The primary nature of these included the misuse of corporate resources (e.g. the storage of personal files on employer's media) and harassment. The paper identified a number of matters to which WARP members had given attention. These included the need for data classification, secure remote access, security testing, log management and the secure use of social networks.

4   The WARP "Vision" and Development

This section examines how the original aims of WARP have developed and progressed since the creation of the programme. As part of this the author sought to identify the source of the WARP concept. This was successful and what follows in this section presents a summary of a structured interview with the originator of WARPs [6].

UNIRAS existed prior to the creation of NISCC. It was initially a reporting system set up by the Central Computer and Telecommunications Agency (CCTA), the UK Government centre for information services until 2001 [8]. This reporting system was developed into a CERT. When NISCC was established in 1999, UNIRAS was integrated into it. UNIRAS became proactive and established a reputation amongst peer CERTs (UNIRAS was the first to identify a variant of the Code Red exploit in 2001).

UNIRAS developed from a team of two to five people. It became responsible for the .gov.uk internet domain. Following a number of defacements of Local Government websites in the UK, UNIRAS was under pressure to provide CERT services to the Local Government sector. This presented a problem as the experience in UNIRAS was of Central Government and Central Government systems, with little knowledge of the business of Local Government. Added to this was the lack of resources, with a small team who were responsible for Critical National Infrastructure and Central Government.

Initial ideas suggested that there was a requirement for something that would involve self-help. The first suggestion was that Local Government required a CERT or CERTs. However, the costs of achieving this were considered prohibitive. The next phase examined the requirements and identified the most expensive parts of a CERT. The main requirements were for the provision of warnings and advice. Since NISCC was the main investor it was considered important that they receive some benefit from the initiative. Hence reporting was added to the requirements. The result of this work produced the concept of a WARP.

Having achieved support from NISCC, London Connects (a collective group of the individual London Councils) were contracted to assist with developing the first WARP. The Information Assurance Advisory Council (IAAC), a cross-sector body that provides strategic guidance to corporate leaders and Government were also involved in providing support. A paper describing the benefits of sharing information and how this can improve security was developed by the partnership [7].

Following a Presidential directive in the US in 1998, Information Sharing and Analysis centers (ISACS) were being developed. At the time that WARPs were being created, NISCC was also developing Information Exchanges. The experience of both ISACS and Information Exchanges was used in the development of WARPs (a view on ISACS was expressed that they were too large to achieve an effective level of information sharing). One of the main aims of WARP was to move away from the CERT model which traditionally issues the same information to all users.

The next phase was to create the first WARP. In partnership with London Connects, this WARP was to support the Local Government community in the thirty-three London Borough Councils. A set of key performance indicators was used to assess the success of the project and these were assessed regularly. Feedback was deemed positive and the view was taken that the success could also be judged from whether the WARP continued or not. Since this time the number of WARPs increased and an annual WARP conference was successful, further demonstrating the significant interest in WARP. The most important action in the development of the WARP programme was supporting the activities required by a WARP with the development of a software package (as discussed in section 2.1). This was provided by Microsoft as a donation to the WARP programme and became the Filtered Warnings Application (FWA).

The WARP programme has to date not developed as rapidly as it could. One of the suggested difficulties is the varying cost estimates for the creation of a WARP (£25 000 - £100 000). Some of the ways in which WARPs could evolve have been discussed. This included work with marketing experts that generated a mission statement that "WARPs would become endemic". The primary obstruction to this was a lack of funding. It was evident that this would not be provided by Government. Hence WARPs will need to be self-sustaining. The possibility of WARPs developing as a franchise was one of the other options discussed.

In terms of the future there is still no "killer app" for WARPs. It is necessary for a large project or a recognised authority to proactively take WARP forward. CERTs could create WARPs. Politics may restrict future opportunities for the development of WARPs: CERTs may be threatened by WARPs. Identifying a suitable Central Government sponsor for WARPs and maintaining a central control has been the most difficult challenge for the WARP programme.

5   Future Challenges

One of the challenges faced by WARPs is that they are operated independently using different methods. Although WARPs share information with each other, each WARP Operator is responsible for the management of the WARP. Some WARPs use the FWA, others operate in an alternative manner. Each WARP develops their own sources of information. Furthermore, there is no central funding for WARP. So each WARP is required to identify their own methods, not only operationally but financially. Achieving sustainability for WARPs remains the greatest challenge. At the time of writing the availability of funding is very limited.

5.1   WARP Governance

It is essential that WARPs are overseen with effective governance and that this includes coordination from an appropriate organization. CPNI provide the main governance for WARPs. It is responsible for the registration and approval of all new WARPs. Each individual WARP will typically operate a steering group. Effective "ownership" of the WARP programme resides with CPNI. Work has taken place to identify whether an alternative governance model may be appropriate in the ongoing development of WARPs. This has included a previous initiative to establish an independent WARP Trust, which was not pursued. WARP member opinion indicates that the involvement of CPNI (or similar authoritative body) is essential. The provision of ongoing governance for WARP represents another future challenge.

6   Conclusions

Any computer network is only as strong as the weakest node on that network. When considered from a global perspective this means that national and international networks may be compromised by any insecure device and this represents a potential threat to critical national infrastructures. Hence a requirement exists to inform and advise a diverse range of computer users on risks and mitigation.

WARP provides a service that fits in between the advisories and advice issued by those responsible in industry and the public sector and individual organisations attempting to comply with the increasing demands of legislation and compliance and the threats presented by increasingly sophisticated hacks and people related issues. It allows these organisations to participate in information sharing in order to be aware of and resolve issues through the experiences of others. From discussion with the originator of the WARP programme in section 4. it is clear that the initiative is yet to fulfill the envisaged potential. He described this in terms of awaiting the "killer app" for WARPs. Moreover there is a suggestion that WARPs may not reach their potential as politically they could be perceived as a threat to CERTs. It is important that CERTs recognize that initiatives like WARP can actually assist with their activity, helping to secure organizations. Equally it is important that WARP Operators cooperate with CERTs. The existing experience suggests that this is something that is happening.

A WARP helps to address one of the key requirements of effective information security: ongoing awareness. WARPs help to maintain general awareness whilst providing alerts containing specific warnings and advice on mitigation. Section 2 identifies some aspects of WARPs that are working well and others that provide opportunities for further development. The Warning functionality of WARP appears to be well-developed. Whilst outside of the operation of a WARP, it would be useful to assess the level of response to WARP alerts: for example, what action is taken on receiving an alert and how widespread is the action? The Advice functionality of WARP is provided mainly through face to face meetings. Whilst this will be ongoing there are opportunities to use technology in order to enhance communication. The Reporting Point functionality is under-developed and requires greater clarity. In particular the relationship between WARP and CERT with respect to incident reporting. The implementation of procedures to address this is required.

Alongside specific developments to WARP it is important to assess the overall effectiveness of the programme in order to identify the factors that will aid the further growth. Section 3 in this paper begins to address this and there is an opportunity for further dedicated research to identify definitive and quantitative benefits of WARPs.

WARP has demonstrated a potential to operate across sectors and the adoption of the model outside of the UK suggests a further trans-national capability. Indeed, work referenced in this paper suggests an appropriateness of WARPs for developing countries. There will be challenges to overcome if this potential is to be realised. These will include linguistic and cultural adaptation. Most national cyber security strategies require systems for warning, advising and reporting. WARPs are a proven method for achieving these aims, having operated and experienced growth since inception in 2003.

References

1. CERT, National Computer Security Incident Response Teams, http://www.cert.org/csirts/national/contact.html
2. CERT, CSIRT FAQ, http://www.cert.org/csirts/csirt_faq.html#1
3. FIRST, FIRST History, http://www.first.org/about/history

4. CPNI, "WARPs Introduction",
   http://www.warp.gov.uk/Index/indexintroduction.htm
5. CPNI, "WARPs explained",
   http://www.warp.gov.uk/Index/indexwarpexplained.htm
6. Burnett, P.: Discussion on the development of WARPs (telephone). Personal Communication (February 01, 2012)
7. Information Assurance Advisory Council. Sharing is Protecting. A review of Information Sharing, Cambridge, UK (2003),
   http://www.warp.gov.uk/downloads/IAAC%20NISCC%20Sharing %20is%20Protecting%20v21.pdf
8. JANET, Web Archive (2012),
   http://www.webarchive.ja.net/services/publications/glossary/ glossaryc.html
9. Mitre Corporation. Common Vulnerabilities and Exposures,
   http://cve.mitre.org/
10. Ellefsen, I., Von Solms, S.: The Community-oriented Computer Security, Advisory and Warning Team. IST-Africa, 1–8 (2010)
11. Proctor, T.: The Development of Warning, Advice, and Reporting Points (WARPs) in UK National Infrastructure. In: Proceedings: 6rd International Conference on Critical Information Infrastructure Security, Lucerne, Switzerland, September 8-9 (2011)

Towards an Empirical Examination of IT Security Infrastructures in SME

Ramona Groner and Philipp Brune

Hochschule Neu-Ulm - University of Applied Sciences
Wileystraße 1, 89231 Neu-Ulm, Germany
ramonacarmengroner@gmx.de, Philipp.Brune@hs-neu-ulm.de
http://www.hs-neu-ulm.de

Abstract. Despite the availability of numerous techniques for information security management and implementation, still many small-to-medium sized enterprises (SME) lack a holistic IT security infrastructure. There have been proposed various reasons for this, ranging from lacking security awareness to the complexity of solutions. However, it remains an open issue how an IT security infrastructure suitable for SME should be designed. This paper presents a research model describing the dependencies between security threats, requirements, and the related framework components. It also accounts for the adoption of security solutions in SME and the impact of human and technical factors. The model allows to quantitatively study the influences on security requirements and the adoption of the respective technologies. This is partially demonstrated by an empirical study conducted among south german SME. The obtained results reveal the current security technology adoption by SME and emphasize the need for an appropriate IT security infrastructure framework.

Keywords: Security Requirements, Security Awareness, Security Architectures, Network Security, Security Infrastructure Adoption, Risk Management.

1 Introduction

In recent years, information security in small-to-medium sized enterprises (SME) has gained increasing attention by the research community. Since SME differ from larger organizations in different ways, like i.e. enterprise culture and limited personal and financial resources, implementing information security measures is especially challenging for them [1,2,3]. Some case studies carried out for SME in different countries indicated their vulnerability to security attacks and the inadequacy of existing countermeasures [4,5,6,7]. Thus, considerable amount of research so far addresses the conditions and pitfalls for implementing information management security systems (ISMS) in SME [8,9,10,3,11]. However, when it comes to the implementation of information security measures on the IT infrastructure level in SME, the existing literature is sparse. In general, many

A. Jøsang and B. Carlsson (Eds.): NordSec 2012, LNCS 7617, pp. 73–88, 2012.
© Springer-Verlag Berlin Heidelberg 2012

studies revealed that SME face the same common challenges regarding the implementation of IT security measures, namely a lack of knowledge in the field and the strongly limited financial resources available [1,2].

To improve this situation, on the technical level a cost-effective, easy to maintain and flexible IT security infrastructure framework especially suited for SME is needed. In the following, IT security infrastructure denotes the sum of all hard- and software components implementing information security requirements on the network and infrastructure layer (thus, in particular below the business application layer). To develop such a framework, first the relevant requirements and boundary conditions have to be determined. This may be equivalently expressed in terms of the following research questions:

- How are information security threats actually perceived by IT stakeholders in SME?
- What is the status quo regarding the actual implementation of IT security infrastructure components in SME (the degree of security technology adoption)?
- How does the perceived quality regarding the fulfillment of non-functional requirements influence the adoption of these IT security infrastructure components?
- Which requirements exist in SME regarding suitable IT security infrastructure components and how important are the respective requirements considered?

To answer this questions, in this paper a quantitative research model is proposed, which is intended to be used to empirically study and better understand information security in SME. To demonstrate the feasibility of the approach, the application of the model to a proof-of-concept empirical study among SME from southern Germany is presented.

The structure of the paper is as follows: In section 2, the related work is discussed in detail. Section 3 describes the proposed research model, and section 4 the conducted empirical study among south german SME. Section 5 explains the data analysis, and in section 6 the results of the empirical investigation of the model and their implications are discussed. We conclude with a summary of our findings.

2   Related Work

Various real-world case studies examining information security, its implementation, improvement and related aspects in SME have been published so far. A considerable amount of this work is devoted to the implementation of ISMS in SME, like e.g. the implementation of an ISMS in a Luxembourg SME [10] or the general difficulties of ISMS implementations in SME [8]. Other studies focus on the cultural aspects of information security in SME in Australia [12], a method to foster information security culture in SME [13], or the higher vulnerability of SME regarding security attacks due to a lack of financial resources and knowledge [4,6,7]. Cultural aspects of information security have also been studied in the literature. [14] examines the information security cultures of four different professions. Key success factors for security during information system implementation have been analyzed [15]. [16] describes a theoretical and methodological framework analyzing the security awareness of different stakeholders. "'Financial restrictions, limited resources and adequate know-how"' are considered as the common factors limiting IT security in SME [17].

Regarding methodologies and solutions for improving information security in SME, most existing work focuses in the organizational level, namely the implementation of ISMS in SME. The feasibility of different security standards like ISO/IEC 27001 and ISO 9000 for SME has been evaluated [9]. However, for most SME, the implementation of an ISMS standard like ISO/IEC 27001 is not feasible. The gap between the currently implemented IT security measures and the ISMS standard requirements is too big. In [11], a method to reduce this gap is presented. Sanchez et al. propose a methodology for the implementation of ISMS in SME, which takes into account the special requirements of SME compared to big companies [3]. In particular, the authors claim that in most SME security is not included in the corporate strategy and that they do not want to pay for security. Thus, their "'Methodology for Security Management and Maturity in Small and Medium-sized Enterprises (MSM2-SME)"' is an ISMS implementation method especially adapted to SME [18]. The method is currently applied by different SME and constantly improved.

However, considering the IT infrastructure layer and the actual technical implementation of information security in SME, only partial aspects have been studied in the literature so far. The vulnerability to hackers and viruses in SME has been analyzed and it has been shown that they have more security issues than larger enterprises [5]. For virtual enterprises, there exists a proposal for a communication infrastructure including communication security aspects (privacy, integrity and authentication) [19]. [20] describes a strategy to reduce spam mail within enterprises. In general, most SME do not have a large IT staff with sufficient IT security knowledge, and they are also not willing to spend time and money to more secure systems [1,2].

Since the creation of a homogeneous security infrastructure within an enterprise is not an easy task due to a lot of different applications which have individual structures and business risks [21], up to now no holistic IT infrastructure framework for SME exists. To develop such a framework, the model presented in the following is intended as a first step allowing to better understand the security requirements of SME.

3   Research Model

The proposed research model is intended to combine elements from technology acceptance [32] and information systems adoption research (see [22] and references therein) with security requirements engineering [23], targeting at the actual implementation of the technical components of an IT security framework for SME.

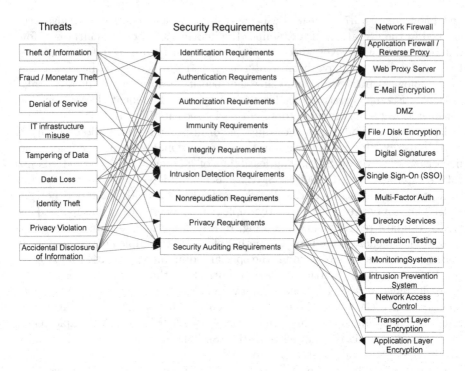

Fig. 1. Overall structure of the proposed model describing the relationships between threats, security requirement types and related IT infrastructure components

Fig. 1 illustrates the basic structure of the model. It was derived from previous works [23,24,25,26] as well as from interviews and discussions with experts in the IT security field and combined to form a holistic model. The boxes in the left column represent the potential threats to information security in an organization. Threats to enterprise information security have been studied already for a long time[27,25,24]. Therefore, the classification of threats in the proposed model in particular reflects Whitman's seminal work [24] as well as its recent update [26].

The threats lead to different types of IT security requirements shown in the middle column. These requirement types were chosen according to systematic classification proposed by [23]. The arrows pointing from the threats to the requirement types describe which threats are assumed to influence the respective requirement types. Obviously, the requirement types as proposed by [23] are of different quality (i.e. functional and non-functional) and not completely independent of each other. This is reflected in the model structure by threats or groups of threats influencing multiple different but interdependent requirement types in a similar way.

As denoted again by arrows, the requirement types are assumed to influence the actual implementation of the different IT security infrastructure components (soft- and hardware) listed in the boxes in the right column. The model takes into account all common IT security components on the network- and IT infrastructure layer widely used today [24,25]. All relationships denoted by arrows are assumed to express a linear proportionality.

The idea behind this structure is that the perceived risks related to the threats will determine the importance of the related requirement types as perceived by the stakeholders, which in turn will influence the actual implementation of the related IT security components. Here it is assumed that in organizations the importance and priority of security requirements will not be the result of the bare existence of information security threats, but of the relevant decision makers perception of the actual risks related to them. While threats denote an existing possibility for compromising enterprise information security, the related risks describe the probability of a respective exploit by an attacker and the magnitude of its consequences [28]. The perceived risk with respect to a threat then denotes the subjective assessment of its risk [29].

E.g., the model proposes that the perceived risk with respect to the "theft of information" threat governs the perceived importance of the identification, authentication, authorization, intrusion detection and security auditing requirement types. These requirement types are then implemented by IT security infrastructure components, i.e. identification requirements are implemented by application firewalls, web proxy servers, single sign-on (SSO), multi-factor authentication, directory services or network access control (NAC).

In Fig. 2 the detailed model for obtaining the perceived importance of the different requirement types is illustrated. This figure examplifies the full proposed causal relationships of the model for one selected threat (data loss) and one security infrastructure component (directory services). For each threat the perceived risk for the different stakeholder groups (namely management, employees and IT staff) is determined. Here, the perceived risks here are treated as directly measurable external variables, thus the model does not take into account the factors influencing the risk perception of the stakeholders. It is assumed that the perceived risks are correlated for the different stakeholder groups, since these groups influence each other in their opinions. The perception of the risks is assumed to significantly influence the perception of the importance of the related requirement types. This is indicated by the respective arrows in the figure.

As stated above, the valuation of the importance of the different requirement types is assumed to determine the perceived importance and thus the adoption of the IT security infrastructure components specified by these requirements (as shown by the respective arrows in Fig. 1).

In addition, the adoption of each IT security infrastructure component is assumed to depend on the stakeholders' perception of its respective quality attributes, namely on its technical complexity, ease of use and benefit/cost-ratio. The dashed arrows describe symbolically all further dependencies in the model according to Fig. 1.

Thus, by quantitatively measuring the perception of the technical complexity, ease of use and benefit/cost-ratio as well as the actual adoption of the different IT security infrastructure components and of the perceived risks related to the different security threats in Fig. 1, the model allows to obtain the perceived

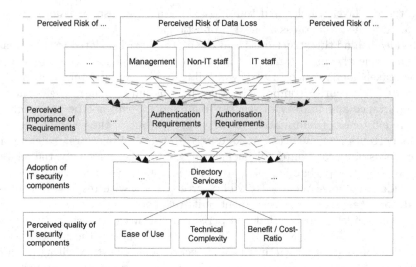

Fig. 2. Proposed causal relationships of the model for one selected threat and security infrastructure component (dashed arrows indicate further dependencies)

importance of the security requirement types and the magnitude of their mutual influences. For this purpose, an empirical study was carried out among SME in southern Germany.

4   Empirical Study

To evaluate the practical value of the proposed research model, it was used for an empirical study. Therefore, a survey was performed among companies from the region of the city of Ulm in southern Germany, mostly of them SME. However, also few larger companies still considered frequently as "medium-sized" in Germany were included in the survey. Ulm is located in between Stuttgart and Munich and its economic structure is dominated by highly innovative, internationally oriented SME from the IT, manufacturing and automotive sectors.

The survey was carried out using a questionnaire designed according to the research model. This questionnaire was sent to about 20 randomly chosen companies, mostly SME. From 15 of these companies, in total 33 participants filled out and sent back the questionnaire. However, some questionnaires were not filled out completely.

In Table 1 the distribution of the returned questionnaires according to certain grouping criteria is shown. Since some participants did not answer the questions on company size and number of employees, the numbers do not sum up to 33 for all criteria. While it was possible to obtain results for all enterprises sizes, obviously the number of returned questionnaires is not equally distributed among different industry sectors and positions of the participants. For the latter two,

Table 1. Number of questionnaires returned by employees from south german companies (mostly SME) grouped by different criteria

Criteria	Returned Questionnaires
No. of Employees:	
< 10	6
< 50	6
< 100	5
< 500	6
≥ 500	8
Industrial Sector:	
IT supplier / service provider	14
Services	10
Manufacturing	6
Position of Participant:	
Non-IT Staff	7
IT staff	15
Management / CEO	11

a bias towards IT-oriented companies and IT staff is observed. In general, this indicates the higher awareness of these target groups with respect to IT security and related issues.

Due to the sensitive nature of the IT security-related information collected with the questionnaire, the full anonymity of the participants needed to be ensured. It should be by no means possible to reveal the identity of the participants or the respective companies. Therefore, the questionnaire was distributed and collected in paper form, since an online survey may have beared the risk of traceability from the participants perspective.

In the questionnaire, participants were asked questions to measure their perception of the security threats, of the quality attributes of the different IT security infrastructure components and the actual degree of implementation of these components in the respective companies. Since not all participants were assumed to be able to give meaningful answers to all of these questions, the questionnaire was split into two sections. In the first section, only questions were asked regarding statistical information about the company and the participants role in there as well as their perception of the different security threats. This section was assumed to be filled out by everyone. The second section contained all the questions for measuring the quality attributes of the different IT security infrastructure components and the actual degree of implementation of these components. This section was assumed to be filled out only by IT staff members. The answers to all quantitative questions needed to be given on a five-grade scale ranging from 1 (low) to 5 (high).

The purpose of this survey was to collect data for an initial empirical study of the model. The number and distribution of the returned questionnaires does currently not allow to obtain statistically significant results or perform a statistical validation of the model. The data analysis presented in the following therefore is of merely descriptive nature. However, since the results are plausible from a practitioners perspective, they still provide important insights about the current state and quality of IT security requirements, their actual implementation and the influences on the adoption of common IT security infrastructure components in SME.

5   Data Analysis

As in structured equation modeling (SEM) [30], for performing the data analysis the model is expressed as two coupled linear systems of equations of the form

$$y_i = \sum_j a_{ij}x_j$$

$$z_i = \sum_j b_{ij}y_j + c_{i1}w_{i1} + c_{i2}w_{i2} + c_{i3}w_{i3} . \tag{1}$$

Here, x_i, z_i and w_{ij} denote the independent variables which were measured by the survey. The variables x_i denote the perceived risks with respect to the different security threats, z_i the degrees of adoption of the different IT security infrastructure components, and w_{ij} $(j = 1, 2, 3)$ the perceived quality attributes (namely technical complexity, ease of use and benefit/cost-ratio) of these components. The dependent variables y_i denote the perceived importance of the different security requirement types. The linear coefficients a_{ij}, b_{ij} and c_{ij} thus describe the different relationships (arrows) between the observed and dependent variables of the model.

In principle, these coefficients can now be determined by fitting the linear system of equations to the values of the independent variables obtained from the questionnaires by using multivariate linear regression. Expressing the proposed model in the form of equations (1) results in a linear system of equations with 57 variables and 133 degrees of freedom in total. However, to perform a statistically significant fit the number of observations (returned questionnaires) needs to be 5-10 times larger then the number of degrees of freedom of a model [31]. With only 33 questionnaires returned, thus it was obviously impossible to validate the full model within the present empirical study.

However, due to the structure of the two linear systems of equations in (1), these may be decoupled into separate independent subsystems with a reduced number of degrees of freedom. E.g, with respect to the linear relations between the measured variables w_{ij} and z_i the term $d_i = \sum_j b_{ij}y_j$ forms only an arbitrary constant offset. Thus, the second equation in (1) in fact denotes one independent linear equation

$$z_i = c_{i1}w_{i1} + c_{i2}w_{i2} + c_{i3}w_{i3} + d_i \tag{2}$$

for each IT infrastructure component (labeled by i). Each of these independent equations contains only 4 degrees of freedom and thus can be fitted with sufficient accuracy using the available data.

In addition, since due to the proposed structure of the model some of the coefficients a_{ij} and b_{ij} are assumed to be zero from the beginning, also the first equation of (1) could be splitted into independent subsystems that were fitted separately. In combination with neglecting for now the distinction between the participants' positions (stakeholder groups) regarding their risk perception (in contrast to Fig. 2) this allowed to obtain further results with sufficient accuracy. Nevertheless, it was not possible to obtain values for all variables.

The multivariate linear fit was carried out using the minimum least squares method. For cost reasons the respective numerical calculations were performed with the popular open source statistics software "R" (`http://www.r-project.org`) in combination with the "lavaan" (latent variable analysis) package (`http://lavaan.ugent.be`). The partial results obtained from this analysis are presented in the following section.

6   Results

In Table 2 the average results for the actual adoption of the the different IT security infrastructure components (corresponding to the mean values $< z_i >$ of the variables z_i in equation (2)) as obtained from the empirical study are presented. The third column shows the respective standard deviations. The results for the average adoption are on a scale from 1.0 to 5.0 (high).

It is obvious from these results that while most IT security infrastructure components have a medium adoption in SME and similar companies in southern Germany today, the one of document encryption solutions, single sign-on,

Table 2. Average adoption values of IT security infrastructure components with the respective standard deviations as obtained from the survey among SME and similar companies in southern Germany. The numbers for the average adoption are on a scale from 1.0 (low) to 5.0 (high).

Component	Avg. Adoption	Std. Dev.
Network Firewall	5.0	0.2
Application Firewall	3.5	1.8
Web Proxy Server	4.2	1.4
Email Encryption	2.3	1.8
DMZ	4.2	1.5
Digital Signatures	2.7	2.0
Disk / File Encryption	2.1	1.8
Single Sign-On	2.3	1.9
Directory Services	4.8	0.9
Penetration Testing	1.9	1.6
Network Access Control	2.7	2.0
Monitoring Systems	3.8	1.7
Transport Layer Encryption	3.5	1.9
Application Layer Encryption	1.6	1.3
Multi-Factor Authentication	1.9	1.7
Intrusion Prevention System	2.9	1.9

penetration testing, application layer encryption and multi-factor authentication is significantly lower. In contrast, network firewalls, directory services and web proxy servers have a very high adoption and thus may be considered already as standard IT security components today.

In Fig. 3 the results for the coefficients c_{ij} obtained by fitting the reduced, independent linear systems of equations (2) are plotted in a cobweb chart. The values of the coefficients c_{ij} describe the influences of the respective quality attributes ease of use (blue line), technical complexity (red line) and benefit/cost-ratio (green line) on the adoption of the respective IT security infrastructure component at each radial line. Negative values denote an inverse influence. Therefore, one might expect the coefficients to be positive in general for the attributes benefit/cost-ratio and ease of use, but negative for technical complexity, since a higher technical complexity should prohibit the adoption of a component.

Obviously, this is the case for some but not all of the IT security infrastructure components in Fig. 3. E.g. in case of multi-factor authentication, technical complexity has a high positive influence on the adoption of the component. This effect might occur due to the reason that either a higher technical complexity was associated with a superior functionality by some participants and thus considered positive, or that some participants who already implemented multi-factor authentication considered the actual technical complexity even higher after adopting the component. Both reasons would result in a positive influence of technical complexity on the adoption. Similar reasons might lead also to the observed inverse effect of a negative impact of ease of use or benefit/cost-ratio on the adoption.

Both effects are in particular observed for multi-factor authentication, which is also one of the components with the lowest adoption. This is reasonable, since the multi-factor authentication requires major changes to an IT infrastructure, i.e. to acquire the necessary hardware security tokens and to adapt existing applications to support them. This suggests the need for easier to adapt and less expensive solutions for that purpose and indicates a direction for further research [33].

In contrast, for the adoption of disk/file encryption the benefit/cost-ratio has the highest positive impact, whereas ease of use seems not very important and the effect of technical complexity is negative as expected. However, file encryption with an average adoption of 2.1 is also comparably seldom used. This may indicate that due to the technical complexity the benefit of file encryption is underestimated.

A second part of the model was evaluated using the assumption that every IT security requirement type is influenced by its related security threats in the same intensity. This is equivalent to reducing the first equation in eqs. (1) to

$$y_i = a_i \sum_j x_j \ , \ a_i = \frac{1}{N_i} \tag{3}$$

with N_i being the number of security threats related to y_i. The division by N_i is required for normalizing the results. By inserting the mean values of the

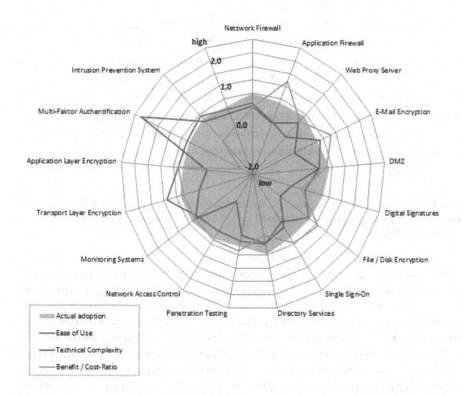

Fig. 3. Linear regression results for the coefficients describing the effect of the quality attributes ease of use (blue line), technical complexity (red line) and benefit/cost-ratio (green line) on the actual adoption of the IT security infrastructure components as measured by the survey. The values for the coefficients are plotted using the given radial scale with the center corresponding to -2.0. The adoption values (grey area) are shown in this chart for a qualitative comparison only. They are plotted using a different, compressed scale, but also with increasing values corresponding to a larger radius.

measured perceived risks for the variables x_i in equation (3) after obtaining the coefficients a_i by the linear regression fit, the estimates for the perceived importance of the security requirement types shown in Fig. 4 were calculated. All values are on a scale between 1.0 (low) and 5.0 (high).

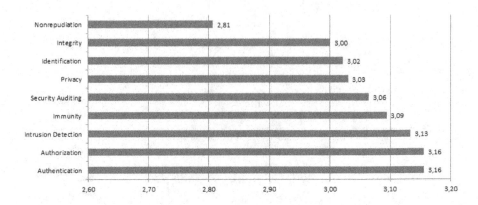

Fig. 4. Importance of the various IT security requirement types on a numerical scale from 1.0 (low) to 5.0 (high) as obtained from the multi-variate linear regression fit of the empirical data

Fig. 4 clearly shows that most requirements show medium importance values between 3.00 and 3.16, only nonrepudiation is considered significantly lower with a value of 2.81. Authentication and authorization requirements are considered most important by the participants. However, this contradicts with the observation that security components like single-sign on or multi-factor authentication, which help to implement these requirements, have a comparably low adoption in the evaluated companies. In contrast, components like digital signatures and intrusion prevention systems, which are assumed to be governed by non-repudiation requirements show a higher degree of adoption despite the lower importance of these requirement type. This indicates that there is a partial mismatch between the actual threat perception and the implemented IT security measures. A reason could be that the implementation of security solutions is not primarily made according to the security threats, but may be influenced by other external factors not covered by the model yet.

Finally, the assumptions made above have been combined to obtain at least values for the full influences on some of the IT security components. It turned out that with the present empirical data this was possible only for very few of components. However, the fit could be performed for the network firewall component, so the numerical analysis of the model could be exemplified for this frequently used component. Fig. 5 shows the variables and relationships influencing the adoption of network firewalls. The values for the influence factors obtained from the multi-variate linear regression fit of the model are shown. The thickness of the respective relationships additionally visualizes these values.

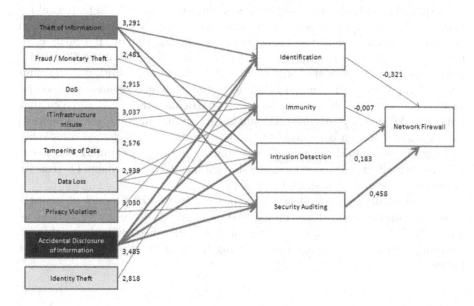

Fig. 5. Magnitude of the influences on the adoption of network firewalls (numerical scale from 1.0 (low) to 5.0 (high)) as obtained from the multi-variate linear regression fit of the empirical data

While the magnitude of most of these influences is reasonable and plausible, the negative influence of immunity and identification requirements on the adoption of network firewalls is counter-intuitive and thus considered to be an artifact due to the reduced set of statistical observations. Thus, the purpose of the fit shown in Fig. 5 is mainly to illustrate the quantitive numerical analysis of the model in principle.

To obtain valid results for the full model, a strongly extended empirical survey with a much higher number of participants is necessary in the future.

7   Conclusion

In conclusion, we have presented a proposal for a research model to quantitatively study the security requirements of SME. Based on this model, a first empirical study among companies (mostly SME) from the city of Ulm region in southern German was conducted. Using paper-based questionnaires, a completely anonymous survey was achieved.

By expressing the research model as linear system of equations and fitting its coefficients to the observations from the survey using multivariate linear regression, it is in principle possible to validate the model statistically. Unfortunately, due to the limited number of participants in this survey the model could neither be completely analyzed nor statistically validated so far.

Despite this fact, the available results of the survey allowed to fit partial aspects of the model using descriptive statistics. From these partial evaluation already reasonable insight was gained in the actual adoption of IT security components by SME and the requirements influencing it. In general, all IT security requirements were considered only of medium importance, resulting from a similar medium perception of major IT security threats. Thus, an adequate security awareness seems to still not established. In particular, the study revealed that important IT security solutions like single sign-on and multi-factor authentication still suffer from a comparably low adoption due their technical complexity and high implementation costs. This supports the original claim of this paper that further efforts are needed to develop an easier to implement IT security infrastructure framework suitable for SME.

To statistically verify and maybe improve the proposed model, a strongly extended empirical field study among SME is required. In this context, the presented field study serves also as a test run which delivered valuable insights for planning the extended survey and designing the final questionnaire in the near future.

References

1. Milne, D., McCarthy, J., Mills, B.: SME Security in the Digital Age. In: 2nd International Conference on Information Warfare and Security, Monterey, pp. 263–270 (2007)
2. Beachboard, J., Cole, A., Mellor, M., Herandez, S., Aytes, K.: Improving Information Security Risk Analysis Practices for Small- and Medium-Sized Enterprises. Issues in Informing Science and Information Technology 5, 73–85 (2008)
3. Sánchez, L.E., Parra, A.S., Rosado, D.G., Piattini, M.: Managing Security and its Maturity in Small and Medium-sized Enterprises. Journal of Universal Computer Science 15(15), 3038–3058 (2009)
4. Gupta, A., Hammond, R.: Information systems security issues and decisions for small businesses. Information Management & Computer Security 13(4), 297–310 (2005)
5. Jennex, M.E., Walters, A., Addo, T.B.A.: SMEs and Knowledge Requirements for Operating Hacker and Security Tools. Innovations Through Information Technology, 276–279 (2004)
6. Kimwele, M., Mwangi, W., Kimani, S.: Adoption of information technology security policies: Case study of Kenyan small and medium enterprises (SMEs). Journal of Theoretical and Applied Information Technology 18(2), 1–11 (2010)
7. Fong, M.W.L.: Chinese SMEs and Information Technology Adoption. Issues in Informing Science and Information Technology 8, 313–322 (2011)
8. Coles-Kemp, E., Overill, R.: The Design of Information Security Management Systems for Small-to-Medium Size Enterprises. In: 6th European Conference on Information Warfare, Shrivenham, pp. 47–54 (2007)
9. Barlette, Y., Fomin, V.V.: Exploring the suitability of IS security management standards for SMEs. In: 41st Annual Hawaii International Conference on System Sciences (2008)

10. Valdevit, T., Mayer, N., Barafort, B.: Tailoring ISO/IEC 27001 for SMEs: A Guide to Implement an Information Security Management System in Small Settings. In: O'Connor, R.V., Baddoo, N., Cuadrago Gallego, J., Rejas Muslera, R., Smolander, K., Messnarz, R. (eds.) EuroSPI 2009. CCIS, vol. 42, pp. 201–212. Springer, Heidelberg (2009)
11. Valdevit, T., Mayer, N.: A Gap Analysis Tool for SMEs Targeting ISO/IEC 27001 Compliance. In: 12th International Conference on Enterprise Information Systems, Funchal, vol. 3, pp. 413–416 (2010)
12. Dojkovski, S., Lichtenstein, S., Warren, M.: Developing Information Security Culture in Small and Medium Size Enterprises: Australian Case Studies. In: 6th European Conference on Information Warfare and Security, Shrivenham, pp. 55–65 (2007)
13. Dojkovski, S., Lichtenstein, S., Warren, M.J.: Fostering Information Security Culture in Small and Medium Size Enterprises: An Interpretive Study in Australia. In: 15th European Conference on Information Systems, St. Gallen, pp. 1560–1571 (2007)
14. Ramachandran, S., Rao, S.V., Goles, T.: Information Security Cultures of Four Professions: A Comparative Study. In: 41st Annual Hawaii International Conference on System Sciences, pp. 454–464 (2008)
15. Thong, J.Y.L., Yap, C., Raman, K.S.: Top Management Support, External Expertise and Information Systems Implementation in Small Businesses. Institute for Operations Research 7(2), 248–267 (1996)
16. Tsohou, A., Karyda, M., Kokolakis, S., Kiountouzis, E.: Analyzing Information Security Awareness through Networks of Association. In: Katsikas, S., Lopez, J., Soriano, M. (eds.) TrustBus 2010. LNCS, vol. 6264, pp. 227–237. Springer, Heidelberg (2010)
17. Park, J., Hong, C., Yeo, S., Kim, T.: IT Security Strategies for SME's. International Journal of Software Engineering and Its Applications 2(3), 91–98 (2008)
18. Sánchez, L.E., Santos-Olmo, A., Fernández-Medina, E., Piattini, M.: Building ISMS through the Reuse of Knowledge. In: Katsikas, S., Lopez, J., Soriano, M. (eds.) TrustBus 2010. LNCS, vol. 6264, pp. 190–201. Springer, Heidelberg (2010)
19. Osório, A.L., Barata, M.M.: Reliable and secure communications infrastructure for virtual enterprises. Journal of Intelligent Manufacturing 12, 171–183 (2001)
20. Siponen, M., Stucke, C.: Effective Anti-Spam Strategies in Companies. In: 39th Annual Hawaii International Conference on System Sciences (2006)
21. Conklin, W.A., Dietrich, G.: Systems Theory Model for Information Security. In: 41st Annual Hawaii International Conference on System Sciences, pp. 265–274 (2008)
22. Venkatesh, V., Morris, M.G., Davis, G.B., Davis, F.D.: User acceptance of information technology: Toward a unified view. MIS Quarterly 27(3), 425–478 (2003)
23. Firesmith, D.G.: Engineering Security Requirements. Journal of Objects Technology 22(1), 53–68 (2003)
24. Whitman, M.E.: Enemy at the Gates: Threats to Information Security. Communications of the ACM 46(8), 91–95 (2003)
25. Yeh, Q., Jung-Ting Chang, A.: Threats and countermeasures for information system security: A cross-industry study. Information & Management 44, 480–491 (2007)
26. Whitman, M.E.: The Enemy at the Gates II: The Enemy Within. In: Proc. of the 15th Colloquium for Information Systems Security Education (CISSE), Fairborn, Ohio, pp. 75–80 (2011)

27. Loch, K.D., Carr, H.H., Warkentin, M.E.: Threats to information systems: Todays reality, yesterdays understanding. MIS Q. 16(2), 173–186 (1992)
28. Rayner, S., Cantor, R.: How fair is safe enough? The cultural approach to societal technology choice. Risk Anal. 7, 3–9 (1987)
29. Weinstein, N.D.: Unrealistic optimism about future life events. J. Pers. Soc. Psychol. 39(5), 806–820 (1980)
30. Kline, R.B.: Principles and Practice of Structural Equation Modeling, 3rd edn. The Guilford Press, New York (2010)
31. Jahn, S.: Strukturgleichungsmodellierung mit LISREL, AMOS und SmartPLS (2007), http://www-user.tu-chemnitz.de/ stjah/Jahn202007-Strukturglei chungsmodellierung%20mit%20LISREL,AMOS%20und%20SmartPLS.%20Eine%20Einf %81hrung.pdf
32. Davis, F.D.: Perceived usefulness, perceived ease of use, and user acceptance of information technology. MIS Quarterly 13(3), 319–339 (1989)
33. Yu, J., Brune, P.: No Security by Obscurity - Why Two Factor Authentication Should Be based on an Open Design. In: International Conference in Security and Cryptography, Seville, pp. 418–421 (2011)

How to Select a Security Requirements Method? A Comparative Study with Students and Practitioners

Fabio Massacci and Federica Paci

Department of Information Engineering and Computer Science, University of Trento
name.lastname@unitn.it

Abstract. Most Secure Development Software Life Cycles (SSDLCs) start from security requirements. Security Management standards do likewise. There are several methods from industry and academia to elicit and analyze security requirements, but there are few empirical evaluations to investigate whether these methods are effective in identifying security requirements. Most of the papers published in the requirements engineering community report on methods'evaluations that are conducted by the same researchers who have designed the methods.

The goal of this paper is to investigate how successfull academic security requirements methods are when applied by someone different than the method designer. The paper reports on a medium scale qualitative study where master students in computer science and professionals have applied academic security requirements engineering methods to analyze the security risks of a specific application scenario. The study has allowed the identification of methods' strenghts and limitations.

1   Introduction

The OWASP CLASP project [20], Microsoft SDL [15], and Cigital's Touchpoints [13] are examples of Secure Development Software Life Cycles (SSDLCs) whose target is the development of secure software. Those processes identify as preliminary step the collection of software's security requirements. Security management standards such as ISO-2700x, COBIT [9], or the NIST standard [17] propose very similar processes where the initial phase is the collection of requirements.

A number of academic methods [6,16,4,14,11,10] have been proposed to elicit and analyze security requirements, but there are few empirical and comparative evaluations that help to select a method rather than another. A number of papers in the academic literature usually present a single, not repeatable experiment according to the terminology from [3] where the designer to show the effectiveness of a proposed method, applies the method to a more or less complex scenario.

However, the only way to investigate the actual effectiveness of academic security requirements methods is to conduct empirical studies.

A. Jøsang and B. Carlsson (Eds.): NordSec 2012, LNCS 7617, pp. 89–104, 2012.
© Springer-Verlag Berlin Heidelberg 2012

This paper presents a qualitative study that we have conducted to investigate whether academic methods are effective in identifying security requirements, and what and why makes these methods effective.

The study involved master students in computer science and professionals in IT Audit for Information Systems who have no previous knowledge in the methods. The empirical evaluation consists of an initial *Training* phase where the participants are instructed about a specific security requirements and risk analysis method, and an *Application* phase where the groups of participants apply the method to identify the security issues of real industrial application scenarios. Each group represents a team of security practitioners that are hired by a company to analyze the security risks of the company using one of the security requirements methods under evaluation. We have collected data on the methods' effectiveness using different data sources. We have video-audio recorded the participants during the application of the methods, we collected the artifacts generated by each group, and administered a number of questionnaires during the different phases of the study execution. We have also conducted focus group sessions with the groups at the end of the Application phase. The analysis of the collected data has allowed us to identified strenghts and limitations of the methods under evaluation.

In the next section (§2), we describe the design our study to compare the different security requirements and risk analysis methods. Then, we introduce the first run of the study that was conducted in 2011 (§3), and the participants and designers that we have recruited (§4). In Section 5, we describe the results of the data analysis. At the end we present related works (§6), discuss the threats to validity in (§7), and conclude the paper (§8).

2   Research Design

We have used qualitative research as main research method because it is suitable to answer research questions of the type *how, what, why*. In our study we want to investigate *how* well do academic security requirements methods actually work when applied by someone different than the designer, *what* aspects make these methods work, and *why*. Thus, we formulate our research questions as follows:

- **RQ1:** *How effective are academic methods to elicit risk and security requirements when applied by a person different than the designer?*
    - **RQ1.2:** *Can a novice to an academic security requirements engineering method easily apply it?*
- **RQ2:** *Which factors do make the methods effective? Which one don't?*
- **RQ3:** *Why these factors make the methods effective? Why they don't?*

2.1   Evaluation Protocol

Since we run the study with subjects novice to the methods, we have distilled an evaluation protocol that consists of the following phases:

Table 1. Main actors of the evaluation protocol

Role	Description
Customer	provides the application scenario for the analysis. It is responsible of providing to participants all the relevant information about the scenario.
Method designer	gives tutorials on the method to aprticipants and remains available for questions connected to the method.
Observer	has to take notes about the behavior of the groups during the Application phase and mediates the interaction between the participants and the method designers.
Participant	conducts the analysis of risk and security issues of the scenario provided by the customer, by using one specific method provided by one method designer. The participant should not have any prior knowledge about the assigned method.
Organizer	is in charge of the evaluation, keep the contacts among the actors, and organize the data collection and analysis.

- **Training.** Participants attend training sessions, in the form of tutorial lectures, about the method they are going to work with. After the training session, participants receive an information package containing the scenario and the instructions on the materials they are asked to produce during the analysis. Participants then are given some time to get familiar with the method.
- **Application.** Participants work in groups and apply the method that was assigned to them on a scenario provided by customers; the group collaboration can take place both face-to-face or remotely by using multiple communication channels (e.g. mail, chat, video conferencing facilities) for supporting the group-work. The Application phase ends with the delivery, by each group of participants, of a final executive report.
- **Analysis.** The organizing team takes care of the data analysis and of the comparative evaluation of the methods. A report of the results of the evaluation is shared with all designers.

The main actors involved in our protocol are illustrated in Table 1. During the Training phase, designers and participants are the only actors that really need to be involved. Collection of material can be done easily by video or audio recording, in particular if we use classical lecture style presentation. On-line, web-based tutorials allow for even richer data collections by means of logs and screen recordings.

The Application phase is the moment where customer and observers play a major role in the process. The customer is there to answer all possible questions that may arise out of the participants analysis (starting from "which legislation does apply?" to "do you already have a SSL server?"). observers are also important. Even if we audio-video record the groups at work, there are "social" events that can be better captured by human observers. A simple example is a change in the group internal organization that was agreed during a coffee break; when participants return to the experiment, two people work on the mitigation strategy while one works on the risk assessment. As a result, the audio recording shows 50 minutes of silence out of which a final executive reports is produced.

Table 2. Data sources

Data Source	Description
Questionnaires	Questions ranged from information about participants' knowledge of IT security and risk assessment methods and their evaluation of the different methods.
Audio/Video Recordings	Audio-video files of the Application phase and Focus Groups discussions. Video and audio recording are transcribed and annotated to identify common patterns of behavior.
Method's Artefacts	Graphs, drawings, diagrams, notes, produced by the groups during Application phase.
Post-it Cloud	Post-it where participants were required to list the five aspects they consider to be particularly positive or negative about the method and about the evaluation procedure.
Focus Group Discussions	Participants discuss with method designers a number of topics related to the method, its application on the given scenario and the process of evaluation.
Group Presentations	Presentations given by groups in front of the method designers, the members of the organizing team, and all the other participants.
Final Reports	A 10-page final recommendation including some information about the analysis

Different types of data (listed in Table 2) should be collected during the study by using the techniques and instruments typically used in the Social Sciences for observing and measuring participants' behavior, attitudes and opinions.

3   The Actual Protocol Run

The first study took place in May 2011 as shown in Figure 1, while a second study is taking place at the time of writing.

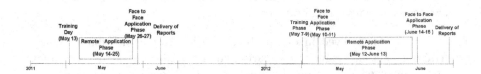

Fig. 1. Chronology of the comparative case study

During the *Training* day, we have introduced the participants to the aims, procedure, the expected outcomes of the study, and to the application scenario. The chosen application scenario was about the Healthcare Collaborative Network (HCN) by IBM [1], which is a "health information infrastructure for interconnecting and coordinating the delivery of information to participants in the collaborative network electronically". HCN was applied to a fictional Healthcare system based in Cityville (France). In the fictional set up, the CEO of the Healthcare System (the customer) hired the teams of analysts (the participants) to analyze the security and risk issues of HCN when applied to the context of Cityville.

The participants, during the Training day, received from the customer two chapters of the HCN book (Ch.1 and Ch.6). Moreover the participants received a 1-hour seminar about HCN, which was given by one member of the organizing team. We have divided participants in groups and assigned them to a security engineering method. Each group was formed by three or four participants: three professionals and one master student. Once divided in groups, the participants were required to attend the tutorials given by method designers about the method they would have used for the analysis of the application scenario. Each tutorial had a duration of approximately 2,5 hours. The *Application* phase lasted from the 14th to the 25th of May: the members of the groups worked remotely using collaborative tools (mainly BSCW and Marratech). During this phase, the groups received additional material about the application scenario: the material was a 2-page long note from the CEO informing the participants (the CEO's fictional consultants) about additional requirements from their client, the Health Care Authority. The remote Application phase has been followed by a two day face-to-face Application phase which took place in Paris. The first day of the face-to-face Application phase was organized into five group work sessions. Each session had duration of 75 minutes. On the second day, groups were asked to give a brief presentation of their work to an audience including organizers, method designers and other students. Participants were also asked to provide their feedbacks via questionnaires and focus group discussion conducted by the observers. Feedbacks were related to the assigned security engineering methods and the organization of the study. At the end of the Application phase, each group has to deliver a 10-page final report that was evaluated by the method designers.

In the 2012 study we have made some changes such as more time for the training phase, and the explicit participation of two industry representatives as customers.

4   Recruiting Participants and Method Designers

We have invited a number of research groups to join the activity (travel partly at our expenses). The selection of the security requirements methods to be evaluated was driven by three main factors: the number of citations, the fact that research on the method is still ongoing, and availability of the method designers. Out of the various oral and email invitations, only four groups accepted to participate in 2011. The most frequent justification has been lack of human resources ("PhD student terminated his studies"), followed by "no longer active in the field". The four security methods that have been the object of study for the comparative evaluation in 2011 are Coras, Secure Tropos, Problem Frames and SI*. Coras is a model-driven method for risk analysis proposed by SINTEF [12]. Problem Frames [6] is a framework for security requirements elicitation and analysis developed at Open University. Secure Tropos [16] is a methodology designed at Univerity of East London; the methodology supports capturing,

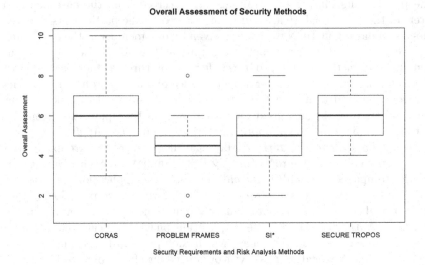

Fig. 2. Overall Security Methods Assessment (scale 1-10)

analysis and reasoning of security requirements from the early stages of the development process. SI* [4] is a formal framework developed at the University of Trento for modeling and analyzing security requirements of an organization. Forty-nine participants were involved in 2011: thirty-six participants were professionals with a minimum of five years of working experience in the field of Auditing in Information Systems. The professionals were attending the Master Course in Audit for Information System in Enterprises at Dauphine University. Thirteen participants were master students in Computer Science from the University of Trento with a background in Security Engineering and Information Systems. We have decided to have both junior and senior participants because involving only students in empirical research is known to be a major threat to external validity [19]. Therefore, by involving professionals, we wanted to avoid this issue.

5   Data Collection and Analysis

In this section we report some of the preliminary findings deriving from the analysis of the data collected by means of the questionnaires, the focus groups and the post-it notes fill out by the participant. Then, we compare the the coverage of security requirements derived from the analysis of groups' final reports with the feedbacks given by the participants about methods coverage.

5.1   Rating Tasks and Data Distribution

Participants were asked to give a final vote to the methods on a scale from 1 to 10 representing the overall level of appreciation of the methods. Figure 2 shows the distribution of the participants's responses to the overall assessment of each method. There is no statistically significant difference among the methods: the median evaluation is barely sufficient (solid line for each box). Each method also had both supporters and detractors (as one can seen from the whiskers), with the exception of the Problem Frames method that had a more concentrated distribution around the median.

A more refined analysis of the responses of the participants on the conceptual model, the analysis capabilities, and the tool support for each of the methods, provide a clearer separation among the methods. The flattened distribution obscures these important details: each method has strenghts and limitations which tend to balance each other.

For the conceptual model and the analysis, participants specified the level of appreciation in the scale 0 (Dislike), 1 (Like it the least), 2 (Like it a little), 3 (Like), 4 (Fairly Like), and 5 (Like it the most). Figure 3 shows that the least liked conceptual model belongs to the Problem Frames method while the one more appreciated by the participants is SI*'s conceptual model.

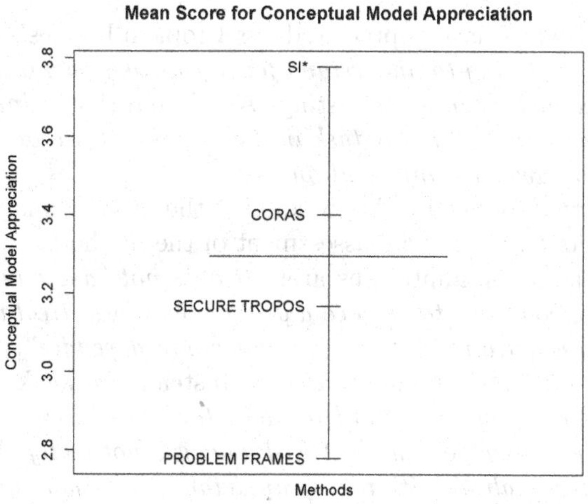

Fig. 3. Conceptual Model Appreciation

The participants helped to identify the key features of the SI* conceptual model: "*Considers dependencies between actors (social aspects). Effective to clarify responsibility of all the actors. Takes into account trust relations*", "*Study of relations between goals and agents*", and "*Easy to show the permission level*". Regarding Coras, the participants have not reported negative or positive aspects. On the contrary, the participants have spotted several weaknesses of Secure Tropos and Problem Frames's conceptual models. For the participants, Secure Tropos conceptual model "*does not have any mechanism to analyze alternative solutions to achieve a goal or to enforce treatments*", "*Difference between goals and objectives is not clearly defined.*", "*Ambiguity in assigning constraints between depender and dependee.*", and "*Hard goals Vs soft goals are ambiguous*".

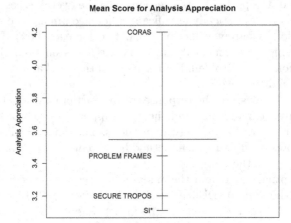

Fig. 4. Analysis Appreciation

Instead, the participants have appreciated less Problem Frames's conceptual because: "*Difficult/ confusing to understand few terms like warrants, formal arguments*", "*Resource nodes cannot be distinguished*", and that "*Unfortunately you don't see the actor connected to the task in the process. Based on my experience, it is very useful to have such information*".

Figure 4 shows that for Secure Tropos and SI* the security analysis is a critical aspect that impacts on the overall assessment of the methods.

Secure Tropos analysis' limitations are: "*It does not have any mechanism to analyze alternative solutions to achieve a goal or to enforce treatments*", "*Ambiguity in assigning constraints between depender and dependee*", "*No automatic analysis process, "Lack manual for guidance*". Instead, the weak aspects of SI*'s analysis are: "*Time consuming. Hard to make the links between the model and the risks maybe due to lack of time*", " *Risk analysis not really obvious. Method complicates the risk analysis with too many details. Does not cover all kinds of risks. Difficulty to find all the risks - thanks to the chart*"; "*Trust relations should support high level of detail*"; "*Starts with the actors and not the goal analysis. Should support goal prioritizations*"; " *Focuses only on some elements in the case, for example: no place for physical asset* ", and "*Too precise - going down to too many levels of details*". Coras and Problem Frames analysis have been appreciated by the participants because they provide a detailed step-by-step process. Participants said that Coras is "*Step by step procedure. Very detailed step with specific explanation*" while Problem Frames has" *Clear and organized steps to analyze problem domain. Structured.*"

About the tool, participants have been asked to evaluate the usability choosing a value in the scale from 0 (Unusable), 1 (Not easy at), 2 (Extra effort needed), 3 (Easy), 4 (Fairly Easy), and 5 (Very Easy). As shown in Figure 5, usability is a factor that could have influenced the overall assessment of the methods since the majority of the participants have negatively evaluated the usability of the tools.

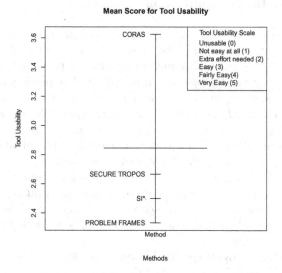

Fig. 5. Tool Usability Assessment

The concerns given by the participants during focus groups discussions and on post-it notes allowed us to understand which are the features of the tools that determine their poor usability. participants have reported several bugs of the Secure Tropos tool. To mention some: " *Problem in saving projects when the size of diagram increases*", " *Unreliable system - Impossible to open the project, once it is closed*", " *Cannot select multiple components to manipulate. For example: to delete a goal, you have to also delete the dependencies*", " *Its an incomplete system which does not have many features like select, cut, copy, duplicate.. etc*", and " *Difficult to modelise/draw a diagram with a complex scenario.* SI*'s tool has received mixed comments: "*Good tool and useful to modelize - Clear presentation of the diagram. Simple graphic diagrams. Friendly graphic formalism. Easy to draw diagrams*", and "*The tool is too abstract, it is possible that the analysts drop some part and don't go into detail.* Also the comments given by the participants on Problem Frames tool are mixed: some of them reported that is a" *nice tool for modeling basically the security issues*", while others mention missing features:"*in other tools we can have decompositions like 'OR' but in this, I can't find it*". The participants have expressed their concerns also on Coras tool, which has been rated the more usable tool among the four methods: they said that the tool " *not enough help to troubleshoot software problem*", " *difficult to understand diagrammatic representation.*", " *no reasoning services in the tool (automation computing of likelihood) support*", and that the " *tool is too complex with only fixed determined models (threat, treatment, asset diagrams)*".

5.2   Data on Methods' Application

During focus groups discussions, participants were asked to evaluate the coverage of the security requirements elicited because of the application of the methods.

participants who applied Coras mentioned that it provides*"..powerful and good coverage in case right people are involved"*. Other participants also said that*"the coverage may depend on the way you apply the method than on the method itself"*, and that *"the concept of the asset we found before, if you are the right guy you will get good coverage otherwise it is very difficult"*.

Problems Frames provides good coverage according to participants's feedbacks: one participants said *"I think the method provides wide coverage on different aspects .... And also we can identify what are the assets that we need to protect, and why we need to protect it, not exactly how but what and why we need to answer. So it provides a good coverage to understand the problem"*; another Partcipant said that the*"Method is good in providing coverage but is not good at providing all kinds of treatments"*.

participants did not provide specific feedbacks on the coverage of Secure Tropos. Instead, on SI* participants asserted that leads to the identification of general security requirements: *"we found a set of general security requirements that every organization would have. Maybe they are 70% relevant but not sure"* and that *"our requirements are not ambiguous but probably they are too global, too large, and so we don't define precise recommendations to have a complete view"*.

In order to see if the participants' feedbacks on security requirements coverage were well founded, we have also analyzed the final report delivered from the groups: for each method, we have retrieved the security requirements and the security recommendations identified by the group as result of the method application.

Figure 6 shows that each method lead to the identification of different requirements. The groups working with Coras and Secure Tropos have focused on Availability, Confidentiality, and Integrity. The groups who have applied Problem Frames instead have identified Integrity and Confidentiality as main security requirements. Finally, the groups working with SI* have focused mostly on Integrity and Privacy. Figure 7 shows that Access Control and Training are the most frequent proposed security solutions across all the methods. These results are quite obvious since Access Control and Training are two of the most common security solutions and they can be applied to any system.

However, what we noticed is that the security solutions identified were quite generic and sometimes not linked to the security requirements at all. This is true in particular for Secure Tropos and SI*. In the final recommendations deriving by the application of Secure Tropos, Confidentiality and Integrity have been recognized as important requirements but there no security recommendations on how they have to be preserved. The same is true for SI*, where Integrity is one of the important security requirements but no security solutions on how to preserve it have been found in the reports. Instead, for the groups working on Coras, it seems that the security solutions proposed in the final recommendations have been easily derived from the treatments identified during the risk analysis.

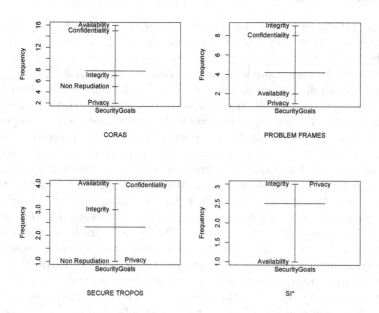

Fig. 6. Security goals frequency for each method

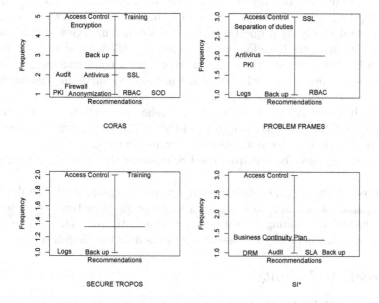

Fig. 7. Security recommendations frequency for each method

6   Related Works

In a mapping study on empirical evaluation conducted in 2009 [3], only the 13% of the papers reporting research in Requirements Engineering were based on a case study.

For instance, [2] is an example of an observational study, while [18] is a good illustration of controlled experiments in security. Two usability studies have been performed to assess how easily models used in risk analysis can be understood [5,8]. Yskout et al.[21] have proposed a methodology to preserve trust properties in a software design. They validated the methodology via an empirical study involving 12 subjects. The results show that their approach does provide an edge in terms of reduced effort required to evolve a software architecture.Heyman et al. [7] have performed an assessment of the quality of about 200 security patterns by means of panel judgment. The main findings are that, often, the same pattern is re-published under a different name, and that the average quality of the documentation for security patterns is low. The closest work to ours is the one by Opdahl et al. [18]. They have carried out two controlled experiments (with 28 and 35 participants, respectively) to compare two methods for early elicitation of security requirements, namely attack trees and misuse cases. They assessed the effectiveness and coverage of these methods. The main differences between the study we present in this paper and the experiments conducted by Opdahl et al. are: a) our study involved not only master students but also professionals to limit threats to external validity; b) the groups of participants have applied only one method among the one under evaluation and not all the methods as in the study by Opdahl et al.; c) our study was a qualitative study, and thus to collect data we have not only used questionnaires but we also interviewed the participants. Other initiatives have focused on gaining knowledge and understanding the secure implementation of software products with empirical means. These usually include tapping the "wisdom of the masses" by surveying development groups to determine what the typical practices are that one should follow to come up with secure software. The most comprehensive such survey as of today is the Building Security In Maturity Model (BISSIM3) [13] which observed and analysed real-world data from 42 leading software development companies, 9 of which were Europeans, the rest from the US. However the level of granularity is too coarse.

Compared to these proposals, the comparative empirical study we describe in this paper does not aim to evaluate a single security method or to survey the best practice in building secure software. Our initiative aims at comparing different methods when they are used by subjects different than inventor.

7   Threats to Validity

- **Construct Validity.** Threats to construct validity are related to decide to which extent what was to be measured was actually measured. The main threat to construct validity in our case studies regards the design of the research instruments: our main measurement instruments are interviews and questionnaires. Three researchers have checked that only questions of relevance to the research questions were included in the interview guide and in the questionnaires; therefore we believe that our research instruments measure what we want to measure. Moreover, to reduce this threat we have gathered data using other data sources like audio-video files, post-it notes, and participants' reports on methods'application.

- **Internal Validity.** A threat to internal validity is that the time spent in training participants was not enough for them to apply the method and understand the application scenarios. To mitigate this threat, method designers and customers should be available to answer questions that participants may arise during the application of the methods. Another threat is represented by participants' previous knowledge of other methods. For example, in one group it was decided to use COBIT to identify the security requirements for the application scenario, rather than the method assigned to the group. In this case, the feedbacks provided by the group have no value because the method was not applied.

  One additional threat is that the time participants spent on the methods'application was too short to let them provide insigthful feedbacks on methods' effectiveness. We are aware that the opinions of the participants may have been different if they would have applied the method over a longer period of time.

- **External Validity.** We have evaluated the effectiveness of the security requirements and risk analysis methods with both master students and professional from different countries, and we have applied the methods in different contexts - Smart Grid and Healthcare. This give use some confidence that our hypothesis and conclusions on methods' effectiveness have a medium degree of generalizability.

- **Conclusion Validity.** An important threat to the conclusion validity of our studies is that our sample is relatively small in statistical terms. In fact, for each method the sample consists of twelve participants. In order to increase the statistical significance of the emerging hypothesis and insights on methods' effectiveness, we are conducting another case study to have a bigger data sample.

8   Lessons Learned and Conclusions

The first study we have conducted allowed us to collect a set of insightful comments about the Coras, Secure Tropos, Problem Frames and SI* and to identify their strenghts and limitations.

Coras overall has been the most appreciated method because it provides a step-by-step process and the conceptual model comprises concepts that are easy to understand. However, the usability of the tool needs to be improved with automatic reasoning support for example automatic likelihood and consequence computation or treatments selection. An important aspect that came out is that it leads to a complete identification of security risks only when experts are involved in the risk analysis.

Secure Tropos requires improvements in all its aspects: the definition of some of the concepts in the conceptual model needs to be revised to avoid ambiguity on when to use a concept or another; the steps of the process to elicit functional and security requirements needs to be clearly defined; the tool requires to improve the functionalities to create, delete and copy diagrams. SI* has to improve the process to elicit requirements under two aspects: the steps of the process are not clear and need to be detailed and the risk analysis has to be simplified because it is overcomplicated and it does allow to identify all the possible risks. Also the SI* tool needs to improve the visual notion of the diagrams. Last and least, Problem Frames strenghts are the process because it is very detailed and it leads to identify which assets need to be protected, and the tool because it allows to model basic security issues. However, the conceptual model for security argumentation needs to be better defined.

The study also helped us to understand a number of aspects to improve the evaluation protocol for the next edition of the challenge, which is currently taking place in May and June 2012. We list the main lesson learned below.

- **Don't (try to) collect too much data.** When we initially designed the protocol, we followed the design principles recommended in most statistics and action research texbooks and tried to collect everything that could be collected (audio, video, photos of artifacts, computer diagrams, question-naires for each possible phases of the experiment etc.) in order to eliminate all possible confounding factors. We found out this was a mistake. At first the sampling disturbs the natural flow of the study. Second, participants developed an uneasy feeling of being stalked or got simply tired of filling questionnaires. This study requires participants to be intellectually moti-vated, concentrated and challenged[1].
- **Take time to explain orally everything.** Another title could be "don't assume people read the consent information sheet". This is particularly im-portant for audio and video recording. Does the participant understand whether they are being monitored and for which purposes? If they have not read the information sheet carefully, after some time they might feel monitored and withdraw from the study.
- **Write simple scenarios and ask a customer to join.** Participants will always ask unexpected questions about the scenario. Following the experi-ence of our first small-scale trials, we have tried to offset in advance the questions raised by participants by choosing a 100+ pages with details and a long description of business and high-level security requirements by the CEO. It turned out to be a mistake. Most people didn't read them carefully. The description of the application scenario should be kept short and pro-vide only key information. Rather a customer should be present during the Application phase to answer participants' questions.

---

[1] Humans or mice do not usually withdraw from medical or biology experiments be-cause they find it boring or feel stalked (they either die or their therapy is somehow modified).

- **Define collectively the rules of engagement:** Do observers and method designers know which questions by the participants they can answer during the Application phase? Since method designers represent themselves and are not under the control of the experimenters they might answer the question of the participants by doing the particular fragment of the model for them. It is therefore important that this issue is discussed and understood by everybody.
- **Beware temptations to use background knowledge.** In one group the participants decided that COBIT would have yielded to better result and silently switched to it. It should be made clear that the evaluation is not about the method results itself but on the application of the method.

In summary we think that this was a very challenging and interesting study. It has been the first time that more than 40+ CS students and practitioner consultants tried to apply security requirements engineering methods in a *comparative* settings. The results of the analysis are still preliminary but this could be the first step towards the development of a scientific protocol for the empirical evaluation of security requirements engineering methods.

Acknowledgments. This work is partly supported by the projects EU-FP7-IST-NoE-NESSOS, EU-EIT-ICTLabs, EU-FP7-SEC-SECONOMICS, PAT-TRISE.

References

1. Healthcare Collaborative Network Solution Planning and Implementation. Vervante (2006)
2. Asnar, Y., Giorgini, P., Massacci, F., Saidane, A., Bonato, R., Meduri, V., Ricucci, V.: Secure and dependable patterns in organizations: An empirical approach. In: Proc. of RE 2007, pp. 287–292 (2007)
3. Condori-Fernandez, N., Daneva, M., Sikkel, K., Wieringa, R., Dieste, O., Pastor, O.: A systematic mapping study on empirical evaluation of software requirements specifications techniques. In: Proc. of ESEM 2009, pp. 502–505 (2009)
4. Giorgini, P., Massacci, F., Mylopoulos, J., Zannone, N.: Modeling security requirements through ownership, permission and delegation. In: Proc. of RE 2005, pp. 167–176 (2005)
5. Grondahl, I.H., Lund, M.S., Stolen, K.: Reducing the effort to comprehend risk models: Text labels are often preferred over graphical means. Risk Analysis 31(11), 1813–1831 (2011)
6. Haley, C., Laney, R., Moffett, J., Nuseibeh, B.: Security requirements engineering: A framework for representation and analysis. IEEE Transactions on Software Engineering 34(1), 133–153 (2008)
7. Heyman, T., Yskout, K., Scandariato, R., Joosen, W.: An analysis of the security patterns landscape. In: Proc. of the 3rd Int. Workshop on Soft. Eng. for Secure Systems, SESS 2007, p. 3. IEEE Computer Society (2007)
8. Hogganvik, I., Stølen, K.: A Graphical Approach to Risk Identification, Motivated by Empirical Investigations. In: Wang, J., Whittle, J., Harel, D., Reggio, G. (eds.) MoDELS 2006. LNCS, vol. 4199, pp. 574–588. Springer, Heidelberg (2006)

9. ITGI. CoBIT - Framework Control Objectives Management Guidelines Maturity Models, 4.1 ed. The IT Governance Institute (2007)
10. Jürjens, J.: UMLsec: Extending UML for Secure Systems Development. In: Jézéquel, J.-M., Hussmann, H., Cook, S. (eds.) UML 2002. LNCS, vol. 2460, pp. 412–425. Springer, Heidelberg (2002)
11. Lodderstedt, T., Basin, D., Doser, J.: SecureUML: A UML-Based Modeling Language for Model-Driven Security. In: Jézéquel, J.-M., Hussmann, H., Cook, S. (eds.) UML 2002. LNCS, vol. 2460, pp. 426–441. Springer, Heidelberg (2002)
12. Lund, M.S., Solhaug, B., Stolen, K.: A guided tour of the coras method. In: Model-Driven Risk Analysis, pp. 23–43. Springer (2011)
13. McGraw, G., Chess, B., Migues, S.: Building Security In Maturity Model (BSIMM3), 3rd edn. Cigital Inc. (2011)
14. Mead, N.R., Stehney, T.: Security quality requirements engineering (square) methodology. SIGSOFT Softw. Eng. Notes 30(4), 1–7 (2005)
15. Microsoft Security Development Life Cycle. Microsft sdl website (2011), http://www.microsoft.com/security/sdl/default.aspx
16. Mouratidis, H., Giorgini, P., Manson, G.: Integrating Security and Systems Engineering: Towards the Modelling of Secure Information Systems. In: Eder, J., Missikoff, M. (eds.) CAiSE 2003. LNCS, vol. 2681, pp. 1031–1031. Springer, Heidelberg (2003)
17. NIST Comp. Security Division. Recommended security controls for federal information systems and organizations. Tech. Rep. 800-53, U.S. Nat. Inst. of Standards and Technology, Rev. 3 (2009)
18. Opdahl, A.L., Sindre, G.: Experimental comparison of attack trees and misuse cases for security threat identification. Inf. Softw. Technol. 51(5), 916–932 (2009)
19. Potts, C.: Software-engineering research revisited. IEEE Softw. 10(5), 19–28 (1993)
20. The Open Web Application Security Project. Owasp website (2011), http://www.owasp.org
21. Yskout, K., Scandariato, R., Joosen, W.: Change patterns: Co-evolving requirements and architecture. Soft. and Sys. Modeling J. (2012)

There Is Safety in Numbers: Preventing Control-Flow Hijacking by Duplication

Job Noorman, Nick Nikiforakis, and Frank Piessens

IBBT-DistriNet, KU Leuven
job.noorman@student.kuleuven.be,
{nick.nikiforakis,frank.piessens}@cs.kuleuven.be

Abstract. Despite the large number of proposed countermeasures against control-flow hijacking attacks, these attacks still pose a great threat for today's applications. The problem with existing solutions is that they either provide incomplete probabilistic protection (e.g., stack canaries) or impose a high runtime overhead (e.g., bounds checking).

In this paper, we show how the concept of program-part duplication can be used to protect against control-flow hijacking attacks and present two different instantiations of the duplication concept which protect against popular attack vectors. First, we use the duplication of functions to eliminate the need of return addresses and thus provide complete protection against attacks targeting a function's return address. Then we demonstrate how the integrity of function pointers can be protected through the use of data duplication. We test the combined effectiveness of our two methods and experimentally show that they provide an almost complete protection against control-flow hijacking attacks with only a low runtime overhead in real-world applications.

Keywords: control-data attacks, duplication, return addresses, function pointers.

1 Introduction

All but the simplest of programs contain non-straight-line code, i.e. code for which the control-flow is not fixed at compile time. The control-flow of those programs will be dictated by data structures located somewhere in memory. These control structures normally take the form of a memory address where the next instruction to be executed is located; the most common examples are return addresses and function pointers. If the program contains some kind of vulnerability that gives the attacker the opportunity to write arbitrary data to a control structure, he will be able to hijack the control-flow.

The problem of control-flow hijacking has been known for a long time; the Morris worm [28] in 1988 was the first popular attack to exploit a stack-based buffer overflow to this end. As such, this problem has gained much attention from the academic world and numerous solutions have been proposed. The most

A. Jøsang and B. Carlsson (Eds.): NordSec 2012, LNCS 7617, pp. 105–120, 2012.
© Springer-Verlag Berlin Heidelberg 2012

widely adopted solution for protecting return addresses is the use of stack canaries (e.g. StackGuard [9] for GCC). While very effective, stack canaries are no silver bullet for the problem of return address smashing. The reason for this is threefold. Firstly, stack canaries can only detect return address smashing through a buffer overflow. If the attacker manages to overwrite the return address through an indirect pointer overwrite [6], he will be able to bypass the protection mechanism. Secondly, the effectiveness of stack canaries relies on a secret value that is located somewhere in memory. If the attacker somehow gains access to this memory location by either overwriting it or disclosing its contents, the protection becomes useless. For instance, prior research has shown that buffer over-reads and format-string vulnerabilities can be used to uncover secrets hidden on the stack or heap of a protected application [31]. Lastly, most implementations will not protect every function by default but rather use a heuristic to decide which functions to protect. This heuristic usually takes the form of only protecting functions that have a stack-allocated character buffer of a certain minimum size and is used to minimize the performance overhead of stack canaries. A recent exploit of LibTIFF [24] used an overflow in an integer array and, as such, was not detectable by stack canaries.

A second attack vector that is used to hijack the control flow of a program, are function pointers. The protection of function pointers, however, has gained much less attention than the protection of return addresses, probably because of their relatively infrequent use in applications. One proposed technique to protect function pointers is the use of encryption by PointGuard [8]. Here, pointer values are encrypted (using XOR with a secret value) when stored and decrypted when used. This technique, like stack canaries, relies on a secret value that the attacker cannot know for the protection to remain effective. Again, it has been shown that this protection may be circumvented in the presence of a buffer over-read vulnerability [31].

In this paper, two techniques are introduced that use duplication to prevent control-flow hijacking. The first technique is a novel compile-time solution of protecting return addresses. Our system duplicates functions in such a way that makes return addresses unnecessary for the program to run correctly. Since instead of trying to *protect* return addresses we completely *remove* them from the program, there simply is no return control-structure left to be attacked. Therefore, this technique provides a more thorough solution to the problem of return address smashing than any popular countermeasure that tries to protect return addresses, including stack canaries. As an added benefit, this technique proves to have little or no overhead since there are no runtime checks to be performed. In fact, programs protected by this scheme in some cases outperform their unprotected versions.

The second technique this paper introduces uses the duplication of control data to protect function pointers. Function pointers used by a program are duplicated in a protected storage so that they can be checked for corruption when used. This technique is similar to that of the Return Address Defender [7], but applied to function pointers instead of return addresses. Because of the infrequent use of function pointers (as opposed to return addresses), the runtime overhead of our technique has proven to be small for most programs.

The rest of this paper is structured as follows: Section 2 gives the general principles of how duplication can be used to prevent control-flow hijacking and shows the design of two different instantiations of this principle. Section 3 gives a short overview of how these instantiations were implemented. In Section 4, we evaluate the two introduced techniques in terms of effectiveness in protecting programs and their overhead on the runtime performance and program size, followed by a discussion of some issues we encountered in Section 5. Section 6 discusses related work and we conclude in Section 7.

2 Design

2.1 Using Duplication for Protection

There are two ways in which duplication can be used to protect control data in memory: (a) duplicate the control data itself so that it becomes more difficult to overwrite all copies, or (b) duplicate some other part of the program so that the control data is not needed any more. Using (a) is highly generic: any kind of data can be protected in this way. How well this protection works, however, depends on how the duplicated control data is protected since an attacker might be able to find a way to overwrite both copies and circumvent the protection. Also, this technique will always cause runtime overhead on the protected program.

Technique (b), on the other hand, offers full protection of the control data by completely removing it. Another asset of this technique is that it does not rely on any runtime checks so it might be possible to implement it without any runtime overhead on the protected program. Unfortunately, it is not possible to protect all types of control data by this scheme. The next sections explain instantiations of both schemes.

2.2 Protecting Return Addresses

Idea. The key idea of our approach is that return addresses are only needed if a function is called from more than one place. Indeed, if a function has only one call site, the return instruction can be replaced by a jump instruction to a hard coded label just after the call site. Figure 1 illustrates this. The transformed function always semantically behaves the same as the original as long as it is only called from one call site.

The whole purpose of having functions, however, is to enable code-reuse. Therefore, most programs will likely not have many functions that are only called from a single call site. This is where function duplication comes in: if we make as many copies of a function as it has call sites, all return instructions in those copies can be eliminated.

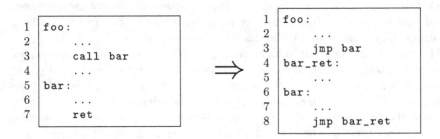

Fig. 1. Transforming a return instruction into a jump

Duplicating Functions. To duplicate functions in such a way that every function has only one call site, information is needed about which function calls are made in a program. More specifically, we need to know for each function by which functions it is called. This information is available in the call graph of the program. A call graph is a directed graph in which every function of the program is represented by a node and there is an edge from node A to node B if function A calls function B. For example, the call graph of the program in Fig. 2 is shown in Fig. 3a.

```
1   static void foo() {}
2   static void bar() {foo();}
3   void baz() {bar();}
4   void qux() {bar();}
```

Fig. 2. An example C program

There is one special node visible in this call graph: the external node. A node has an incoming edge from the external node if it might be called from an unknown function. In this example, the functions baz and qux have external linkage (i.e., not declared with the static keyword in C) which means they might be called from functions not available at the time of compilation. This is important information since it means that we cannot eliminate return instructions in functions that are called from the external node. Indeed, it is impossible to compute, at the time of compilation, where these functions should return to.

Through the use of the information available in the call graph, the process of duplicating functions is straightforward. Starting from the external node, every node is visited once. If a node is visited that has more than one incoming edge, it is copied as many times as there are incoming edges and the call graph is updated accordingly. For the example C program shown in Fig. 2, the nodes corresponding to the function baz and qux are visited first. Since both have only one incoming edge, nothing needs to be done. Next, the node for the function bar is visited, which has two incoming edges. Duplicating this function introduces a new function and the original call sites are updated. This is illustrated in Fig. 3b. Note that due to this transformation, the function foo, which originally had only one call site, now has two. The node for bar_clone, which has only one incoming edge, is visited next. Then foo is visited which needs to be duplicated. When this is done, the process is complete. The resulting call graph is shown in Fig. 3c.

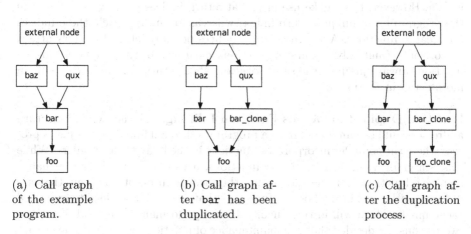

(a) Call graph of the example program.

(b) Call graph after bar has been duplicated.

(c) Call graph after the duplication process.

Fig. 3. Example call graph transformation

At this point, the program has been transformed to a version that is semantically equivalent to the original but has only functions that are called by at most one other function. This means the principle explained in the previous section can be applied in a straightforward way. First, we add a label after all call instructions, which will allow the called function to jump back to this point. Then, in the called function all return instructions are replaced by direct jumps to the inserted label.

Recursive Functions. The aforementioned technique of function duplication does not work for recursive functions, since recursive functions cannot be duplicated in a way that makes them have only one call site. The same property holds for groups of mutually recursive functions. As a result, we cannot know at compile time where a recursive function will return to. To solve this problem, this decision has to be postponed to runtime.

The approach taken in our solution is the following: first, the functions in the call graph are grouped in sets of mutually recursive functions; these sets are the strongly connected components of the call graph[1]. Then duplication is performed as usual but instead of duplicating functions, these sets are duplicated. The result of this step is a call graph in which each mutually recursive group of functions

---

[1] A strongly connected component of a directed graph is a maximally sized subgraph in which each node can reach all other nodes.

has only one call site from outside this group. This assures that each function has the lowest possible number of call sites.

When eliminating return instructions, each call to a function having more than one call site will push a different return index on the stack. When the called function needs to return, it will pop this index and use it to decide where to return to. If an invalid index is encountered when returning, the program is aborted. Note that this approach is similar is the one taken by Li et al. in [15]. However, they make use of global return indices (i.e., every call site in the program has a unique return index) whereas in our approach, these indices are local to functions. Also, since return indices possibly introduce a new attack vector, only (mutually) recursive functions make use of these indices; normal functions always jump to the same location when returning. We discuss this in more detail in Section 5.

Function Duplication versus Function Inlining. Another way that return addresses could be eliminated from a program is through function inlining, a process where the compiler incorporates functions in the body of their callers. While this is a viable approach for simple functions, it cannot be used for (mutually) recursive functions. At the same time, the incorporation of functions that are not frequently used in the body of functions that are, will likely lead to increased cache misses which will in turn incur a higher performance overhead. For these two reasons, we decided that the maintenance of functions as stand-alone chunks of code with hard-coded return addresses is the best of the two approaches and thus favored it over function inlining.

2.3   Protecting Function Pointers

For the protection of function pointers, we have taken the approach of duplicating the pointers themselves. The source code of a program is automatically transformed so that when a value is stored in a function pointer, it is duplicated in another part of memory and when it is loaded, the loaded value is compared with the duplicated value. If these values do not match, the program is aborted.

Although duplication alone would provide some protection – the attacker would need to find a way to overwrite two distinct memory locations with the same value – our technique additionally protects the memory locations where duplicates are stored. Two different techniques for protecting these duplicates are provided by our solution: (a) the use of unwritable guard pages around the storage, or (b) making the entire storage location unwritable while it is not needed. While (b) is clearly the most secure of the two, it also incurs the most overhead since two calls to `mprotect` (thus, two system calls) are needed whenever a pointer is stored: one to unlock the storage and one to lock it again. Note that no system calls are needed when a pointer is loaded since the storage remains readable at all times.

3   Implementation Details

The techniques presented in this paper have been implemented using the LLVM Compiler Infrastructure [17]. Compilation of a program using LLVM is a three-step process: (a) a frontend translates the source language in the LLVM Intermediate Representation (IR), (b) architecture independent optimizations are run on the IR, and (c) a backend translates the IR to target instructions and runs architecture dependent optimizations.

3.1   Protecting Return Addresses

The technique of duplicating functions to protect return addresses has been implemented as two passes in LLVM. The first pass is a transformation of the IR to bring the program in the form discussed in Section 2.2: every function has only one call site. Because it transforms the IR, it is completely independent of the source language and the target architecture. Unfortunately, the IR has some restrictions which make it impossible to eliminate return instructions at this point. More specifically, the IR does not allow jumping outside of functions, which is exactly what is needed to replace return instruction by jumps.

The solution to this problem is to eliminate return instructions in the backend where it is possible to insert arbitrary instructions of the target architecture. The downside of this approach is that the implementation is not architecture independent any more. Currently, support has been implemented for x86 (32 and 64 bit), which is the platform of choice for most desktop and server environments.

3.2   Protecting Function Pointers

The implementation of our protection of function pointers contains two parts: a secure storage mechanism and a program transformation that inserts calls to this storage. The secure storage is implemented as a fixed-size hash map to provide fast insertions and lookups of pointers. The hash map maps the address of a memory location to the value of the function pointer at that memory location. The size of the storage, as well as the desired protection mechanism, can be configured through environment variables.

The transformation of the program is implemented as a pass in LLVM. It is a transformation of the LLVM IR so it is completely independent of the source language or target architecture. The transformation itself is straightforward: all loads and stores of function pointers are replaced with calls to the secured storage. This is illustrated in Fig. 4. There are three transformations visible in this figure: (a) assignments to a function pointer are replaced by a call to __store_ptr(). This function stores the pointer in the protected storage as well as in the original location. (b) Calls of a function pointer are replaced by a call to __load_ptr() which loads the pointer from the storage and checks for equality with the value at the original location. The pointer is loaded in a register and then this register is used to call the function. (c) If the lifetime of the protected pointer ends, its storage space is released with __free_ptr(). Currently, this is only implemented for stack based function pointers.

```
1  void foo();
2
3  void bar()
4  {
5      void (*f)() = foo;
6      f();
7  }
```

⟹

```
1   void foo();
2
3   void bar()
4   {
5       void (*f)();
6       __store_ptr(&f, foo);
7       register void (*tmp)() =
8           __load_ptr(&f);
9       tmp();
10      __free_ptr(&f);
11  }
```

Fig. 4. Transformation used for pointer duplication

4   Evaluation

4.1   Security Evaluation

We evaluated the provided protection of our solutions using RIPE [36], an open source testbed for quantifying the protection of any given countermeasure. RIPE performs a plethora of different attacks on itself and reports each attack's success or failure. For example, it is able to perform direct (e.g., buffer overflows) and indirect attacks on return addresses, function pointers and longjmp buffers[2] located in all memory segments (e.g., stack, heap and BSS). All experiments were performed on a Linux system configured to not use any protection mechanisms.

The results of RIPE are shown in Table 1. For the protection of return addresses, it is clear that our proposed technique of duplicating functions is more effective than stack canaries[3]. This is because, as explained in Section 1, stack canaries fail to protect against indirect pointer overwrite attacks while our technique does protect against such attacks.

The table also shows that using the pointer duplication technique is very effective: on its own, it protects against more than half of the attacks that were possible in the unprotected version of RIPE. The reason that the protection of function pointers seems to be more effective than that of return addresses is that RIPE is able to perform more attacks on the former. When combining our two techniques, the only attacks that still succeed are attacks abusing longjmp buffers. Given the fact that newer versions of libc actively protect this type of structures, the same LLVM-compiled and protected binary produces zero successful attacks on a more modern system.

---

[2] Longjmp buffers are used to store the program state (e.g. program counter and stack pointer) between calls of setjmp() and longjmp() and are a popular attack vector.

[3] We use the stack canary implementation of LLVM which is similar to StackGuard.

Table 1. The number of successful attacks in RIPE when using different protections

Protection type	Successful attacks
No protection	540
Stack canaries (1)	520
Duplicated functions (2)	470
Duplicated function pointers (3)	230
(1) + (3)	210
(2) + (3)	180

4.2   Performance Evaluation

In our evaluation, we compare the runtime performance of applications protected by our techniques to that of unprotected applications. Duplicated function pointers are protected by guard pages to give a baseline of the overhead incurred by this countermeasure. We also show the performance of each application when protected by stack canaries since our proposed technique of duplicating functions is an alternative to that approach.

Two types of performance benchmarks are used: First, we compare the runtime performance of our system using SPECint2006 [29] with the reference workload. Second, we evaluate the performance of popular server applications following the same approach used by Lvin et al. [18].

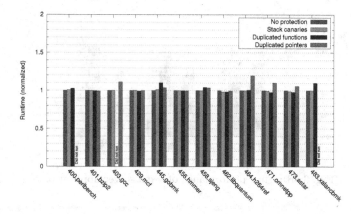

Fig. 5. Runtime performance of the SPECint2006 benchmark suite

SPECint2006. Figure 5 presents the normalized runtimes of the 12 programs of SPECint2006. For some of the programs, we were unable to produce valid runs: (a) 403.gcc did not compile when using duplicated functions because of out-of-memory issues (b) 400.perlbench and 483.xalancbmk did not run using duplicated function pointers because of false positives. These issues will be further discussed in Section 5.

As observable in Fig. 5, function duplication incurs no overhead for most programs and even causes a slight speed-up in some applications. There are some programs for which there is overhead when using duplicated functions but this overhead is less than 10% in all cases. The use of duplicated function pointers can cause a higher overhead for applications that make heavy use of function pointers. The most affected program, 464.h264ref, has an overhead of approximately 20%. While this is a non-negligible overhead, it is also obvious that all other applications that make more moderate use of function pointers have a much lower overhead.

Server Applications. The performance of three different server applications was measured: the thttpd web server, the bftpd FTP server and the OpenSSH server. For the first two, we measured the time it takes for 50 simultaneous clients to make 100 requests each. For OpenSSH, we measured the time needed to authenticate, spawn a shell and disconnect.

Figure 6 shows the results of these experiments, normalized with the programs' unprotected versions. The overhead incurred by duplicating functions is negligible. The overhead due to function pointer duplication is less than 2% in almost all cases with the exception of the OpenSSH server where the overhead is 6%.

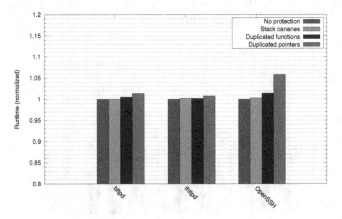

Fig. 6. Runtime performance of some server applications

4.3 Code-Size Evaluation

The duplication of all functions so as to eliminate the need of return addresses leads of course to the expansion of the code section of a program. The average size of the SPECint2006 binaries, before function duplication is 2MB. After the application of our duplication algorithm, the average size is 156 MB. While this may appear as a very high overhead, it is important to remember that this is the size of the program on disk. Given the capacity of today's commercial off-the-shelf hard disks, we believe that the difference in size is unimportant.

The enlarged code section will still be loaded as individual memory pages by the operating system, and each page will be in-turn swapped-out when it is no longer necessary. This behavior allows for the majority of the code to be off-memory, on-disk while still maintaining low performance overheads, as shown in Section 4.2.

5   Discussion and Future Work

Return Address Protection. In principle, the technique of function duplication offers complete protection from return address smashing since the return addresses are simply removed from the program. However, special care has to be taken to ensure that the entire attack surface is covered. As explained in Section 2.2, return addresses cannot be removed from functions that have external linkage. This means that there will always be one copy of such functions that will not benefit from our protection. Fortunately, this problem can easily be solved by postponing the function duplication step to link time where the linkage type of all function can be changed to internal.

Functions that are called though function pointers pose a similar problem as those with external linkage. For these functions it is also impossible to know at compile time where they will return to, so we need to keep one copy of each which still uses a return address. Unfortunately, there seems to be no easy way to solve this problem, leaving those functions unprotected in our current implementation. It should be noted, however, that these function *are* protected when a direct call to them is made. This means that if such a function contains a vulnerability, it can only be exploited when it is called through a pointer.

Since our solution to the problem of recursive functions, discussed in Section 2.2, introduces state on the stack, one might wonder whether this state could become a new attack vector. As mentioned earlier, our approach is similar to that used in [15] with the difference that the indices used by us are local to functions instead of global to the program. Because the indices are local to functions, the number of possible legal values an attacker could overwrite an index with, is very limited making it practically impossible to construct exploits of any real value. If the index on the stack is not in the range of values expected by the program, the process aborts thus any in-place attacks are terminated.

Lastly, note that our system focuses on the protection of return addresses instead of the detection of buffer overflows. Since the return addresses cannot be modified by an attacker, applications may be able to execute correctly even in the presence of an overflow that would normally hijack or crash the program.

Memory Usage. While duplicating functions, memory usage can be problematic: some programs may fail to compile due to out of memory errors. However, since most software is provided in binary form, a vendor can provide the necessary resources once upon compilation and then ship the compiled and protected binary to all users. Nevertheless, to make our countermeasure as widely applicable as possible, we currently provide two possible solution to this problem. The first is the ability to manually exclude functions from the duplication process. While not optimal, this approach can be used by seasoned developers who understand which functions are the least likely to contain vulnerabilities. One of our goals however, is to make the protection of return addresses fully automatic. Hence, we are currently implementing an automatic safety analysis framework to eliminate the need of manual intervention.

In our current implementation, a function is considered unsafe if it might do anything that alters memory in an unexpected way. This approach is already more sophisticated than the heuristics used in most stack canary implementations, which only check for the presence of character buffers on a function's stack frame. Our framework takes into account the fact that the return address of a function other than the current one may be overwritten by writing through a compromised pointer [6]. This means that any store through a pointer may only be considered safe if it can be proven where that pointer points to and that the corresponding memory location is large enough to store the value being stored.

The results of this framework are looking promising in the sense that a lot of functions can already correctly be detected as being safe. However, a significant amount of work still lies ahead since the number of functions that can be eliminated from duplication is still not enough to make all complex programs compile in a safe way.

Memory Aliasing. Most low-level programming languages allow casting of pointer types. This makes it impossible to know in some cases whether or not a store to a memory location stores a function pointer. In our current implementation, we simply ignore loads of pointers to which no corresponding store has occurred which means that such pointers are not protected.

One way to protect those pointers is by observing that, if a function pointer is aliased by another pointer, this pointer is a `void` pointer in most cases. This means that we could duplicate all `void` pointers in addition to function pointers although this would likely incur a higher runtime overhead than the current function pointer duplication.

6   Related Work

In general, there are three categories of countermeasures against popular control-flow hijacking attacks: (a) specifically trying to protect return addresses and function pointers, (b) more generally trying to counter vulnerabilities that enable the overwriting of sensitive control-data structures, and (c) minimizing the usefulness of being able to overwrite a control-data structure. Our function-duplication technique belongs to category (a). Here we will discuss some of the most well-known existing countermeasures in all three categories.

A popular way of detecting attacks against a function's return address is through the use of stack canaries. Most modern compilers have implemented some form of stack canaries (e.g., StackGuard [9] for GCC). ProPolice [11] is a re-implementation of StackGuard with the addition of security-enhancing features such as variable reordering. While more robust than StackGuard, ProPolice also cannot detect a return-address overwrite, happening through an indirect pointer overwrite.

Another way of protecting return addresses is by using a shadow stack. Return addresses will be pushed on both the normal and the shadow stack and then checked for equality when used. This approach is used by the Return Address Defender [7] and Libverify [4] and in both cases, the mechanism necessary to protect the shadow stack incurs a significant performance overhead. StackShield [35] follows a similar approach with a return-address shadow stack, but also attempts to protect function pointers by verifying that they do not point within the program's stack, heap or data segment. Recent attacking techniques however, like return-to-libc [10] and return-oriented-programming [26], that do not need to inject new code in a process' address space circumvent this countermeasure.

Function pointers can be protected much in the same way as return addresses. PointGuard as discussed in Section 1, is a technique specifically designed to protect function pointers. ValueGuard, by Van Acker et. al [34], protects all data items from overflows, including function pointers. This is done by placing canaries before every item, similar to the StackGuard approach. Unfortunately, the large number of checks causes this technique to incur a large runtime overhead.

The most common vulnerability that leads to the attacker being able to overwrite the return address or a function pointer located on the stack is a stack-based buffer overflow. A popular way of defending against buffer overflows is through the use of bounds-checkers, systems that discover the correct bounds of each object and terminate programs that write out-of bounds. These systems provide strong security guarantees and researchers have therefore proposed a plethora of bounds-checkers [3, 12, 13, 14, 19, 20, 30]. These security guarantees however, usually come at the cost of high runtime overheads. Today, the fastest implementation of a bounds checker has a runtime overhead of about 60% [2].

The third type of protection tries to prevent the usefulness of overwriting a return address. An attacker can make the most out of overwriting a return address if he can point it to code he supplied himself. The easiest way to do this is to inject code together with the new value for the return address which means this code will end up on the stack. An obvious way to prevent such an exploit is to make the stack non-executable [33]. Another common way to mitigate such exploit is Address Space Layout Randomization (ASLR) [5, 32]. Both approaches however, have their limitations: a non-executable stack will not prevent overwriting the return address with the location of existing code in the program's address space and ASLR can be de-randomized [23, 27] or bypassed altogether [25].

When a control-flow hijacking attack is being carried out, the attacked program inevitably diverges from its normal control-flow. A number of countermeasures have been proposed that use this fact to detect control-flow hijacking attacks. One way to detect such divergences is to monitor the system calls made by the program. Systrace [22], by Provos, automatically builds system call policies during training sessions. If, during a normal run, a system call is encountered that is not specifically allowed by the policy, the user is asked if the call should be allowed. Linn et al. proposed statically analyzing binaries to discover from which addresses system calls are made [16]. These locations are then transfered to the kernel which enforces them on subsequent system calls.

The previous techniques only try to enforce normal program behavior at its boundaries, i.e., the behavior that is exhibited towards the kernel. Abadi et al. have proposed a more complete technique for insuring the integrity of control-flow within programs [1]. They statically create the program's Control-Flow Graph (CFG), which contains all control transfers the program can legally make. Then, the binary is instrumented so that every control transfer is checked at runtime to correspond to an edge in the CFG. A similar approach is taken by Philippaerts et al. in [21]. Here, control-data is masked before being used in order restrict the addresses it can hold.

7   Conclusion

The market penetration of personal computing devices, and the expansion of server-side computing resources to handle the fast-growing client population, has made the task of protecting vulnerable software and private user-data more relevant than ever. In this paper we reviewed the shortcomings of popular countermeasures against control-flow hijacking and introduced the concept of program-part duplication as a means of securing the control-flow of a potentially vulnerable program.

We instantiated the duplication concept and introduced a novel technique that duplicates the functions in a program in such a way that return addresses are no longer needed, providing a complete protection against return address smashing attacks. Additionally, we described a generic method which uses duplication to protect all types of control-data and demonstrated how this method can be used to protect function pointers. The evaluation of our techniques showed that they provide a very effective protection while incurring only a minimal runtime overhead in real-life applications, making them applicable to both desktop and server environments.

Acknowledgments. This research was done with the financial support from the Prevention against Crime Programme of the European Union, the IBBT, the IWT, the Research Fund KU Leuven, and the EU-funded FP7 project NESSoS.

References

1. Abadi, M., Budiu, M., Erlingsson, U., Ligatti, J.: Control-flow integrity principles, implementations, and applications. ACM Trans. Inf. Syst. Secur. 13(1), 4:1–4:40 (2009)
2. Akritidis, P., Costa, M., Castro, M., Hand, S.: Baggy bounds checking: an efficient and backwards-compatible defense against out-of-bounds errors. In: Proceedings of the 18th Conference on USENIX Security Symposium, SSYM 2009, pp. 51–66. USENIX Association, Berkeley (2009)

3. Austin, T.M., Breach, S.E., Sohi, G.S.: Efficient detection of all pointer and array access errors. In: ACM Conference on Programming Language Design and Implementation (1994)
4. Baratloo, A., Singh, N., Tsai, T.: Transparent run-time defense against stack smashing attacks. In: Proceedings of the 2000 USENIX Technical Conference, San Diego, California, USA (June 2000)
5. Bhatkar, S., DuVarney, D.C., Sekar, R.: Address obfuscation: An efficient approach to combat a broad range of memory error exploits. In: Proceedings of the 12th USENIX Security Symposium, Washington, D.C., pp. 105–120 (August 2003)
6. Bulba and Kil3r. Bypassing Stackguard and Stackshield. Phrack, 56 (2000)
7. Chiueh, T.-C., Hsu, F.-H.: RAD: A Compile-Time Solution to Buffer Overflow Attacks. In: ICDCS 2001, pp. 409–417 (2001)
8. Cowan, C., Beattie, S., Johansen, J., Wagle, P.: PointGuard^{TM}: Protecting Pointers from Buffer Overflow Vulnerabilities. In: Proc. of the 12th Usenix Security Symposium (2003)
9. Cowan, C., Pu, C., Maier, D., Hinton, H., Walpole, J., Bakke, P., Beattie, S., Grier, A., Wagle, P., Zhang, Q.: StackGuard: Automatic Adaptive Detection and Prevention of Buffer-Overflow Attacks (1998)
10. Solar Designer. Getting around non-executable stack (and fix). Posting to BuqTraq mailing list (August 1997), http://seclists.org/bugtraq/1997/Aug/63
11. IBM. Gcc extension for protecting applications from stack-smashing attacks, http://www.trl.ibm.com/projects/security/ssp/
12. Jones, R.W.M., Kelly, P.H.J.: Backwards-compatible bounds checking for arrays and pointers in C programs. In: 3rd International Workshop on Automatic Debugging (1997)
13. Kendall, S.C.: Bcc: Runtime Checking for C Programs. In: USENIX Summer Conference (1983)
14. Lhee, K.-S., Chapin, S.J.: Type-Assisted Dynamic Buffer Overflow Detection. In: 11th USENIX Security Symposium (2002)
15. Li, J., Wang, Z., Jiang, X., Grace, M., Bahram, S.: Defeating return-oriented rootkits with "Return-Less" kernels. In: Proceedings of the 5th European Conference on Computer Systems, EuroSys 2010, pp. 195–208. ACM, New York (2010)
16. Lin, C., Rajagopalan, M., Baker, S., Collberg, C., Debray, S., Hartman, J.: Protecting against unexpected system calls. In: Proceedings of the 14th USENIX Security Symposium, Baltimore, Maryland, USENIX Association (August 2005)
17. LLVM Developer Group. The LLVM Compiler Infrastructure, http://llvm.org/
18. Lvin, V.B., Novark, G., Berger, E.D., Zorn, B.G.: Archipelago: trading address space for reliability and security. SIGOPS Oper. Syst. Rev. 42, 115–124 (2008)
19. Oiwa, Y., Sekiguchi, T., Sumii, E., Yonezawa, A.: Fail-Safe ANSI-C Compiler: An Approach to Making C Programs Secure: Progress Report. In: International Symposium on Software Security 2002 (2002)
20. Patil, H., Fischer, C.N.: Low-Cost, Concurrent Checking of Pointer and Array Accesses in C Programs. Software: Practice and Experience 27(1) (1997)
21. Philippaerts, P., Younan, Y., Muylle, S., Piessens, F., Lachmund, S., Walter, T.: Code Pointer Masking: Hardening Applications against Code Injection Attacks. In: Holz, T., Bos, H. (eds.) DIMVA 2011. LNCS, vol. 6739, pp. 194–213. Springer, Heidelberg (2011)
22. Provos, N.: Improving host security with system call policies. In: Proceedings of the 12th USENIX Security Symposium, Washington, D.C., pp. 257–272 (August 2003)

23. Roglia, G.F., Martignoni, L., Paleari, R., Bruschi, D.: Surgically returning to randomized lib(c). In: 25th Annual Computer Security Applications Conference (2009)
24. Rosenberg, D.: Breaking LibTIFF,
    http://vulnfactory.org/blog/2010/06/29/breaking-libtiff/
25. Schwartz, E.J., Avgerinos, T., Brumley, D.: Q: Exploit hardening made easy. In: Proceedings of the USENIX Security Symposium (2011)
26. Shacham, H.: The geometry of innocent flesh on the bone: Return-into-libc without function calls (on the x86). In: di Vimercati, S.D.C., Syverson, P. (eds.) Proceedings of CCS 2007, pp. 552–561. ACM Press (October 2007)
27. Shacham, H., Page, M., Pfaff, B., Goh, E.-J., Modadugu, N., Boneh, D.: On the Effectiveness of Address-Space Randomization. In: Proceedings of the 11th ACM Conference on Computer and Communications Security, Washington, D.C., pp. 298–307 (October 2004)
28. Spafford, E.H.: The internet worm program: an analysis. SIGCOMM Comput. Commun. Rev. 19, 17–57 (1989)
29. Standard Performance Evaluation Corporation. SPEC CINT2006,
    http://www.spec.org/cpu2006/CINT2006/
30. Steffen, J.L.: Adding Run-Time Checking to the Portable C Compiler. Software: Practice and Experience 22(4) (1992)
31. Strackx, R., Younan, Y., Philippaerts, P., Piessens, F., Lachmund, S., Walter, T.: Breaking the memory secrecy assumption. In: Proceedings of the Second European Workshop on System Security, EUROSEC 2009, pp. 1–8. ACM, New York (2009)
32. The PaX Team. Documentation of ASLR in PaX,
    http://pax.grsecurity.net/docs/aslr.txt
33. The PaX Team. Documentation of PAGEEXEC in PaX,
    http://pax.grsecurity.net/docs/pageexec.txt
34. Van Acker, S., Nikiforakis, N., Philippaerts, P., Younan, Y., Piessens, F.: Value-Guard: Protection of Native Applications against Data-Only Buffer Overflows. In: Jha, S., Mathuria, A. (eds.) ICISS 2010. LNCS, vol. 6503, pp. 156–170. Springer, Heidelberg (2010)
35. Vendicator. Stack Shield technical info file v0.7 (January 2001),
    http://www.angelfire.com/sk/stackshield/
36. Wilander, J., Nikiforakis, N., Younan, Y., Kamkar, M., Joosen, W.: RIPE: Runtime Intrusion Prevention Evaluator. In: Proceedings of the 27th Annual Computer Security Applications Conference, ACSAC. ACM (2011)

Coinductive Unwinding of Security-Relevant Hyperproperties

Dimiter Milushev and Dave Clarke

IBBT-DistriNet, KU Leuven, Heverlee, Belgium

Abstract. Unwinding relations have been widely used to prove that finite systems are secure with respect to a variety of noninterference policies. The latter are prominent instances of security-relevant hyperproperties. As hyperproperties are defined on potentially infinite systems, a new mathematical development is needed in order to (re)use unwinding relations for generic verification of security-relevant hyperproperties. In this paper we propose a framework for coinductive unwinding of security relevant hyperproperties. To illustrate the usefulness of the framework, we show that Mantel's Basic Security Predicates (BSPs), the noninterference policies they compose, as well as their respective unwinding relations, have a meaningful coinductive reinterpretation. We prove that in a number of cases the coinductive variants of the unwinding relations imply the respective coinductive variants of the BSPs. Moreover, the latter can be used to compose high-level security-relevant hyperproperties for both finite and infinite systems. A number of the unwinding theorems also hold as expected. In conclusion, the proposed framework and results are useful both theoretically in the study of hyperproperties and in practice for verification of hyperproperties on potentially infinite systems.

1 Introduction

Unwinding is a well-known technique used to prove that systems are secure with respect to a variety of noninterference policies, which essentially regulate the flow of information within a system. The original term and idea of unwinding date back to the work of Goguen and Meseguer [3]. As they describe it, unwinding is the process of translating a security policy, first, into local constraints on the transition system, inductively guaranteeing that the policy is satisfied, and second, into a finite set of lemmas such that any system that satisfies the lemmas is guaranteed to satisfy the policy. The idea is intuitively appealing because the connection between the transitions of the system and the higher level policy, often expressed as difficult to check relations on execution traces, is given by an *unwinding theorem*.

There is a substantial amount of work on unwinding of information flow policies [3,5,15,13,10,16]. Each of these results are developed for a specific definition(s) and hence they lack modularity. This is unfortunate, as it results in the need to reprove many similar results. In an attempt to remedy this, Mantel [7,8] introduced a *modular* framework in which most well-known information flow

A. Jøsang and B. Carlsson (Eds.): NordSec 2012, LNCS 7617, pp. 121–136, 2012.
© Springer-Verlag Berlin Heidelberg 2012

policies can be composed from a set of *basic security predicates* (BSPs). A major advantage of Mantel's framework is precisely its modularity: BSPs common to different definitions need to be verified only once per system; the same holds for unwinding relations. Interestingly, some BSPs are equivalent to, and can be constructed as, conjunctions of unwinding relations, whereas other BSPs are over-approximated by conjunctions of unwinding relations. Mantel's unwinding relations are noteworthy for at least two major reasons. First, because they can be *arbitrary* relations rather than equivalence relations, as are typically found in the literature. And second, because they can be specified *locally*, on states of the system, as opposed to the more traditional, global, trace-based unwinding relations. In addition to the local unwinding relations for his BSPs, Mantel presented *unwinding theorems* for most known possibilistic security policies.

Later on, Clarkson and Schneider introduced the notion of *hyperproperties* [2] in order to formalize security policies. A *hyperproperty* is a set of sets of (infinite) execution traces, or alternatively a property on trace sets or a second-order predicate over execution traces. Hyperproperties generalize properties and are expressive enough to capture most interesting security policies on systems, including notions of noninterference, but also many other policies. The notion of a hyperproperty is intuitively appealing, because it represents the set of systems permitted by some policy. Unfortunately, a generic verification methodology for hyperproperties does not exist. In this work, we make a step towards such a methodology based on unwinding.

The problem of directly using Mantel's framework for verification of hyperproperties, in particular for security-relevant ones, is that the framework is geared towards reasoning about only terminating behaviors (finite systems). In order to enable reasoning about infinite systems, particularly about systems having confidential events occurring infinitely often, we illustrate the need of and propose a new mathematical development. We present a coinductive reinterpretation of Mantel's unwinding relations, BSPs and security-relevant hyperproperties. The security relevant hyperproperties are different than the respective policies studied by Mantel, required by the fact that systems are possibly infinite. This results in different definitions of the BSPs and the respective unwinding relations. Another consequence is that security policies have different semantics on finite systems compared to the ones presented by Mantel. Further, we show that the respective variants of a number of the unwinding theorems hold as expected. Our contribution opens the door to verification of nontrivial, potentially infinite systems w.r.t. security relevant hyperproperties. Moreover, it reuses key ideas from Mantel's framework, which is both well-established and conceptually appealing. Finally, it sheds light on the significance of *incremental hyperproperties*, recently proposed by Milushev and Clarke [12].

The rest of the paper is structured as follows. Section 2 provides some background material and motivation. Section 3 introduces the proposed coinductive variants of some well-known holistic security hyperproperties and their respective BSPs. Section 4 presents the proposed coinductive variants of the unwinding relations of selected BSPs. Section 5 presents the coinductive versions of three types of theorems: firstly, theorems connecting unwinding relations and BSPs, secondly, ones connecting BSPs and holistic hyperproperties and thirdly, a version of Mantel's unwinding theorems, which can be used directly for verification. In Section 6 we discuss our main contributions and compare them with related work. Finally, we conclude by summarizing our results and sharing some ideas for future work. The proofs and more examples can be found in the accompanying technical report [11].

2   Background and Motivation

2.1   Background

Let A be a fixed alphabet of abstract observations, sometimes called *events*. A *string* is a finite sequence of elements of A. The set of all strings over A is denoted A^*. A *stream* of A's is an infinite sequence of elements of A. The set of all streams over A is $A^\omega = \{\sigma \mid \sigma : \{0, 1, 2, \ldots\} \to A\}$. A stream σ can be specified in terms of its first element $\sigma(0)$ and its stream derivative σ', given by $\sigma'(n) = \sigma(n+1)$; these operators are also known as *head* and *tail*. A *trace* is a finite or infinite sequence of elements of A. The set of all traces over A is denoted $A^\infty = A^* \cup A^\omega$. Let 2 be any two element set, for instance $2 = \{true, false\}$. A *system* is a set of traces. The set of all systems is $\mathsf{Sys} = 2^{A^\infty}$, the set of infinite systems is $\mathsf{Sys}_\omega = 2^{A^\omega}$.

Properties vs. Hyperproperties. Clarkson and Schneider present a theory of policies based on properties and hyperproperties [2]. A *property* is a set of traces. The set of all properties is $\mathsf{Prop} = 2^{A^\infty}$. A *hyperproperty* is a set of sets of traces or equivalently a set of properties. The set of all hyperproperties is $\mathsf{HP} = 2^{2^{A^\infty}} = 2^{\mathsf{Prop}} = 2^{\mathsf{Sys}}$. Note that our definition, unlike the original one, does not require all traces to be infinite; as a result termination-sensitive definitions can be expressed in a more natural fashion.

Partial Automata. We model systems as partial automata [14]. A *partial automaton* with input alphabet A and a start state is defined *coalgebraically* as a 4-tuple $\langle S, o, t, s_0 \rangle$, where set S is the possibly infinite state space of the automaton, the observation function $o : S \to 2$ says whether a state is accepting or not, the function $t : S \to (1 + S)^A$ gives the transition structure and s_0 is the initial state. Notation S^A stands for the set of functions with signature $A \to S$; $1 + S$ is notation used for the set $\{\bot\} \cup S$: whenever the function $t(s)$ is undefined, it is the constant function mapping A to $\bot$; if $t(s)$ is defined for some $a \in A$, then $t(s)(a) = s'$ gives the next state.

Let $A^* \cdot \delta = \{w \cdot \delta \mid w \in A^*\}$ be the set of finitely deadlocked words. Note that $\delta \notin A$ is a special symbol to signify divergence. The collection of all languages acceptable by partial automata is $A_\delta^\infty = A^* \cup (A^* \cdot \delta) \cup A^\omega$. For words $w \in A^*$ and sets $L \subseteq A_\delta^\infty$, define the *w-derivative* of L to be $L_w = \{v \in A_\delta^\infty \mid w \cdot v \in L\}$. Finally, let $t|_Z$ be the projection of a string t to elements from some set Z.

Trees. Following our recent work [12], we model system behavior as potentially infinite trees instead of as sets of traces. A *tree* is obtained from a language (or set of traces) by continuously taking derivatives with respect to elements of A. The start state of the system corresponds to the root of the tree and vertices correspond to sets of traces (languages).

We define a particular pair of functions $\langle o, t \rangle$ allowing us to switch perspective from seeing a system as a set of traces to seeing it as a partial automaton. It should be noted that such a pair of functions induces a unique tree, giving the behavior of the automaton and the set of traces (see [14] and [12] for details). Let $C \in$ Sys, $a \in A$ and $\sigma \in A^\infty$. First, define an auxiliary function $test :$ Sys $\rightarrow$ $(A \rightarrow 2)$ as follows:

$$test_a(C) \,\hat{=}\, \exists \sigma \in C \,.\, \sigma(0) = a.$$

Now, we can define the functions o and t as follows:

$$o(C) \,\hat{=}\, \epsilon \in C \qquad t(C)(a) \,\hat{=}\, \begin{cases} \{\sigma' \mid \sigma(0) = a\} & \text{if } test_a(C) \\ \bot & \text{if } \neg test_a(C). \end{cases}$$

Auxiliary Definitions. We can straightforwardly extend *test* to an obvious inductive definition of predicate $test^* :$ Sys $\rightarrow$ $(A^* \rightarrow 2)$ on words. For $a \in A$, $w \in A^*$ and ϵ the empty trace:

$$\frac{o(X)}{test^*_\epsilon(X)} \qquad \frac{test_a(X) \qquad test^*_w(X_a)}{test^*_{a \cdot w}(X)}$$

We also need a coinductive definition of trace inclusion in trees:

$$\frac{o(S)}{\epsilon \in S}\; coind \qquad \frac{test_a(S) \qquad w \in S_a}{a \cdot w \in S}\; coind$$

Note that coinductive definitions are indicated as *coind* on the right side of their respective inference rules.

Incremental Hyperproperties as Coinductive Predicates on Trees. Our recent work [12] introduced and formalized the notion of *incremental hyperproperties*. Such a hyperproperty is the greatest fixed point of a monotone function over Sys^n, given in a fragment of Least Fixed Point Logic called $\mathcal{IL}$. More informally, incremental hyperproperties are *coinductive tree predicates* or alternatively coinductively defined relations on the state space of the system. The original notion of hyperproperties [2] is also formalized and called *holistic hyperproperties* [12].

2.2 Motivation

Many typical security-relevant policies (for instance all the ones presented in [8]) reason about finite only traces. As a result, such definitions are termination insensitive: informally, this implies that all diverging computations are considered to be "the same". This is clearly not satisfactory when reasoning about potentially infinite systems, such as servers, embedded systems, operating systems etc. Moreover, the typical termination insensitive definitions allow leaks through *covert channels*. For instance, consider the simple system $S_1 = \{(hl)^\omega, l^*\}$, where $A = L \cup H$, $L = \{l\}$ and $H = \{h\}$ (*low* and *high* events). Clearly, termination insensitive definitions (such as NF_o introduced in Section 3.1) distinguish this system as trivially *secure*: as only one of the traces is in A^* and it has low events only. However, the system is intuitively not secure as termination is low-observable. In general, theoretical machinery is needed in order to reason about potentially infinite behaviors allowed by system specifications. Such machinery, at least for reasoning about security-relevant hyperproperties in general, is currently lacking. This is the main motivation of this work.

3   Coinductive Interpretation of Security-Relevant Hyperproperties

Security-relevant policies (notably notions of noninterference) have traditionally been defined using a model of finite traces, as well as inductively defined relations on those traces using existential and universal quantification. In order to be able to reason about potentially infinite behavior, the above mentioned relations have to be lifted to potentially infinite traces. Thus, a coinductive (re)interpretation of the well-known notions of noninterference is needed in order to reason about the same policies on (potentially) nonterminating systems. The reason is that when computations do not terminate, there is no longer a well-ordering and hence inductive definitions are ill-formed.

The coinductive interpretation of well-known, holistic, security hyperproperties requires coinductively defined predicates on traces and sometimes functions (often treated as relations). We start off by giving the needed definitions. Note that set $Z \subseteq A$ used below is assumed to be *non-empty*.

Definitions. Coinductively define predicate $no_Z : A^\infty \to 2$ (parameterized by set Z), which states that there are no events from set Z in a trace:

$$\frac{}{no_Z(\epsilon)} \; coind \qquad \frac{a \in A \setminus Z \qquad no_Z(x)}{no_Z(a \cdot x)} \; coind$$

Note that $no_Z(t)$ is the coinductive version of predicate $t|_Z = \epsilon$. Next, inductively define $w \rightsquigarrow_Z a \cdot w'$ (w Z-reveals a with tail w'):

$$\frac{}{\epsilon \rightsquigarrow_Z \epsilon} \qquad \frac{a \in Z}{a \cdot w \rightsquigarrow_Z a \cdot w} \qquad \frac{b \in A \setminus Z \qquad w \rightsquigarrow_Z a \cdot w'}{b \cdot w \rightsquigarrow_Z a \cdot w'}$$

We also need a coinductive relation ev_Z, relating any trace to its projection onto Z. Technically, the relation is a partial function, filtering out events from set Z, and will be defined and used as one, mainly to keep the connection to $t|_Z$.

$$\frac{}{ev_Z(\epsilon) = \epsilon} \; coind \qquad \frac{w \rightsquigarrow_Z a \cdot w' \qquad ev_Z(w') = u}{ev_Z(w) = a \cdot u} \; coind$$

Finally, coinductively define *weak bisimulation* (parameterized by set Z) $\approx_Z$: $A^\infty \times A^\infty \to 2$ as follows:

$$\frac{}{\epsilon \approx_Z \epsilon}\ coind \qquad \frac{w \rightsquigarrow_Z a \cdot w' \qquad u \rightsquigarrow_Z a \cdot u' \qquad w' \approx_Z u'}{w \approx_Z u}\ coind$$

Note that the inductive/coinductive part of the definition avoids the potential fairness problem where τ^ω is equivalent to any trace.

Next, we present definitions adopted from Mantel's MAKS framework [8]. For a partition of alphabet A as $A = A_v \cup A_n \cup A_c$, define a *view* to be a tuple $V = (A_v, A_n, A_c)$ corresponding to *visible, neither* visible *nor* confidential (i.e. neutral) and *confidential* events. Let $\mathcal{H}$ denote the view $(L, \emptyset, H)$ where H and L are the sets of *high* and *low* events, and the set of neutral events is empty. Let sets I and O represent inputs and outputs such that $I \subseteq A$, $O \subseteq A$ and $I \cap O = \emptyset$. Let $\mathcal{HI}$ denote the view $(L, H \setminus HI, HI)$, where HI is the set of high inputs, i.e. $H \cap I$. Let the set of all views be $\mathcal{V}$ and ρ be a function from *views* to subsets of A, i.e. $\rho : \mathcal{V} \to 2^A$. An event is defined to be ρ-admissible in a tree T after a possible finite trace β for some view $V = (A_v, A_n, A_c)$ if $Adm_V^\rho(T, \beta, e)$ holds, where $Adm_V^\rho(T, \beta, e)$ is defined:

$$Adm_V^\rho(T, \beta, e) \ \hat{=}\ \exists \gamma \in A^*.(\gamma \cdot e \in T \wedge \gamma \approx_{\rho(V)} \beta).$$

Intuitively, ρ can give a finer grained distinction of events than a view. For instance, one policy might be defined as follows: given some view (A_v, A_n, A_c) and from observing events in A_v one should not be able to deduce occurrence/nonoccurrence of ρ-admissible events in A_c (or some subset of it).

3.1 Coinductive View on Some Well-Known Holistic Security-Relevant Hyperproperties

The definitions presented next are well-known from the literature, but we present their respective variants on potentially infinite systems (as hyperproperties).

Noninference. This policy will be called NF_o (original NF) and is originally defined on finite systems as follows [17]:

$$NF_o(X) \ \hat{=}\ \forall x \in X.\ x|_L \in X.$$

The coinductive variant of *noninference* is called NF and given using ev_Z:

$$NF(X) \ \hat{=}\ \forall x \in X.\ ev_L(x) \in X.$$

Generalized Noninference. This policy is originally proposed by Zakinthinos and Lee [17] and given as follows:

$$GNF_o(X) \ \hat{=}\ \forall x_0 \in X\ \exists x_1 \in X.\ (x_1|_{HI} = \epsilon \wedge x_1|_L = x_0|_L).$$

Our coinductive interpretation of *generalized noninference* GNF is given here:

$$GNF(X) \ \hat{=}\ \forall x_0 \in X\ \exists x_1 \in X.\ (no_{HI}(x_1) \wedge x_1 \approx_L x_0).$$

For the following policies, we only give the coinductive definitions.

Generalized Noninterference. Using coinductive relations on traces, we define *generalized noninterference GNI* as a hyperproperty:

$$GNI(X) \; \hat{=} \; \forall x_1 \in A^* \, \forall x_2, x_3 \in A^\infty \, . \, [(x_1 \cdot x_2 \in X \wedge x_3 \approx_{A \backslash HI} x_2) \rightarrow$$
$$\exists x_4 \in A^\infty. \, (x_1 \cdot x_4 \in X \wedge x_4 \approx_{L \cup HI} x_3)].$$

Note that the equality of projections is replaced by our coinductively defined $\approx_Z$ relation.

Perfect Security Property. Finally, we present our coinductive variant of the *perfect security property PSP* (proposed by Zakinthinos and Lee [17]):

$$PSP(X) \; \hat{=}' \; (\forall x \in X. \, ev_L(x) \in X) \wedge (\forall \alpha \in A^\infty \forall \beta \in A^*.$$
$$[(\beta \cdot \alpha \in X \wedge no_H(\alpha)) \rightarrow \forall h \in H. \, (\beta \cdot h \in X \rightarrow \beta \cdot h \cdot \alpha \in X)]).$$

We have presented only a few of the information flow definitions in order to illustrate what is needed to represent them as hyperproperties. It is relatively straightforward to convert any of the ones not presented here. Nevertheless, the examples are enough to cover a number of important BSPs and unwinding relations, as well as to raise some interesting questions, which will be presented in the following sections. Moreover, the examples suggest a possible technique to adapt Mantel's unwinding relations to reason about security-relevant hyperproperties and a connection with incremental hyperproperties, namely that an H'-simulation [12], implying that an incremental hyperproperty H' holds, is a(n) (conjunction of) unwinding relation(s). This is further elaborated in Section 4.

3.2   Coinductive View on BSPs

Mantel introduces the MAKS framework [8,7], which can represent most well-known possibilistic security policies as conjunctions of Basic Security Predicates. Mantel classifies his BSPs in two dimensions. In the *first dimension* fall BSPs that essentially hide the *occurrence* of A_c-events, whereas in the *second dimension* are BSPs that hide the *non-occurrence* of A_c-events. Mantel's BSPs and security policies are defined on finite traces only. In this section we present a coinductive perspective on a number of the BSPs, parameterized by a *security view* (see Section 3). Although we have changed the definitions, we have kept their original names. We start with some BSPs from the first dimension.

Removal of Events. Predicate $R_V(T)$ requires for any trace $\sigma \in T$ the existence of another trace γ which has no events from A_c and which has the same A_v-events (essentially allowing "corrections" of A_n-events). Our definition is:

$$R_V(T) \; \hat{=} \; \forall \sigma \in T \, \exists \gamma \in T \, . \, (no_{A_c}(\gamma) \wedge \sigma \approx_{A_v} \gamma).$$

Note that we have replaced the relations on traces in the original work with coinductive ones, similarly to the modifications of the definitions from Section 3.1. Interestingly, such a straightforward modification will not be possible for the rest of the BSP definitions we explore.

Stepwise Deletion of Events. The original definition [8] changes any trace σ in a candidate set T by deleting the *last* occurrence of a confidential event and requires that the resulting trace can be corrected (by possibly inserting/deleting events in A_n if it is not empty) resulting in a possible trace γ in T. If we *naively* convert Mantel's definition to potentially infinite traces, we get the following:

$$DN_V(T) \; \widehat{=} \; \forall \alpha \in A^\infty \; \forall \beta \in A^* \; \forall c \in A_c \, . \, [(\beta \cdot c \cdot \alpha \in T \wedge no_{A_c}(\alpha)) \rightarrow$$
$$\exists \alpha' \in A^\infty, \beta' \in A^* \, . \, (\beta' \cdot \alpha' \in T \wedge \alpha' \approx_{A_v} \alpha \wedge no_{A_c}(\alpha') \wedge \beta' \approx_{A_v \cup A_c} \beta)].$$

This definition would work as expected on finite traces. Unfortunately, it is not well-suited for infinite traces. To illustrate this, consider the following example:

Example 1. Let $V = (A_v, A_n, A_c)$ be a view such that $A_v = \{l_1, l_2\}$, $A_n = \emptyset$ and $A_c = \{h_1, h_2\}$. Consider system $S_1 = \{(l_1 h_1 h_2 l_2)^\omega\}$. Intuitively system S_1 is not secure, as every time l_2 is observed it is clear that h_1 and h_2 must have occurred. Unfortunately, the definition of DN_V does not capture this intuition, as system S_1 is trivially secure w.r.t. the definition. The reason for this problem is that *confidential events appear infinitely often*, thus there is no suffix t for which $no_{A_c}(t)$ holds.

Potentially infinite traces are allowed in many useful systems (operating systems, reactive and embedded systems etc.) and oftentimes there is no last confidential event, as confidential events might occur infinitely often. Thus the definition needs to be changed. The following definition fixes the problem:

$$D_V(T) \; \widehat{=} \; \forall \alpha \in A^\infty \; \forall \beta \in A^* \; \forall c \in A_c \, . \, [\beta \cdot c \cdot \alpha \in T \rightarrow$$
$$\exists \alpha' \in A^\infty, \beta' \in A^* . \, (\beta' \cdot \alpha' \in T \wedge \beta' \approx_{A_v \cup A_c} \beta \wedge \alpha' \approx_{A_v \cup A_c} \alpha)].$$

This definition deletes *any* occurrence of a confidential event in a trace and then perturbs the resulting trace. Unfortunately, on finite traces the definition is not semantically equivalent to the original one. To see this consider the following:

Example 2. Let $V = (A_v, A_n, A_c)$ be a view such that $A_v = \{l_1, l_2\}$, $A_n = \emptyset$ and $A_c = \{h_1, h_2\}$. Consider system $S_2 = \{l_1 h_1 h_2 l_2, l_1 h_1 l_2, l_1 l_2\}$. It is easy to check that $D_V(S_2)$ does not hold (because $l_1 h_2 l_2$ has to be in S_2, but it is not). Nevertheless S_2 is secure w.r.t. Mantel's original definition, as well as w.r.t. our naive definition DN_V.

It should be noted that the definition D_V (proposed here and used throughout the work) is stronger (it requires more possible traces and hence higher uncertainty for the attacker) than DN_V. In other words, $D_V(X) \rightarrow DN_V(X)$. Moreover, D_V properly rejects systems exhibiting the pattern of S_1 as insecure; to see one reason why, note that $l_1 h_2 l_2 (l_1 h_1 h_2 l_2)^\omega \notin S_1$.

Backwards Strict Deletion. The next BSP is called *BSD*. The intuitive idea is that the occurrence of an A_c-event should not be deducible. The difference with D_V is that the part of the trace that has already occurred (β) cannot be changed. Our coinductive definition of $BSD_V(T)$ is given as:

$$BSD_V(T) \; \hat{=} \; \forall \alpha \in A^\infty \; \forall \beta \in A^* \; \forall c \in A_c \;.\; [\beta \cdot c \cdot \alpha \in T \rightarrow$$
$$\exists \alpha' \in A^\infty.\, (\beta \cdot \alpha' \in T \wedge \alpha' \approx_{A_v \cup A_c} \alpha].$$

Note that a similar modification as to D_V is needed here and the reason again is to enable tackling systems which do not have a last confidential event.

Although the BSP definitions have changed, the following theorem establishes a connection between the BSPs, familiar from Mantel's work.

Theorem 1. *Let $V = (A_v, A_n, A_c)$ be a view and T be a set of traces. Then the following implications hold: $BSD_V(T) \rightarrow D_V(T)$ and $D_V(T) \rightarrow R_V(T)$.*

Strict Deletion. Our version of this BSP is again different than Mantel's: as in the previous definition, it does not search for the last A_c-event, hence it works on infinite traces. Our coinductive version of $SD_V(T)$ is given next:

$$SD_V(T) \; \hat{=} \; \forall \alpha \in A^\infty \; \forall \beta \in A^* \; \forall c \in A_c \;.\; [\beta \cdot c \cdot \alpha \in T \rightarrow \beta \cdot \alpha \in T].$$

The rest of the presented BSPs are from the second dimension, hiding the *non-occurrence* of A_c-events.

Backwards Strict Insertion. This BSP is in a sense dual to BSD_V— instead of deleting an A_c-event, it requires the possible insertion of such an event. Of course, we have again modified the definition to a coinductive one and it does not search for the last A_c-event, hence it works on infinite traces. The same also holds for all the following definitions. Our coinductive version of $BSI_V(T)$ is:

$$BSI_V(T) \; \hat{=} \; \forall \alpha \in A^\infty \; \forall \beta \in A^* \; \forall c \in A_c \;.\; [\beta \cdot \alpha \in T \rightarrow$$
$$\exists \alpha' \in A^\infty.\, (\beta \cdot c \cdot \alpha' \in T \wedge \alpha' \approx_{A_v \cup A_c} \alpha)].$$

Backwards Strict Insertion of Admissible Events. This BSP is similar to BSI_V, but it hides the non-occurrence of *admissible* events only. Our coinductive version of $BSIA_V^\rho(T)$ is given as follows:

$$BSIA_V^\rho(T) \; \hat{=} \; \forall \alpha \in A^\infty \; \forall \beta \in A^* \; \forall c \in A_c \;.$$
$$[(\beta \cdot \alpha \in T \wedge Adm_V^\rho(T, \beta, c)) \rightarrow$$
$$\exists \alpha' \in A^\infty.\, (\beta \cdot c \cdot \alpha' \in T \wedge \alpha' \approx_{A_v \cup A_c} \alpha)].$$

Strict Insertion. This BSP requires the possibility to insert any A_c-event at any place in a stream, it is strict because neither the past nor the future part of the trace may be changed. Our coinductive version of $SI_V(T)$ is given as follows:

$$SI_V(T) \; \hat{=} \; \forall \alpha \in A^\infty \; \forall \beta \in A^* \; \forall c \in A_c \;.\; [\beta \cdot \alpha \in T \rightarrow \beta \cdot c \cdot \alpha \in T].$$

Strict Insertion of ρ-Admissible Events. This BSP requires the possibility to insert any ρ-admissible A_c-event at any place (where admissible) in a stream. Our coinductive version of $SIA_V^\rho(T)$ is given as follows:

$$SIA_V^\rho(T) \;\widehat{=}\; \forall \alpha \in A^\infty \; \forall \beta \in A^* \; \forall c \in A_c \,.$$
$$[(\beta \cdot \alpha \in T \wedge Adm_V^\rho(T, \beta, c)) \rightarrow \beta \cdot c \cdot \alpha \in T].$$

Insertion of ρ-Admissible Events. This BSP is similar to SIA_V^ρ, except that the definition is not strict (perturbations of the front and back parts of the trace are possible). Our coinductive version of $IA_V^\rho(T)$ is given as follows:

$$IA_V^\rho(T) \;\widehat{=}\; \forall \alpha \in A^\infty \; \forall \beta \in A^* \; \forall c \in A_c.$$
$$[(\beta \cdot \alpha \in T \wedge Adm_V^\rho(T, \beta, c)) \rightarrow$$
$$\exists \alpha' \in A^\infty . \exists \beta' \in A^*. \, (\beta' \cdot c \cdot \alpha' \in T \wedge \alpha' \approx_{A_v \cup A_c} \alpha \wedge \beta' \approx_{A_v \cup A_c} \beta)].$$

4 Coinductive Interpretation of BSP Unwinding Relations

Instead of verifying BSPs directly or via global unwinding conditions, Mantel proposes the use of *local* unwinding conditions [7]. Essentially, the existence of an *unwinding relation(s)* satisfying a set of unwinding conditions has to be shown in order to prove that a number of BSPs hold and hence a particular policy is respected. In this section, we present a coinductive reinterpretation of Mantel's unwinding relations, which is needed in order for them to be suitable for non-terminating systems. We also show that the relations are instances of our H'-*simulation* relations [12].

The coinductively defined unwinding relations are presented next. The first relation is historically called *output-step consistency* and denoted osc_V. Defined coinductively, an osc_V-*simulation* is a relation R such that for all $X, Y \in$ Sys if $(X, Y) \in R$, then

$$o(X) \leftrightarrow o(Y) \bigwedge \forall a \in A \setminus A_c. \, (test_a(X) \rightarrow$$
$$\exists \sigma \in (A \setminus A_c)^*.(test^*{}_\sigma(Y) \wedge \sigma \approx_{A_v} a \wedge (X_a, Y_\sigma) \in R)).$$

An osc_V-simulation relation R is denoted $osc_V(R)$. We will often overload notation and state $osc_V(X, Y, R)$ iff $osc_V(R)$ and $(X, Y) \in R$.

Next, define an lrf_V-*simulation* as follows: a relation R such that for all $X, Y \in$ Sys if $(X, Y) \in R$, then

$$o(X) \leftrightarrow o(Y) \bigwedge \forall a \in A_c. \, (test_a(X) \rightarrow (X_a, Y) \in R).$$

Next, define an lrb_V-*simulation* relation as follows: a relation R such that for all $X, Y \in$ Sys if $(X, Y) \in R$, then

$$o(X) \leftrightarrow o(Y) \bigwedge \forall a \in A_c. \, (test_a(Y) \wedge (X, Y_a) \in R).$$

Next, define $En_V^\rho(X, s, a)$, saying whether event a is enabled in state s of system X w.r.t. a set of admissible events given by function ρ (see Section 3):

$$En_V^\rho(X, s, a) \;\hat{=}\; \exists \beta, \gamma \in A^*.[test^*{}_\beta(X) \;\wedge\; s = X_\beta \;\wedge\; o(s) \;\wedge\; \gamma \approx_{\rho(V)} \beta \;\wedge$$
$$test^*{}_\gamma(X) \wedge o(X_\gamma) \wedge test_a(X_\gamma) \wedge o(X_{\gamma \cdot a})].$$

Finally, define an $lrbe_V^\rho$-*simulation* relation as follows: a relation R such that if $(X, Y) \in R$, then

$$o(X) \leftrightarrow o(Y) \bigwedge \forall a \in A_c. \; (En_V^\rho(T, Y, a) \to (test_a(Y) \wedge (X, Y_a) \in R)).$$

Next, we show that the relations defined in this section are indeed H'-simulations. First, recall that incremental hyperproperties are coinductive predicates on trees [12]. Formally, an H'-*simulation* is an n-ary relation R such that $R \subseteq \Psi_{H'}(R)$. An H'-simulation corresponds to a monotone operator $\Psi_{H'}$ whose greatest fixed point is the coinductive predicate H'. Hence showing the existence of such a relation is sufficient to show that H' holds [12]. Because of the way the relations are defined, it is obvious that $R \subseteq \Psi_{H'}(R)$ holds; informally, $\Psi_{H'}$ is the "step" of the relation. Thus, the relations are indeed H'-*simulation* relations.

5   Coinductive Interpretation of the Theory

We have taken a coinductive perspective on Mantel's unwinding relations [8]. The high-level goal is to properly incorporate the unwinding relations in our framework in order to facilitate the verification of security-relevant hyperproperties. To show that we have succeeded in this, we present three types of theorems, very similar to the ones initially introduced by Mantel in his framework: firstly, theorems connecting unwinding conditions and BSPs, secondly, ones connecting BSPs and holistic hyperproperties and finally, a version of Mantel's unwinding theorems.

The fact that we can prove these theorems implies that our definitions of unwinding relations, BSPs and holistic hyperproperties are reasonable and, more importantly, that our framework is suitable for the verification of a number of security-relevant policies via unwinding.

5.1   Unwinding Conditions to BSPs Theorems

The following two lemmas prove the intuition of osc_V-simulation relations: states related by such a relation are indistinguishable to the A_v part of the view.

Lemma 1. *Let* $R \subseteq \mathsf{Sys} \times \mathsf{Sys}$ *be an arbitrary relation and* T, S *arbitrary systems. If* $osc_V(T, S, R)$ *holds for some* $T, S \in \mathsf{Sys}$ *then we have*

$$\forall \alpha_1 \in (A \setminus A_c)^*.(test^*{}_{\alpha_1}(T) \;\to$$
$$\exists \alpha_2 \in (A \setminus A_c)^*. \; (test^*{}_{\alpha_2}(S) \wedge \alpha_1 \approx_{A_v} \alpha_2 \wedge (T_{\alpha_1}, S_{\alpha_2}) \in R)).$$

Lemma 2. *For all $T, S \in \mathsf{Sys}$ if there exists $R \subseteq \mathsf{Sys} \times \mathsf{Sys}$ s.t. $osc_V(T, S, R)$ holds, then the following is valid:*

$$\forall \alpha_1 \in (A \setminus A_c)^\infty.(\alpha_1 \in T \; \rightarrow \; \exists \alpha_2 \in (A \setminus A_c)^\infty.(\alpha_2 \in S \wedge \alpha_1 \approx_{A_v} \alpha_2)).$$

The next result gives logically sufficient conditions (conjunctions of unwinding relations) for a number of BSPs. This is not surprising (Mantel presents a similar result), but it is nevertheless important, because the definitions have changed.

Theorem 2. *Let $R \subseteq \mathsf{Sys} \times \mathsf{Sys}$ be an arbitrary relation and T an arbitrary system. The following implications are valid:*

1. $lrf_V(T, T, R) \wedge osc_V(T, T, R) \rightarrow BSD_V(T)$
2. $lrf_V(T, T, R) \wedge osc_V(T, T, R) \rightarrow D_V(T)$
3. $lrf_V(T, T, R) \wedge osc_V(T, T, R) \rightarrow R_V(T)$
4. $lrbe_V^\rho(T, T, R) \wedge osc_V(T, T, R) \rightarrow BSIA_V^\rho(T)$
5. $lrb_V(T, T, R) \wedge osc_V(T, T, R) \rightarrow BSI_V(T)$.

The following theorem gives a conditional completeness result (when $A_n = \emptyset$) for some BSPs. Further results on this have been left out due to space limitations.

Theorem 3. *Consider a view (A_v, A_n, A_c) s.t. $A_n = \emptyset$. The following are valid:*

1. $BSD_V(T)$ *implies there exists a relation $R \subseteq \mathsf{Sys} \times \mathsf{Sys}$ s.t. $lrf_V(T, T, R)$ and $osc_V(T, T, R)$ hold.*
2. $BSIA_V^\rho(T)$ *implies there exists a relation $R \subseteq \mathsf{Sys} \times \mathsf{Sys}$ s.t. $lrbe_V^\rho(T, T, R)$ and $osc_V(T, T, R)$ hold.*

5.2 Coinductive Version of BSPs to Holistic Hyperproperties Theorems

This section presents useful results, relating BSPs and the holistic, security-relevant hyperproperties, introduced in Section 3.1. First, recall that $\mathcal{HI} = (L, H \setminus HI, HI)$. The instantiation of BSD_V with view $\mathcal{HI}$ is given as follows:

$$BSD_{\mathcal{HI}}(T) \;\hat{=}\; \forall \alpha \in A^\infty \; \forall \beta \in A^* \; \forall c \in HI \,.\, [(\beta \cdot c \cdot \alpha \in T \rightarrow$$
$$\exists \alpha' \in A^\infty.\, (\beta \cdot \alpha' \in T \wedge \alpha' \approx_{L \cup HI} \alpha)].$$

The instantiation of BSI_V with view $\mathcal{HI}$ is given as follows:

$$BSI_{\mathcal{HI}}(T) \;\hat{=}\; \forall \alpha \in A^\infty \; \forall \beta \in A^* \; \forall c \in HI \,.\, [(\beta \cdot \alpha \in T \rightarrow$$
$$\exists \alpha' \in A^\infty.\, (\beta \cdot c \cdot \alpha' \in T \wedge \alpha' \approx_{L \cup HI} \alpha)].$$

The following result establishes the connection between certain BSPs and *GNI*.

Theorem 4. *For all $T \in \mathsf{Sys}$ we have $BSD_{\mathcal{HI}}(T) \wedge BSI_{\mathcal{HI}}(T)$ iff $GNI(T)$.*

The next theorem establishes that the holistic hyperproperty noninference is equivalent to the BSP removal of events, instantiated with view $\mathcal{H}$.

Theorem 5. *For all $T \in$ Sys we have $R_{\mathcal{H}}(T)$ iff $NF(T)$.*

The following result claims that the holistic hyperproperty *GNF* is equivalent to the BSP removal of events, this time instantiated with view $\mathcal{HI}$.

Theorem 6. *For all $T \in$ Sys we have $R_{\mathcal{HI}}(T)$ iff $GNF(T)$.*

Finally, we have proven Theorem 7, representing *PSP* as a conjunction of BSPs.

Theorem 7. *For all $T \in$ Sys we have $BSD_{\mathcal{H}}(T) \wedge BSIA_{\mathcal{H}}^{\rho_A}(T)$ iff $PSP(T)$.*

5.3   Coinductive Version of Mantel's Unwinding Theorems

Finally, we present the coinductive unwinding theorems for a number of known security-relevant hyperproperties. These unwinding theorems allow the specification and verification of the high-level policy by reasoning about the local states of the candidate system. Interestingly, there is a completeness result only for the definition of *PSP*. Similar theorems have been shown before, but for different unwinding relation, BSP and hyperproperty definitions and different models (for instance see the MAKS framework [8]).

Noninference *NF*. We have proven an unwinding theorem for *NF*, giving logically sufficient conditions. Because we only have an implication, there may be secure systems for which the needed unwinding relation does not exist.

Theorem 8 (Unwinding of *NF*). *If there exists a relation $R \subseteq$ Sys $\times$ Sys such that $lrf_{\mathcal{H}}(T,T,R) \wedge osc_{\mathcal{H}}(T,T,R)$, we have that $NF(T)$ holds.*

Generalized Noninference *GNF*. Further, we have proven an unwinding theorem for *GNF*, again giving logically sufficient conditions. Unfortunately, such conditions are again not necessary.

Theorem 9 (Unwinding of *GNF*). *If there exists a relation $R \subseteq$ Sys $\times$ Sys such that $lrf_{\mathcal{HI}}(T,T,R) \wedge osc_{\mathcal{HI}}(T,T,R)$, we have that $GNF(T)$ holds.*

Generalized Noninterference *GNI*. We have also been able to prove an unwinding theorem, giving logically sufficient conditions for *GNI*.

Theorem 10 (Unwinding of *GNI*). *If there exist relations $R, Q \subseteq$ Sys $\times$ Sys such that $lrf_{\mathcal{HI}}(T,T,R) \wedge osc_{\mathcal{HI}}(T,T,R)$, as well as $lrb_{\mathcal{HI}}(T,T,Q) \wedge osc_{\mathcal{HI}}(T,T,Q)$, we have that $GNI(T)$ holds.*

Perfect Security Property *PSP*. The *Perfect Security Property* is special, as there are necessary and sufficient conditions. We have been able to show this in our framework as well. First, let $\rho_A(A_v, A_n, A_c) = A_v \cup A_n \cup A_c = A$.

Theorem 11 (Unwinding of *PSP*). *There exist relations $R, Q \subseteq$ Sys $\times$ Sys such that $lrf_{\mathcal{H}}(T,T,R) \wedge osc_{\mathcal{H}}(T,T,R)$, as well as $lrbe_{\mathcal{H}}^{\rho_A}(T,T,Q) \wedge osc_{\mathcal{H}}(T,T,Q)$, iff $PSP(T)$ holds.*

This theorem gives unwinding relations for *PSP*. Moreover (unlike for the other definitions), for *PSP* we know that if no relations $R, Q \subseteq \mathsf{Sys} \times \mathsf{Sys}$ such that $lrf_{\mathcal{H}}(T, T, R) \wedge osc_{\mathcal{H}}(T, T, R)$ exist, the candidate system T is not secure.

6 Discussion

We have presented a new mathematical development enabling the application of unwinding relations for the verification of security-relevant hyperproperties.

First, a novel *coinductive perspective* was taken on the security-relevant hyperproperties themselves, by adapting their definitions to allow reasoning about nonterminating behavior. Such a modification is important not only from a theoretical point of view, but also in practice. As a motivating example, consider systems with nonterminating behavior such that confidential events in all traces occur infinitely often (this is a liveness property). In such situations it is impossible to declare a system secure by examining only finite prefixes. A typical policy, for instance given by Mantel's deletion of events [8] or a naive coinductive interpretation of the latter (*DN_V* from Section 3.2), would not be able to properly reason about such systems. Such policies would simply accept systems having only infinite behavior as being trivially secure (e.g. $S = \{(lhl)^{\omega}, (hll)^{\omega}, (llh)^{\omega}\}$). Intuitively, this is not desirable. As systems, exhibiting infinite behaviors and having no last confidential event, are abundant in practice (databases, operating systems, reactive and embedded systems), they are important for both specification and verification. Since hyperproperties are generic system specifications, it is natural to address the above-mentioned problems by giving them a coinductive semantics and use coinduction as a reasoning tool for such systems.

The only related paper that explores nonterminating behaviors and identifies the need for a coinductive interpretation of noninterference for potentially nonterminating systems is by Bohannon et al. [1]. They introduce the notion of *reactive noninterference* and explore variants suitable for reactive systems. The main similarity with our work is that they use coinductive and inductive/coinductive definitions in order to define relations on streams. They convert their high-level, holistic definition into a relation (called *ID-bisimulation*) on program states; they show that their ID-bisimulation implies the high level, holistic policy. Their ID-bisimulation is essentially an incremental hyperproperty.

Second, we have demonstrated the potential of a modular framework for coinductive reasoning about hyperproperties. This is achieved by combining the framework from our previous work [12] with a coinductive reinterpretation of Mantel's BSPs and unwinding relations. It should be noted that our proposed coinductive variants of the BSPs are not equivalent to Mantel's on finite systems, nevertheless their conjunctions still imply the desired high level policies.

Third, we present a coinductive reinterpretation of Mantel's unwinding relations and argue that they are instances of our H'-simulations [12]. More precisely, an H'-simulation is a (conjunction of) unwinding relation(s). This realizes a connection between unwinding relations and incremental hyperproperties: incremental security hyperproperties can be seen as conjunctions of coinductively-defined unwinding relations, or alternatively as (conjunctions of) our H'-simulations [12], implying the respective high level policies. This is obvious if we consider some of the incrementalizable classes of hyperproperties [12], particularly SHH and OHH. Moreover, other interesting security-relevant hyperproperties, such as separability [17], forward correctability [6], nondeducibility of outputs [4] etc., having known representations as conjunctions of unwinding relations, can benefit from the techniques presented here.

Finally, we have presented a number of *unwinding theorems* for our coinductive reinterpretation of well-known security-relevant hyperproperties.

7 Conclusion

We have proposed a framework suitable for coinductive reasoning about hyperproperties in general and illustrated its usefulness by exploring a new coinductive reinterpretation of known noninterference policies as hyperproperties. The framework is modular, as it permits expressing a number of security-relevant hyperproperties as conjunctions of variants of Mantel's BSPs. We have demonstrated the usefulness of coinductive unwinding relations for reasoning about hyperproperties. In particular, we have presented unwinding theorems for generalized noninterference [9], noninference [17], generalized noninference [17] and the perfect security property [17]. Moreover, we have proven results connecting unwinding relations and BSPs, relating different BSPs and relating BSPs and holistic hyperproperties.

To the best of our knowledge, the results are novel in several ways. First we further develop our recently proposed framework for reasoning about hyperproperties [12] and establish a connection with the most relevant (in our opinion) work on verification via unwinding [7]. We also identify and illustrate the potential of unwinding relations (which turn out to be instances of our H'-simulations) for generic verification of hyperproperties. Further, we argue that coinductively defined hyperproperties are important not only from a theoretical standpoint, but also in practice, due to the abundance of nontrivial reactive systems. Finally, the results shed light on the significance of incremental hyperproperties.

In the future, we envision extending the work in two main directions: formally characterizing the class of security-relevant incremental hyperproperties and applying the framework for reasoning about reactive system security.

Acknowledgements. We thank Dominique Devriese for valuable comments on a draft of this paper and Tatyana Doktorova for helpful suggestions on the presentation. We also thank the anonymous reviewers for the constructive feedback.

References

1. Bohannon, A., Pierce, B.C., Sjöberg, V., Weirich, S., Zdancewic, S.: Reactive noninterference. In: Proceedings of the 16th ACM Conference on Computer and Communications Security, CCS 2009, pp. 79–90. ACM Press, New York (2009)

2. Clarkson, M.R., Schneider, F.B.: Hyperproperties. In: CSF 2008: Proceedings of the 2008 21st IEEE Computer Security Foundations Symposium, pp. 51–65. IEEE Computer Society Press, Washington, DC (2008)
3. Goguen, J.A., Meseguer, J.: Unwinding and Inference Control. In: IEEE Symposium on Security and Privacy, pp. 75–86 (1984)
4. Guttman, J.D., Nadel, M.E.: What Needs Securing? In: Proceedings of the IEEE Computer Security Foundations Workshop, pp. 34–57 (1988)
5. Haigh, J.T., Young, W.D.: Extending the Noninterference Version of MLS for SAT. IEEE Transactions on Software Engineering 13(2), 141–150 (1987)
6. Johnson, D.M., Thayer, J.F.: Security and the Composition of Machines. In: Proceedings of the IEEE Computer Security Foundations Workshop, pp. 72–89 (1988)
7. Mantel, H.: Possibilistic Definitions of Security - An Assembly Kit. In: Proceedings of the 13th IEEE Workshop on Computer Security Foundations, pp. 185–199. IEEE Computer Society, Washington, DC (2000)
8. Mantel, H.: A Uniform Framework for the Formal Specification and Verification of Information Flow Security. PhD thesis, Universität des Saarlandes, Saarbrücken, Germany (July 2003)
9. McCullough, D.: Specifications for Multi-Level Security and a Hook-Up. In: IEEE Symposium on Security and Privacy, pp. 161–166 (1987)
10. Jonathan Millen. Unwinding Forward Correctability. In: Proceedings of the Computer Security Foundations Workshop, pp. 2–10. IEEE (1994)
11. Milushev, D., Clarke, D.: Coinductive unwinding of security-relevant hyperproperties: extended version. Technical Report CW 623, Katholieke Universiteit Leuven (August 2012)
12. Milushev, D., Clarke, D.: Towards Incrementalization of Holistic Hyperproperties. In: Degano, P., Guttman, J.D. (eds.) POST 2012. LNCS, vol. 7215, pp. 329–348. Springer, Heidelberg (2012)
13. Rushby, J.: Noninterference, Transitivity and Channel-Control Security Policies. Technical Report CSL-92-02, SRI International
14. Rutten, J.J.M.M.: Automata and Coinduction (An Exercise in Coalgebra). In: Sangiorgi, D., de Simone, R. (eds.) CONCUR 1998. LNCS, vol. 1466, pp. 194–218. Springer, Heidelberg (1998)
15. Ryan, P.Y.A.: A CSP formulation of non-interference and unwinding. In: Cipher: IEEE Computer Society Technical Committee Newsletter on Security & Privacy, pp. 19–30 (March 1991)
16. Ryan, P.Y.A., Schneider, S.A.: Process Algebra and Non-Interference. Journal of Computer Security 9(1/2), 75–103 (2001)
17. Zakinthinos, A., Lee, E.S.: A general theory of security properties. In: Proceedings of the 1997 IEEE Symposium on Security and Privacy, SP 1997, pp. 94–102. IEEE Computer Society, Washington, DC (1997)

Retooling and Securing Systemic Debugging

Björn Ståhl and Per Mellstrand

Blekinge Institute of Technology
{bsh,pme}@bth.se

Abstract. There are a few major principal tools that have long supported the often frustrating and time-consuming part of software development and maintenance that is debugging. These tools are the symbolic debugger, the profiler, the tracer and the crash dump analyzer. With the advancement of dynamic protection mechanisms directed towards hindering or thwarting exploitation of software vulnerabilities (a subset of possible software bugs), combined with a shift from developers being in charge of the development of one distinct piece of software to, instead, piecing a large assortment of third party components and libraries into a common service or platform, many of the mechanisms that the aforementioned tools rely on have been either eliminated, circumvented or otherwise rendered inefficient. In this article, we present an industrial case illustrating this shift, highlighting specific issues and challenges facing the effective use of aforementioned tools, then look at how recent developments in tracing frameworks can be further improved to remedy the situation. Lastly, we introduce such a tool alongside initial experimentation and validation.

1 Introduction

In its essence, software debugging first concerns the discovery of causal factors (chain of events) behind undesired behaviors and thereafter taking remedial action with the end-goal of preventing said behaviors from reoccurring[6]. The way this plays out in actual software development is, at the very least, two-folded – on the one hand we have the active development or bring-up of an envisioned software-based system (early-stage) where anomalies are uncovered during validation efforts, and on the other we have the reactive response to anomalies experienced by end-users (late-stage). Subsequently, we refer to these two different phases as *program debugging* and *systemic debugging*[1].

Among the notable differences of relevance to the argumentation herein, is that in the program debugging case, the analyst has access to higher precision and accuracy in measurements, more options for controlling environmental factors and for intervening with the subject. Among numerous non-trivial issues that needs to be accounted for in the systemic case, we find obfuscation, encryption, digital-rights management, unknown third party software (including rootkits and viruses) and the work is often closer in nature to reverse-engineering

---

[1] For a lengthier non-academic elaboration of the subject, consult [14].

A. Jøsang and B. Carlsson (Eds.): NordSec 2012, LNCS 7617, pp. 137–152, 2012.
© Springer-Verlag Berlin Heidelberg 2012

challenges than it is to programming ones. For these reasons, this article will assume the systemic debugging perspective.

This article is organized as follows:

In Sect. 2, *Smartphone Transition* we illustrate the breadth of the problem with an industrial case based on a shift from feature phones (i.e. cellphones as static and monolithic embedded systems) into so-called smart-phones (semi-open, heterogeneous and dynamic) focused on the configuration, role and interplay of debugging aids from the perspective of a debugging-focused team of specialist (a so called "tiger team") at Sony Mobile Communications[2].

Then, in *Moving Forward* we examine how recent developments in tracing frameworks can be improved upon to remedy the issues that was brought up in the previous section, and then describe the architecture and design of such a tool.

Lastly, in *Testbed for Systemic Tracing* we introduce the prototype and experimental validation of a free and open tool based on the ideas laid out in *Moving Forward*.

2   Smartphone Transition

Current generation smartphones are interesting from a debugging perspective in that they quite cleanly illustrate an embedded- to open- shift during a compact time-frame. One the one hand, there are older cellphones ("feature phones") as embedded, albeit quite complicated, kinds of systems that have advanced protocols interfacing the large and legacy-rich phone networks. On the other hand, there are smartphones in the sense of semi-open[3] generic mobile computing platforms where the distinguishing features from other devices such as tablets or netbooks are related to form factor, user input methods and other superficial details, rather than the computing that is being performed.

Starting with the feature phone, as representative of a closed but large (millions rather than thousands of lines of source code) monolithic, embedded system; They are closed in the sense that there is limited, regulated or no access for running third party, *foreign*, code on the device. In addition, third party code, when allowed, is limited to a reduced feature set and only portable across a small span of devices. The resources that are available to developers are similarly limited and in addition to some real-time requirements on behalf of the communication protocols, optimizations need to consider not processing power as such but rather energy consumption. Furthermore, the memory space of these phones is not guaranteed to be separated between processes. This means that a wild pointer could, for instance, corrupt long chains of code, data and memory-mapped resources belonging to other parts of the system and tight packing of the memory space makes this statistically more likely than in a system where

---

[2] The views expressed herein are those of the principal authors and do not necessarily represent the views of, and should not be attributed to, Sony Mobile Communications.

[3] Semi-open because these devices are still subject to varying degrees of vendor lock-in along with type approval and other certification processes regulating the rate at which the platform can be updated.

each computing task has a distinct process with a dedicated virtual 32/64-bit memory space. Thus, the execution environment is highly static to the degree that it is trivial to establish a memory map of functions and resources, simply from the output of the static linking stage of a build system. These properties have interesting repercussions for the kinds of anomalies experienced and how long and far-reaching different kinds of errors can cascade into each other before being detected, often producing severe problems (permanent malfunction that results in a 'bricked' device that cannot be returned to a stable state). *Furthermore, the high number (millions) of instances of the same system means that even problems with very low repeatability rates will need to be investigated even when the problem in question cannot be directly reproduced.*

The smartphone transition involved large changes to the aforementioned points. To begin with, the hardware platform is many times more powerful and, in terms of ability, more similar to that of laptops one or two generations back. The software platforms are available under open-source conditions and third-party developers are encouraged to develop and release their software through built-in, regulated, marketplaces as a means to gain users. Subsequently, the end-user is able to fine-tune and customize the software configuration to their hearts' desire. However, these changes and associated economic incentives open up for other, darker areas, such as piracy and various forms of privacy invasions. The industry response from affected or concerned developers is, unsurprisingly, to try and protect the software against such piracy through the usual means and obfuscation, DRM and coupling to external state-holders (e.g. web services) are openly encouraged [1]. Such measures, however, further complicates debugging.

The crucial aspect is that the smartphone developers integrate an array of partially underspecified platforms, often without clear service-level agreements. Thus, it is rather a branded and themed access to these platforms, rather than a feature-specified, controlled and locked one that is being mediated and ultimately sold by the smartphone vendors. Even though the developers behind individual brands have comparably little influence as to the actual software configuration of any specific instance, it is ultimately a notable part of their responsibility to optimize the end-user experience. This calls for both a direct (third party-developer support programs) and indirect (third party software analysis to figure out where and what to optimize) response.

As part of this indirect response, we find the connection between this optimization challenge, the debugging challenge and to other, more subtle ones (e.g. malware analysis), in that the desired capabilities of the supporting tools are remarkably similar. Therefore, we will continue this section by taking a look at available tools, how they fit together in a larger organization and the requirements that exists which limits their use.

2.1 Toolchains

Before looking into the specifics of each separate category of tools, it is worthwhile to note that in the setting described herein, debugging tools are never operated in isolation but are rather integrated into the entire value-chain, with intermediate steps being tightly tracked and controlled with users ranging from novices to specialists. Figure 1 illustrates a drastically simplified such chain, where we can follow how an experienced issue propagate from an end-user (or external voluntary tester with a specialized tracing build) to a service center (performing initial assessment for repair, replacement, snapshotting or special tracking) onwards to specific developer groups within the organization (these include test-departments), and should the issue be of a more complicated nature, onwards to specialized task forces. Thus, it is paramount that any new tool or mechanism doesn't disrupt the flow of such a setup.

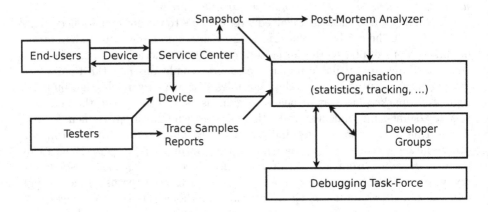

Fig. 1. Simplified example of interaction between tools and organizational units

Comparing debugging to exploitation, the successful exploitation of software vulnerabilities involve controlling the chain of events preceding an undesired behavior, setting up ideal conditions (weakness) for triggering the behavior and for taking advantage of the aftermath in order to circumvent restrictions (dissolve security properties). As such, there is an inherent conflict between the two activities in that successful debugging implies the removal of a weakness, albeit it should ideally be more difficult to exploit a bug than should ever be to fix it. Other than that, there's a surprising amount of overlap in terms of how we figure out the chain of events, and thus, the tools used to assist debugging can also typically be used in developing an exploit. Since dynamic protections are designed to combat the mechanisms used in what would otherwise be successful exploitation of vulnerabilities, relying on the same mechanisms for implementing a debugging tool would imply a forced choice between the one or the other. *Therefore, the first principal problem for all debugging tools is selecting techniques that would assist debugging but not the development of rootkits and exploits.*

Looking at specific categories of tools employed in an organization such as the one described, we find a few major categories being *symbolic debuggers*, *tracers*, *profilers* and *crash-dump analyzers* and will continue this section by highlighting specific issues encountered with each of them.

2.2   Symbolic Debugger

The arguably most powerful of tools in a software analysts' toolsuite is the symbolic debugger; a core component of most IDEs, lurking behind features such as breakpoints and stepping through execution one statement at a time. Part of the utility of a symbolic debugger stem from the ability to use source-code as a form of representation for measurements, and other parts from the ability to not only gather measurements but to actually intervene with the subject and alter its states. In order to achieve this the symbolic debugger needs to be able to exert some level of control of a subjects execution, typically from manipulating code and data in memory with assistance from a designated interface (e.g. POSIX:Ptrace, Win32:CreateRemoteThread, and hardware JTAG). This also makes such interfaces prime candidates for exploitation and all of them have successfully been used in notable exploits in the past. *The principal security challenge for the symbolic debugger is thus hardening of debugging interfaces and improving access control.*

Other challenges include:

1. The presence and ability of a symbolic debugger can be both detected, circumvented (anti-debugging [11]), misdirected ([13]) and is further hindered by common security measures such as ASLR [18], DEP/WX [16], etc.
2. Many low-level dynamic states needs to be tracked in order to retain truthfulness[19], e.g. relocations, trampolines, variable-instruction length decoding, state sensitive instruction sets, etc. If a debugger is missing this property, it is not just useless but also misleading.
3. The debugger kernel has to both track, and be aware, of threading schedulers and other concurrency techniques.
4. The source-code level of representation requires a special build that retains private symbols and, preferably, excludes most or all optimizations.

2.3   Tracer

If the symbolic debugger was a narrow category, the category of tracers is far wider. The term *tracer* refers to all tools that provide some specific traces of execution of a program that are not strictly part of its intended input / output. Subsequently, there is a rich variety in the number of information sources for tracing, e.g. system logs, process signals etc. These also include the venerable "printf" debug output left behind by careless developers. Furthermore, most symbolic debuggers have some trace functionality added through the *call trace*, also called *stack trace*. This means that it will try and extract the sequence of function calls or jumps that led to a triggered breakpoint. This is achieved either by analyzing data on the stack, with varying degrees of difficulty depending on the architecture and on how optimized the code is, or by maintaining a separate stack or log.

Such corner cases aside, tracers are tools with a generic data gathering approach that can take advantage of a wide range of information sources that

are not exclusive to dedicated debugging interfaces and other forms of specialized support. In addition, they are not as strictly bound to a single program as
symbolic debuggers are.

Some key-pointers in relation to tracing tools:

1. The connection between trace samples and the source of the sample is not
   always obvious or tracked. Thus, the data need to be tagged with some
   reference in regards to its source, covering both *where* (instruction, function,
   program, etc.) and *when* (timestamps) the sample was gathered.
2. The imposed overhead varies a lot with the quantity of data and the frequency of samples together with the properties of the interface and the resource that the data comes from.
3. There is no clear or default reference model (e.g. source-code) to appropri-
   ately compare and study.
4. As tracing tools are quite easy to develop, you can quickly end up with a
   large number of unnecessarily specialized tracers, unless the tool-chain is
   heavily moderated.

2.4   Profiler

The profiler as a generic category covers performance measurements, but can be
viewed as a distinct form of a tracer[4] that specializes in performance degradation problems. The implicit assumption is that the performance degradation is
linked to some subsystem where the most execution time is being spent, which
is not always the case with, for instance, resource-starvation linked performance
degradation.

These measurements can be implemented using two trace sources or a single
datasource, a situation which is here referred to as *event-driven* or *sampling-
based*. With event-driven tracing, there is some sort of reference clock (to establish time or cycles that elapse) and two trace points (entry and exit), such as
the function prologue and epilogue in many low-level calling conventions. With
sample-based tracing, some data source is sampled at a certain rate, and changes
(or the lack of changes) to this data source are recorded. An obvious such source,
from a low level perspective (particularly in cases where the code distribution
in memory is well-known and static), would be the instruction pointer/program
counter of a CPU. This even though this may require specialized hardware, but
the idea translates to virtual machines as well.

The shared aspect of these tools, however, (perhaps more so in the event-
driven case) is that the refined use relies heavily on the analyst's skills when it
comes to statistical data analysis and modeling.

Here follows some key-pointers about profilers (and subsequently, about the
use of these tools for debugging performance degradation):

1. Even though the needed precision may vary, the case can, at times, be that
   the degraded performance is not directly linked to just processing power, but

---

[4] Even though it can be integrated as a part of a specialized build of the software.

rather to the relationship between different resource types (communication, processing and storage with their respective latencies).

2. When the environment is heterogeneous rather than uniform, it cannot safely be assumed that performance measurements generalize between different instances of the same system.

3. Some scenarios (specialized builds, event-driven tracers) with adaptive algorithms that alter behavior based on estimated processing power (common in audio and video applications), are particularly prone to suffer observer effect from profilers, and the evaluation criteria used by the algorithm implementation may need to be controlled and manipulated.

2.5   Crash-Dump Analyzer

The last tool category to be covered here is the crash dump (post-mortem) analyzer on which two perspectives are presented. The first perspective is that crash dump analysis is a specialized part of the preexisting functionality of the symbolic debugger, with the difference being that the option to continue execution is not especially useful. The debugger merely provides the analyst with an interactive interface from which to query various states pertaining to a crash (or breakpoint). The other perspective is that a crash dump (snapshot) of processor states can be combined with more domain and application-specific knowledge and quickly generates reports and other documents to a wide assortment of specialists and can thus serve as an important glue between actors in a larger development effort or organization. Both of these are relevant to the extent that they cover a broad and detailed description of the states and data of a system or subsystem that, if the underlying cause is proximate in time to the trigger that generated the snapshot or crash, may encompass sufficient data for successful troubleshooting.

In addition, crash dump analysis, as both a manual process and in the form of automated tools, finds its relevance when the target instance is not immediately accessible at the time it presented some anomalous behavior. This further assumes that these snapshots are both generated and collected. This, in turn, implies that a larger support infrastructure is needed, one that manages all the aspects of collaborating with different stakeholders, and thus ascertains that relevant and intact snapshots are obtained.

Some concluding points in regards to crash dump analyzers:

1. The success of analysis is largely dependent on how intact the underlying data is, meaning that data corruption that specifically affects control structures (metadata) and other key areas rapidly reduces the chances that a snapshot will be useful.

2. The success of analysis is also largely dependent on how encompassing the data is. Some state holders external to the subsystem in question may not be fully retrievable at the point when the snapshot is being generated, such as OS file, socket and pipe descriptors.

3. Crash dump analysis is in many respects similar to computer forensics. Thus, new developments and techniques that benefit the one may well apply to the other.
4. A considerable challenge is to gather only relevant data (both cases) and present only that which is necessary (latter case) for each group of stakeholders, using the most fitting native and non-native representations.
5. The principal problem for the crash-dump analyzer (and to a lesser extent, the tracers) is that of privacy, i.e. how can state relevant for debugging be separated from data that is sensitive to the user.

3   Moving Forward

A major development in terms of tracing is the expansion of (virtual-) machine support in the direction of tracing frameworks [17]. Recent works that does this include dtrace [8], systemtap [2], PinOS [7], and Lttng [10]. The basic idea is that the code is prepared with *instrumentation points*. These can be implemented through, for instance, NOP instructions, which should preferably have been added already during compilation but which may have, of course, been added dynamically. During regular execution, these instructions are executed. By definition, they impose no real change in system or processor state and their only real overhead is the trivial cost of a few more bytes of code. When an instrumentation point is later *activated*, the instruction is changed to a jump to some *stub* code controlled by the tracing framework. Note that at this stage, the change is very similar to how *software breakpoints* in a regular debugger behaves. The key difference lies in what happens after execution has been hijacked.

With the tracing framework, the analyst specifies which tracepoints he or she wants activated, using domain specific language native to the framework. This specification also covers which tracepoint-associated data that should be collected, and how this data should be processed and presented. Thus, among the key differences between the frameworks is the interface specifications for data adjacent to the instrumentation point, and how the gathered information is exported.

A major problem that persists from both tracers and the other tool categories is how the gathered data are represented, particularly when source-code and debug-builds are not available or sufficient. Even though there are polished user interfaces available, such as Apple instruments [4] and the lttng's viewer, the actual presentation consists of fairly simple 2D graphs and histograms, similar to those used by many profilers.

3.1   Trace-Probe Networks

The suggested enhancement to tracing frameworks, concerns loosening the grip and focus on the specifics of how each individual trace probe operates, and instead focus on how they are modeled and how collected traces are represented. This means that they do not all need to operate on the same mechanisms but should instead be configurable to a larger degree. If such restrictions are dropped, it would be easier to apply them to a more heterogeneous environment where the set of available and accessible control mechanisms is constantly shifting. This would also make it unnecessary to rely on being able to modify the code of the system or subsystem that we are interested in observing.

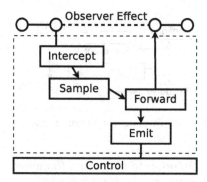

Fig. 2. Key actions for a trace probe

We begin by outlining a more abstract probe and breaking it down into a few key functions, as illustrated in Fig.2.

Probe Design. The first challenge for a tracing probe is *interception*, which concerns the issue of the extent of control needed, in respect to the extent of control that is necessary, in order to gather measurements. If it is dangerous or otherwise unwise to have a probe alter the space in any way, this function may have to be reduced to a statistical approach and external sampling. When control has somehow been intercepted, the target has irrevocably been altered, which is illustrated by the *observer effect*. Preexisting debugging interfaces can, of course, still be used to intercept execution, but there are other tools that can also do the job, tools such as the dynamic linker through facilities such as LD_PRELOAD in the GNU LD linker (and others). Other viable options are more exotic techniques such as those described in [5], as well as the interface for process or raw memory access, specialized drivers, loadable plugins, JIT facilities of virtual machines [15], process parasites[9], packet filter DIVERT rules etc.

After control has been intercepted, it is possible to *sample*, meaning to extract data from the subject. Sampling is closely tied to the chosen interception mechanism because it can provide reasonable assumptions as to the type, size and location of adjacent data. As soon as a sample has been generated, the probe *emits* the sample and *forwards* control back to the target. The task of emitting a sample involves tagging (time-stamps, sequence numbers, etc.), packaging (compression, encryption) and synchronization.

Note that a key-decision in the design and development of each probe, is to establish which functions that should execute as part of the target, and which should be made external. The external part, is referred to as the *control-interface* (labeled as *control* in the figure) and acts as an mediator between the target and the analyst. This part is responsible for all administrative tasks such as attaching and detaching one or more probes (performing the initial interception) to one or several targets.

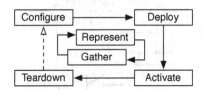

Fig. 3. Coordinating a network of trace probes

Probe Coordination. In order to get such a framework to operate in a more advanced and heterogeneous environment, we need an overarching structure that enables coordination, as illustrated in Fig. 3. This can be implemented recursively by establishing hierarchies of controller-interfaces. Similarly, to the workings of each probe, there are a few key functions that cycle, and they can be divided into an outer, external, ring (*configure, deploy, activate, teardown*) and an inner, local, ring (*represent, gather*).

The first function, *configure*, works as an interactive starting point in that the analyst specifies which configuration of sensors that he or she wants. Such a configuration entails the interception mechanism and its parameters, the direct address of the control-interface and the relative address from there to the target. In this way, this step is comparable to the configuration mentioned earlier in this section. At this point, it is also possible to perform both a sanity check (are all the desired targets reachable, can each control-interface inject the probes in question, etc.), and a test-run to make sure that all probes can perform an intercept to detach sequence. When a workable configuration has been determined, it can be propagated to the control-interfaces in question, i.e. *deploy*.

The inner ring can be activated as soon as samples from trace probes are starting to gather. In the inner ring, there are two key actions that can be alternated interactively. The first one, *gather*, concerns making an informed selection from the data that have been gathered thus far. The second action, *represent*, is necessary in order to make the selected data intelligible by providing visual models to which the data can be attached. These *representations* can be both native (using the symbols and relations from the running configuration) but also non-native with help from a wide range of visualization techniques such as graphs, diagrams, bitmaps and histograms, etc. These representations can also be recorded and distilled into reports akin to the ones previously discussed in the section dealing with crash dump analysis.

The last stage in the outer ring (which subsequently will interrupt the flow of the inner ring) is *tear down*, meaning that all control-interfaces deactivate, disconnect or otherwise disables the probes that they govern, so that the flow of samples is terminated. This action can be followed by a new iteration, i.e. refining the previous configuration based on experiences gained from the previous session.

Discussion. The fact of the matter is that similar approaches have already been realized in a number of other contexts; Network communication for many of the communication protocols widely used when it comes to routers and packet filters (firewalls), has dealt with dynamic systemic debugging challenges for a long time, particularly from a performance perspective. In addition to this, there are many refined monitoring tools that make use of similar principles to the solution that was just discussed. Wikipedia has an extensive summary of such tools at [3] and a comprehensive overview of useful native and non-native representations can be found in [12]. Thus, the principal contribution and step forward would be found in unifying such monitoring systems in iteratively refined epistemic models with configurable non-native forms of representation that compensates for the role of, not only the tracer, but the other principal debugging tools as well and that for systemic debugging purposes, at least, there is a serious need to be able to correlate and evaluate causal links between highly different and non-obvious semantic levels and not just at the more convenient and accessible interfaces (e.g. network communication).

4 Testbed for Systemic Tracing

Moving from the sketch-ideas in Sect. 3 to a working prototype not only for demonstrating the feasibility of the concept as such but also to be used as a stepping stone in bootstrapping a robust systemic tracing tool, involves a few challenges of its own. Aside from the issues put forth in Sect. 2.1, debugger tools suffer from the requirement of truthfulness more than anything else – we need to know that the output being studied is the actual sampled data of the subject rather than partial or full-corruption induced by the tool itself. *A misleading debugging tool is worse than no tool at all.*

We took the set of desired initial features and looked for alternative communities with as large an overlap as possible, ultimately settling on graphical

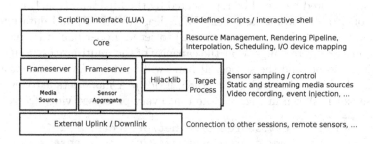

Fig. 4. Overview of Arcan/SenseEye tools

frontends for games, emulators and home-theaters in order to quickly reach a reasonably stable core and API, as the feedback loops in these areas are short and it is comparably easier to find workable qualitative and quantitative evaluation scenarios than it would be for a normal debugging tool, hence more useful data from initial testers. Other aspects of this decision will be covered in Sect. 4.1.

Thus, there are two tools available: Arcan[5], and SenseEye[6] that shares a majority of the same codebase, with the core of Arcan being used as the baseline, subject to only very modest changes to its current design with a priority of the engine remaining portable (Win32/BSD/POSIX) and scripts being compatible with future versions. The other tool, SenseEye is subsequently a fork of the Arcan codebase exposing a different API, more forms of visual representations, and a more capable frameserver / set of hijack features. Since this will cover somewhat unknown territory (domain-specific languages for dynamic real-time monitoring in contrast to a common scripting interface such as LUA), it will be subject to more radical change as things progress.

A quick rundown of the major components can be found in Fig. 4. To map this to the Fig. 3 model, the sensor configuration is specified through the scripting interface (*configure*), and for each specific target (e.g. process, device, dtrace script, ...) a corresponding frameserver is launched, having its privileges dropped to a minimal level (*deploy*) with named shared memory acting as low-level IPC. With the shared memory mapped, a few basic data-structures and synchronization primitives are set up (ring-buffers, event-queues, semaphores, ...) which are polled on a best-effort or rate-limited basis by the main program and then mapped to resources(*represent*) exposed to the Scripting Interface, with a lot of options for caching and post-processing (weighted deltas, GPU shaders for GPGPU style offloading, ...). Failure or misbehavior using semaphore synchronization causes the frameserver to be forcibly terminated (emphteardown).

The *hijacklib* represent a specialized version of the frameserver API in the form of an injectable shared object. The way it is used in Arcan (and in the experimentation further down) is that it intercepts some common symbols related to Audio/Video/Input and either manipulates the data *in situ* before passing it on to the target, or sample and expose to the user script.

4.1 Experimentation

The sensor explored here will be represented by the hijack-lib (Fig.4) used as an example of, if not a worst-case scenario, at least a difficult and data-intensive scenario in terms of observer effect (Fig. 2) to set an upper bound for more specialized sensors and to gauge what the capacity of the multi-process frameserver approach would be, and the subject at hand will be the MAME[7] emulator suite emulating the "Top Gunner" game (1986, Exidy). A more detailed view of the specific sensor is shown in Fig. 5. Note that every processed video-frame would

---

[5] available at http://www.sourceforge.net/projects/arcanfe
[6] available at http://www.sourceforge.net/projects/senseye
[7] http://www.mamedev.org

impose at the very least two additional context switches along with associated inter-process semaphore synchronisation. Also note that there is an element of tampering in this sensor as well since I/O events can be scripted and interleaved with those in the event loop of the target.

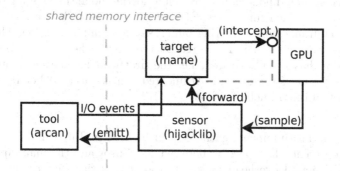

Fig. 5. Overview of Arcan/SenseEye tools

The reasons for using an emulator as an experiment subject for this kind of benchmarking is due to accurate emulation being notably resource intensive (the emulation of very old devices can still saturate even modern CPU cores and at higher resolutions, the emulator fully consumed one of the available CPU cores) but with little to no dynamic / adaptive behavior or external dependencies present and well-defined strict performance characteristics (set number of frames to deliver at precise intervals). The highly interactive gaming element allows for easy quantitative and qualitative evaluation, e.g. are there any discernible differences in gameplay, and would a comparison of instrumented input/output recordings yield any measurable difference?[8]. In contrast, modern gaming engines are highly adaptive to the point that a well-designed engine masks temporary stalls imposed by offsetting image quality which, in addition to ethical cheating/DRM circumvention concerns, make them ill-suited for experimentation. Furthermore, the actual implementation of an interpreting emulator is notably similar to those found in other Virtual Machines (e.g. Dalvik in Android) but with considerably less forgiving constraints.

The reasons for the choice of this particular emulator is its long legacy (in development since 1997), priority on accuracy in favor of speed, well-tested and ported to a large number of different platforms, with source code readily available. The reasons for the specific choice of emulation target is that its distribution and use in this emulator have been sanctioned by the copyright holders and is thus legally available and readily accessible for verification purposes, and the original hardware platform used a vector display which yields a renderpath in the emulator that would be in disfavor of the sensor sampling technique used.

---

[8] The reader is encouraged to download and try it for him/herself.

Setup. The script used to configure the tool is the 'internaltest' part of the main Arcan distribution. Measurements are gathered based on the *clock_gettime* using CLOCK_MONOTONIC_RAW on a 64-bit Linux 3.0 kernel running on a Intel Core2Duo E7500@2.93GHz with frequency scaling and other adaptive hardware tuning disabled. The targeted software itself have not been altered in any way and is thus considered non-cooperative, non-hostile (no antidebugging or similar techniques used). Each run covers 3600 samples (60 seconds runtime) with the timing of each frame stored in a ring-buffer, saved upon termination. The timing for the instrumented run is measured at the point where the corresponding representation has been activated, i.e. the draw-call for the associated video object. The timing for the non-instrumented run is gathered before initiating the readback of the framebuffer from the GPU.

Results. The measurements gathered can be seen in Table. 1. Note that the data-rate represents data passing between the sensor and the main application and that the actual overhead imposed is at least twice that of the specified rate. The standard deviations are set against the reference clock of (16.67 ms per frame). The instrumented delta refers to the average time elapsed between frames.

Table 1. Measuring the observer-effect on an instrumented subject (milliseconds)

Resolution	Data rate (MiB/s)	σ (Non-Instrumented)	σ (Instrumented)	Mean Delta
320x240	17.578	0.662	1.154	16
640x480	70.313	0.576	58.78	20
800x600	109.863	5.523	226	30
1024x768	180.0	3.249	2457	65

Discussion. As evident from Table. 1, the standard deviation from the ideal mean differs quite notably between the instrumented run and the non-instrumented ones, especially as the resolution increase. This is because the sensor was not equipped with any other synchronization options (e.g. dropping or batching frames to account for temporary stalls, pipeline bubbles etc.) thus as soon as one frame starts drifting, it cascades onwards. Using the mean delta between frames, we can see that already at 640x480, every 4th frame would've have to been discarded to maintain transparent sampling of target state without a user noticing.

To translate this sensor into a more serious context, one can think of the sampled framebuffer(emulated video display) as any memory region, heap-allocated or otherwise memory-mapped, and by altering offsets between sample points to, for instance, match minimum page-size combined with abusing certain syscalls (e.g. *write*) quite rapidly map out process memory space layout and access patterns while using GPU shaders with a lookup-table in the host application to efficiently track changes and alternate between non-native representations for real-time analysis. Other fairly trivial use cases for a similar sensor would be to project the sampled buffer into a point-cloud and visually assess distribution for cryptography engineering purposes – most, if not all, necessary code for these suggestions are already in place, with the major point being that this can be done from several processes in parallel, overlay with streaming data from other analysts working in parallel, while the session is being recorded for off-line tracking.

5 Concluding Remarks

In this paper, we have argued that many modern development and protection techniques counteract mechanisms that are needed for crucial debugging tools to be useful in their current state, which further complicates the already difficult task of fixing complex problems in increasingly heterogeneous and dynamic software solutions where multiple stakeholders fight for control over enabling platforms. We have also highlighted the importance of evaluating these tools in the context of the wider organization that will directly or indirectly be forced to operate them. We thereafter presented a taxonomy of problems facing specific debugging tools derived from seminar sessions with domain experts and, using current tracing frameworks as a model, described enhanced tools for enabling systemic tracing which, in essence, would enable *dynamic* monitoring of software-intensive systems for a wide range of purposes, the more interesting of which would be complementing and validating protection mechanisms for existing *static* hierarchical monitoring systems (e.g. SCADA for critical infrastructure). Lastly, we demonstrated the implementation and use of such a tool, with some examples of future work in the near to immediate future.

References

1. Android application licensing, implementing an obfuscator,
   http://developer.android.com/guide/publishing/licensing.html
2. Architecture of systemtap: a linux trace/probe tool,
   http://sourceware.org/systemtap/archpaper.pdf
3. Comparison of network monitoring systems,
   http://en.wikipedia.org/wiki/Comparison_of_network_monitoring_systems
4. Developer tools: Apple developer overview,
   http://developer.apple.com/technologies/tools/
5. Embedded elf debugging,
   http://www.phrack.com/issues.html?issue=63&id=9
6. Araki, K., Furukawa, Z., Cheng, J.: A general framework for debugging. IEEE Softw. 8, 14–20 (1991)
7. Bungale, P., Luk, C.: Pinos: a programmable framework for whole-system dynamic instrumentation. In: Proceedings of the 3rd International Conference on Virtual Execution Environments, pp. 137–147 (2007)

8. Cantrill, B.M., Shapiro, M.W., Leventhal, A.H.: Dynamic instrumentation of production systems. In: Proceedings of the Annual Conference on USENIX Annual Technical Conference, ATEC 2004, pp. 2–2. USENIX Association, Berkeley (2004)
9. "Crossbower": Single process parasite,
   http://www.phrack.com/issues.html?issue=68&id=9
10. Fournier, P.M., Desnoyers, M., Dagenais, M.R.: Combined tracing of the kernel and applications with LTTng. In: Proceedings of the 2009 Linux Symposium (July 2009)
11. Gagnon, M.N., Taylor, S., Ghosh, A.K.: Software Protection through Anti-Debugging. IEEE Security & Privacy Magazine 5(3), 82–84 (2007)
12. Marty, R.: Applied Security Visualization. Addison Wesley Professional (2008)
13. Mateas, M., Montfort, N.: A box, darkly: Obfuscated code, weird languages, and code aesthetics. In: Proceedings of the 2005 Digital Arts and Culture Conference, pp. 144–153 (2005)
14. Mellstrand, P., Stahl, B.: Systemic Software Debugging. Sony Mobile Communications (2012), http://www.systemicsoftwaredebugging.com
15. Olszewski, M., Mierle, K., Czajkowski, A., Brown, A.D.: Jit instrumentation: a novel approach to dynamically instrument operating systems. SIGOPS Oper. Syst. Rev. 41, 3–16 (2007)
16. Raadt, T.D.: Exploit mitigation techniques (2005),
    http://www.openbsd.org/papers/ven05-deraadt/index.html
17. Toupin, D.: Using tracing to diagnose or monitor systems. IEEE Softw. 28, 87–91 (2011)
18. Xu, H., Chapin, S.J.: Address-space layout randomization using code islands. J. Comput. Secur. 17, 331–362 (2009)
19. Zellweger, P.T.: An interactive high-level debugger for control-flow optimized programs. SIGPLAN Not. 18, 159–172 (1983)

Cracking Associative Passwords

Kirsi Helkala[1], Nils Kalstad Svendsen[1], Per Thorsheim[2], and Anders Wiehe[1]

[1] Gjøvik University College, Norway
{kirsi.helkala,nils.svendsen,anders.wiehe}@hig.no
[2] EVRY Consulting, Norway
per.thorsheim@evry.com

Abstract. Users are required and expected to generate and remember numerous good passwords, a challenge that is next to impossible without a systematic approach to the task. Associative passwords in combination with guidelines for the construction of 'Word', 'Mixed', and 'Non-word' passwords has been validated as an effective approach to creating strong, memorable passwords. The strength of associative passwords has previously been assessed by entropy-based metrics. This paper evaluates the strength of a set of collected associative passwords using a variety of password-cracking techniques. Analysis of the cracking sessions shows that current techniques for cracking passwords are not effective against associative passwords.

1 Introduction

Although it is often claimed that password authentication is outdated and inferior to alternative mechanisms [8, 22, 30] it is likely to remain one of the top authentication mechanisms. [12, 21]. Current best practice is described by Smith's paradoxical statement, "the password must be impossible to remember and never written down" [31]. An alternative formulation of this statement is that easily remembered passwords are weak, because they are easy to guess. The background for this work is a desire to undermine this myth. We have previously reported on an experiment [17], which demonstrated that providing users with an appropriate methodology is a key factor to escaping the paradox. We suggested an approach to creating passwords in which users for a given service take an element associated to the service and a personal element as input to the creation process. This process is guided by a small set of criteria, which informs the user if a password is good. In general, these associative passwords were well remembered. We also showed that the strongest passwords were the best-recalled passwords.

The participants in [17] were encouraged to combine an association element and a personal factor. The association could be something he or she received when accessing the site or service on the Internet. The personal factor was to be strictly personal, or something personal related to that service. The guidelines did not specify how these two elements were to be combined or mixed, because the participants, themselves, know what kind of passwords they are most likely to remember. This approach was combined with a second set of guidelines presented

A. Jøsang and B. Carlsson (Eds.): NordSec 2012, LNCS 7617, pp. 153–168, 2012.
© Springer-Verlag Berlin Heidelberg 2012

1. Identify the element associated to the service
2. Identify the personal factor
3. Create a password in one of the listed categories
   (a) Word password:
      i. Minimum 13 characters
      ii. Use many short and modified words
      iii. Remember special characters when modifying
      iv. The longer the password, the less modification is needed

   (b) Mixture password:
      i. Minimum 11 characters
      ii. Use several short (not the same length), modified words together with extra characters from the large character set
      iii. Remember the special characters when modifying

   (c) Non-word password:
      i. Minimum 9 characters
      ii. Use characters from all character sets but in such a way that there are many special characters

Fig. 1. Design guidelines for different password categories [17]

in [14, 16]. In these studies, passwords were divided into three categories and a set of guidelines was derived for each category of password: 'Word', 'Mixture' and 'Non-word'.

In [14], we analysed the strength of passwords based on the amount of information that is revealed, when the structure of a password is known. In our computations, the character set contained all of the visible keyboard keys and the length of a password was between eight and fourteen characters. This gave us 94 bits as maximum entropy for the whole group of passwords. We defined a password to be "good" if its structure revealed less than half of the baseline bits, i.e., 47 bits. A password quality tool [16] transforms entropy measurements to scores. With the scoring system, a password with a score of at least 735 points is a good password. By following the guidelines for the respective category, good passwords can be generated, in terms of the strength of the password. The guidelines are shown in Figure 1 and the following three examples show how an association can be used, together with the password guidelines. All of the passwords that were generated are good passwords[1].

1. Association: Green color on the logo of a bookstore loggin site
2. Personal factor: Princess with a golden ball, 1984 (the first book one of the authors read)

---

[1] Quality scores are approximations, because a word set used in the quality tool is Norwegian and the passwords in the example are based on English.

3. Examples of passwords for each category:

   Word: `Pr1c3ssWith@Gr33nB@ll`   (score: 747)
   Mixture: `Princess#With#@#Green#B@ll` (score: 740)
   Non-word: `GPrreiennc8e4SS`   (score: 850).

We further claim that that by following the recommendations given above, the risk of using same password for a different account can be reduced. Even though a user uses the same password structure, the variations in the type of association element should prevent the revelation of one password from revealing all the others. [17] lists three types of association elements: primary, secondary, and tertiary associations. The two latter ones are difficult to guess because they are not obvious to find on the service sites. However, the primary associations, such as the name of the site, the IP-address, and the logos are easily derivable for an attacker.

The fact that passwords might contain information that can be derived from the login sites or have a repeated structure has been a source of criticism of the security of these generated passwords. Therefore, this paper addresses these possible drawbacks by analysing the security of associative passwords, not only using this password quality tool [16] but also challenging the generated passwords as MD5crypt representatives with the open source password-cracking tool, John the Ripper [28]. MD5 representatives were used in a public challenge to the password-cracking community.

The reminder of this paper is structured as follows. Section 2 provides an overview in the areas password design, password security evaluation, and password cracking. Section 3 introduces and describes the experimentally generated passwords. Section 4 outlines the design of the attacks on the password representatives that is carried out in Section 5. Finally, Section 6 concludes the paper with a discussion of the experimental results and a set of recommendations for good password design.

2   Related Work

Password systems are likely to remain because they are readily accepted by users, they have low initial costs, and alternative authentication mechanisms have higher complexity and cost [11,35]. The problem of poor-passwords is addressed in numerous ways in the literature and extensive analysis of the alternatives has been carried out, i.e., one-time password generators [19,36], mnemonic techniques [20,22,39], and challenge-response protocols [23,24].

When the security of a whole password-based authentication system, both technical, organisational and human aspect of the system have to be considered [25]. If the problem is reduced to an evaluation of the strength of passwords, two approaches can be taken: evaluating the strength of the password per se, or evaluating how resistant it is to attempts at cracking it.

The first approach is applied in systems for proactive password checking, as outlined by Bishop and Klein [10]. It is also the underlying philosophy of the

Table 1. Overview of the collected passwords [17]

Category	Percent	Modified	Good ones Score>735	Good ones of those which satisfy min length
Word	21.3 %	90.6%	8.5%	12.3%
Mixture	47.4 %	91.1%	25.4%	30.9%
Non-word	31.3 %	-	46.8%	59.7%

Table 2. The used modifications

Original	a	d	e	g	h	i, l	o	s	t	u	å	ø
Replaced	4,@	L	3,€	6	|-|	1	0, ø	5, z, $	7	|_|	@, aa,\a	oe, o,@,\o
Original	1	3	&	to	se	og	eight					
Replaced with	i	e	3	2	z	&	8					

NIST Electronic Authentication Guideline [13, 34], where the key metric for password strength is entropy. The main critique against this measurement is the difficulty of estimating the information leakage caused by the user who selects the password, and sparse knowledge of the underlying distribution of the password selection. Helkala and Snekkenes [14, 15] address this challenge by introducing password design strategies that help the user to maximise the password space.

Most of the current methods that are currently used for cracking passwords are based on Helmans crypto analytic principles for time-memory trade-off [18] and Oechslins refined rainbow tables [26]. An updated overview of the field of password cracking, covering brute force attacks, dictionary attacks and probabilistic attacks is given by Weir [37].

3   Description of the Associative Passwords

The distribution of passwords collected in previous work [17] is shown in Table 1. Most 'Word' and 'Mixture' passwords were modified. Capitalisation was the most used modification tool, appearing in 60.0% of the generated passwords. The other modifications, summarised in Table 2, were very similar to Leet alphabets [38], with the addition of Norwegian characters.

3.1   Used Languages

Language on the sites used in the experiment varied, using Norwegian, English, Finnish, and Swedish. Most of the participants had Norwegian as their mother tongue, and their known languages were English and Swedish. Finnish was a foreign language for all participants [17].

We analysed passwords from a linguistic point-of-view. In general, 60.0% of passwords were generated using only Norwegian, 19.9% of the passwords were based on English and 9.3% used Finnish words. Bilingual passwords constituted

Table 3. Association Elements, [17]

Category	Primary	Secondary	Tertiary
Percent	56.8 %	25.7%	17.5%

8.9% of the passwords. Most bilingual passwords were Norwegian-English. When looking at the correspondence to the language used on the site, it was noted that only 32% of monolingual passwords were based on the language of the site. However, if that was Norwegian, then 70% of passwords generated for these sites were based on only Norwegian. If the site was non-Norwegian, 57% of the passwords were still based on only Norwegian. This indicates that users' first option for the language is their mother tongue.

3.2 Association Elements

All generated passwords contained an association element. The association elements were further divided into three main categories: Primary, Secondary, and Tertiary, as described in [17]. Primary association elements can be found on the site itself. Secondary association are elements are related to the service itself, and tertiary association refers to a new association based on the primary or secondary association. The distribution of association categories is shown in Table 3.

From the collected passwords, 85.8% began with a letter and 17% began with the same letter as the name of the site. Among starting letters, 84.1% were upper case letters. 31.3% of all of the passwords contained the name of the site in one form or another. A similar finding was done in the analysis of the passwords leaked from Stratfor in December 2011 [29]. Here the site name "Stratfor" appeared, in one form or another, in each top ten list of cracked passwords of eight to eleven characters. Furthermore, 10.8% of passwords in our dataset included a colour word (in some form or another). 65.5% of these passwords were associated with sites that used strong colour(s).

3.3 Personal Factors

Similar to the association elements, the personal factors were divided into four categories: No factor, Service-related, Site-related and Not-related [17]. 'No factor' means that the participants had not used a personal factor at all. Service-related factors were associations of the services. Site-related factors were association with the layout of the site. The 'Not-related' factor has no relation to either the service or the site. The distribution of personal factors over the categories is shown in Table 4. Personal factors varied considerably and most of them were information that is rather difficult to find. None of the participants selected or created the same personal factor.

Table 4. Personal Factors, [17]

Category	No Factor	Service Related	Site Related	Not related
Percent	15.1 %	13.9%	4.6%	66.5%

3.4   Password Semantics

In [17] password structures were divided into ten different categories, based on how the personal factor and the association element had been used. In general, the participants had interpreted the association element as set of words, while the personal element also contained strings of digits or combination of letters and digits. In order to use the information in attack trials, we did not separate the personal factors and association elements, but referred to them only as words. This led us back to the three categories mention earlier.

Category 1 contains word structures according to the formula

$$Word_1 Word_2 ... Word_n, \tag{1}$$

where n is a number of words in a password. Words are either pure or modified. These passwords belong to Word-password group. "`MyOwnStrongPassword`" is an example of a Category 1 password.

Category 2 contains structures generalised by the formula

$$Nw_0 Word_1 Nw_1 Word_2 Nw_2 ... Word_n Nw_n, \tag{2}$$

where Nw_is are meaningless strings of characters with variable lengths and the characters belongs to the set of visible keyboard characters. If we let Nw_i be nothing, we get the structure of Equation 1 and the passwords are Word passwords. In the case that Nw_i is some other character, the passwords are Mixture passwords. "`My Own Strong Password`" and "`!My#Own#Strong#Password!`" are examples of Category 2 passwords.

Category 3 contains structures that are more complex from the dictionary word perspective, such as "string of letters, digits and symbols from the sentence based on the association elements and personal factors" and "string of syllabus from association elements and personal factors". However, because these structures give "random"-looking strings, they all can be generalised by the formula

$$C_1 C_2 ... C_n, \tag{3}$$

where n is length of the password and C_is are characters from all character sets. These passwords are Non-word passwords. "`!M#0#S# P!`" is an example of a Category 3 password.

4   Designing Targeted Attacks

Social engineering attacks are not a focus of this paper. These attacks cannot be fought by strong passwords, but rather with user awareness and education. In this paper, we discuss the types of attack, which can be carried out from publicly available and generally known information about the password policies and user groups.

Our study supports the idea that users apply languages that they know. In our study, 60% of the passwords were based on the participants mother tongue. The second most popular language was English, which is commonly studied as the first foreign language in Norway. From the perspective of a successful attack, wordlists of the users' mother tongue are a good starting point.

The rules and examples of how to generate passwords, especially visible on login sites, provide information about the structure of passwords. In our case, we have three categories: 'Word', 'Mixture' and 'Non-word', each having its own structure. We assume that this information is also available for an adversary, and the different types of structure can be programmed by using eqs. (1) to (3). In our study, the 'Mixture' password is the most popular type.

Modifications were used in more than 90% of the 'Word' and 'Mixture' passwords. Capitalisation was the most commonly used modification, followed by Leet-language substitutions. However, the Leet- substitutions summarised in Table 2 are commonly known and can therefore be easily programmed into the attack algorithms. Also, as noted in Section 3.2 84% of passwords began with an upper case letter. Therefore, first letter capitalisation should also be included to the modification tasks.

The common wordlists are rather long and therefore, from the attackers point of view, it would be handy to get hold on a reduced but still valid wordlist. In our study, we have used associations from login sites, and almost 60% of the passwords contained primary associations. This means that the words, which are basis for passwords, can be found on the login site. This was assumed beforehand. Therefore, the personal factor was introduced to make the creation of a possible password for the specific site more difficult. However, no personal factor was used in 15.1% of the passwords, and 4.6% of the personal factors were site-related. This means that one fifth of the passwords in this study are only based on words that can be associated with the login site.

5   Cracking Experiments

As discussed in Section 2 , the strength of passwords can be assessed theoretically by evaluating their entropy. This is the basis for the password scores described in Section 1. The other way to evaluate the strength of a password is the empirical approach of cracking the password, and then using the time spent as a measurement of its strength. Current methods for password cracking, mentioned in Section 2 are in typical cases more effective than brute force. The questions addressed in this section are how these tools perform on associated passwords and to what extent the tools can be modified to perform better. Finally, this section also describes the efforts of the password-cracking community on an associated password challenge. The passwords for the challenge are the 508 passwords generated in the study by Helkala and Svendsen [17] and the attacks have been carried out on their MD5crypt and MD5 representatives.

5.1 Using John the Ripper, Part I

In the first three approaches, we used MD5crypt with salt to hash the passwords, because it is supported in the newest Linux-distribution for storing login-passwords. The same salt was used for all the passwords and the machine used for cracking was Intel(R) Core(TM) i7-2760QM CPU @ 2.40GHz with CentOS operating system. The computer had alternative tasks to handle during the experiment, which reduced the cracking speed.

Cracking 1. In the first attempt, we combined English and Norwegian wordlists from Aspell [1] in the newest version of Fedora, because they contained more words than those following CentOS. The wordlists were used to run John the Ripper in "wordlist mode" adapted with MD5 hash rules.

- With this mode, we were immediately able to crack 3 out of 508 passwords.
  - First one was 8 character long password, which only contained digits. The strength-score of the password was 80.
  - Second one was a name of an English town with first letter capitalized. The strength-score of the password was 121.
  - Third password was a name of a Norwegian community with first letter capitalized. The strength-score of the password was 119.

All the cracked passwords were extremely weak - not even close to 735 points - and contained only one pure word with easy and grammatically correct capitalisation. However, there were two other single words with first-letter capitalisation, which were not revealed One was a Norwegian first name (strength 115) and the other was a normal Norwegian word (strength 79). We checked the wordlist and found both of the words on the list. However, the name of the person was misspelled by the user generating the password and the normal word did not have a capitalised version in the wordlist.

Cracking 2. In the second approach, we used John the Ripper in "incremental mode". We let it run for a week at approximately 40M c/s and were able to crack eleven of the remaining 505 passwords. This run is summarised in Table 5, which also display the strength score of the cracked passwords. We observed that these passwords were very weak according to our classification.

All of the identified passwords were shorter than eight characters. There were several other passwords with less than eight characters, but they were not found within the timeframe and had the following properties:

Table 5. Passwords which were cracked by incremental mode

Category	Explanation	Strength	Cracking time
Word	6 characters 2 words: no capitalisation, no modifications	138	18 min 25 sec
Non-word	3 characters, based on 1 word: all letters modified with other uppercase letters	87	36 min 27 sec
Word	4 characters 1 words: first letter capitalised, mod: e → 3	161	1 h 33 min 57 sec
Non-word	4 characters, based on 1 word: all letters modified with other uppercase letters	116	1 h 56 min 53 sec
Mixture	5 characters 1 word: first letter capitalisation and mod: e → 3 non-word part: single digit in the end	171	2 h 37 min 24 sec
Word	7 characters 2 words: first letter capitalisation and mod: a → @	187	4 h 39 min 01 sec
Non-word	4 characters, based on 1 word: all letters modified with other uppercase letters	116 116	4 h 43 min 15 sec 4 h 43 min 15 sec
Non-word	5 characters, based on 2 words: first letters capitalised, every second letter left out	476	8 h 14 min 23 sec
Non-word	6 characters, based on a word: first letter capitalised, every second letter left out	348	2 d 4 h 27 min 25 sec
Word	7 characters 2 words: no capitalisation, no modifications	155	5 d 3 h 57 min 12 sec
Non-word	5 characters, based on 1 word: all letters modified with other uppercase letters	145	6 d 20 h 29 min 14 sec

- 5 character long passwords: two of them were mixture passwords, both having word part first with first letter capitalized and non-word part in the end including a special character. The last of them was totally capitalized non-word password.
- 6 character long passwords: three of them were totally capitalized non-word passwords. The last of one was a word password containing two words, one word was having not so common modification (ø→ @) and both were also modified by capitalization.
- 7 character long passwords: four of them were non-word passwords containing uppercase letters, lowercase letters and digits. The last of them was a 'Mixture' password containing also not so common modification (that might also need a bit more challenging programming task), when "to" inside a word was replaced with "2". The password also ended to non-word part with two digits.

On the eighth day, we decided to stop the program. All the passwords found were very weak and they were also under length threshold of best practice minimum (currently around eight characters). With our categorisation, the minimum length is different for each category. One cannot generate a good password, which is under thirteen characters long, no matter how it is modified. The limit is eleven characters for Mixture passwords and nine characters for Non-word passwords. Because the length alone does not determine strength, one also needs to take

Table 6. Between characters

<no char.>	<space>	,	.	_	−	+	/	\	?	!	#	@	<	>

the character sets that were used into account. Cracking with whole wordlist in the incremental mode would take too much time. Therefore, we concluded that more information on the passwords was needed if they were to be cracked.

Cracking 3. For the third approach with John the Ripper, we refined the wordlist by reducing its size. The participants in [16] had registered their associations, and we used this information to generate a new wordlist. This list contained 247 elements, mostly words, but also digits, symbols and Internet addresses. It should be noted that this list contained all three types of association elements. If an adversary made the list, we can assume that he would have been able to include the primary associations to his list easily. However, including the secondary and tertiary associations would have needed a great deal of guessing. Again, this implies that a potential attacker would have a larger wordlist than the one we used as input.

We also had information about the modified characters presented in Table 2. Based on this, we generated modification rules for John the Ripper. For programming reasons, we only used one-to-one substitutions and excluded substitutions, such as "eight" → "8" and "og" → "&" ("og" is "and" in Norwegian). Because the modifications are very similar to Leet-alphabets, it can also be assumed that the modification types are commonly known and the adversary is able to use same information.

We also noticed that previous cracking mode did not capture 'Mixture' passwords when words were separated from each other by n-length non-word part, where $n = 1, 2, ...$ Therefore, we programmed a cracking mode that uses these 247 words with all their possible modifications and we also separated words with "Between Characters". In our trial, we decided to separate the words with only one character. We observed 15 "Between Characters" in the plaintext passwords. These are shown in Table 6.

We decided to limit the passwords containing one, two or three words, separated with a between character. Finally, the wordlist contained 3 391 490 557 raw combinations. Each of these combinations was to be modified along the modification rules when search was carried out. In our dataset of 508 passwords, 107 (21%) passwords fulfilled this requirement. Five of these had been found earlier and were, therefore, excluded from the search list. The whole run took six days, four hours and twenty-six minutes. The speed at the end was twenty-five million trials per second, and within our run time, we were able to do at least $13 \cdot 10^{12}$ trials.

In this mode, we were able to crack only one additional password: a three-letter word with first letter capitalised. We had expected more. However, we knew that most of the passwords did not contain association elements alone. Comparing the plain text passwords to the association list, we noticed that there were twenty-one passwords left that contained only association elements. Unfortunately, one very obvious association was missing from the association list, which put six passwords out of our reach. If this association word had been in the list, we would have found the additional passwords, which had the structure $Word_1 Word_2$. The strength of these passwords was between 115 and 211 points, meaning that they were weak passwords.

Later, we noticed that our list did not contain all of the grammatically correct forms of a Norwegian word. Through this oversight, this we lost three passwords. Four of the remaining passwords were sentences, which meant that they included other words than those stated as association elements. Three passwords contained modification that did not treat all same letters in a same way, e.g., not all "e"s were substituted by "3" on the same password. One password had strange capitalization: every second last letter was capitalised, and one of these was also modified. That left us four passwords, which we should have been able to crack by writing all of them in small letters and with first letter capitalised, which is the most obvious means of capitalization. Unfortunately, we had forgotten this. These four passwords had strengths of between 160 and 308, meaning that they also were weak passwords.

Observations: Based on the experience from the three attempts of using John the Ripper, we can observe that a precondition for success is to have a sufficiently large but still specified wordlist with all grammatical versions of the words. The list should also contain additional words, such as verbs, prepositions, and pronouns. The cracking mode should include coding for several different rules of structural modification and, at least, the easiest capitalisations. It should also handle passwords containing more than three words. Unfortunately, the equipment at our disposal was not sufficiently powerful to carry out this kind of experiment.

5.2 Cracking Challenge

With the awareness of the limited capacity of the machinery at our disposal and of our limited experience with password cracking prior to this experiment, a somewhat untraditional approach was chosen to further challenge the strength of associated passwords. We decided to challenge the password-cracking community by publishing nine examples of the password MD5 hash without salt on the Security Nirvana blog site [33]. Three of these nine passwords were 'Word' passwords, three were 'Mixture' passwords and three were 'Non-word' passwords. From each category, we included one weak password (scores between 360 - 390 points), one good password (scores between 735 - 860) and one strong one (scores between 1000 - 1500 points). All passwords were also recalled by the users in the previous study [17]. Examples of each category were given on the introduction part of the blog post, but we did not reveal which hash belonged to which category. The published password hashes are shown in Table 7 and the activity on the blog site is documented in Figure 2.

Table 7. MD5 hashes for the Cracking Challenge

Group	MD5 hash
Group A	e231227ca23c28910d562399c51b9a83
	e52d4b9af20c584db9b39d3992d85d8d
	385e9eba54ac21c19ba6005a2de6946e
Group B	56a2ca31a41f9ea2c2c49ff059d2950e
	8d844602aaaa0cb41e89bb2566dc8246
	558483c0f05f0fb9655af6e509c4e4a7
Group C	bf185ae2278ad2e01e6d41e33d7dd261
	ae41ac6534232e73a246a2c00d34fe6a
	43bf1339a5a0a0b47696a042f3157cbf

Observations: At the time of submission of this paper, none of the passwords has been cracked and the challenge is still on going. Even if the lack of reported results from such a challenge has limited scientific value, it allows us to make a valuable observation: Associated passwords generated with the methodology

---

- On May 7 2012, the challenge was given with general information about the password categories
  - Trial 1: Using GPU driver with oclHashcat-plus-64 bit v0.08 [4] and ruleset best64.rule [2]
    Success: Running time 7 seconds. Success rate 0%.
  - Trial 2: Using GPU driver with oclHashcat-plus-64 bit v0.08 [4] with other rule-based attacks found on [6]
    Success: Trials took 15-20 min. Success rate 0%.
  - Trial 3: Hashed were fed to JulGor's findmyhash.py [3], which checks hash-values against common hash databases online
    Success: Success rate 0%.
  - Addition to trial 3: Several other online MD5 crackers were "recommended" in [32]. We tested some of them with the two weakest passwords in the competition (these being a Word-password with four English words with the first letter capitalised and a Mixture password with the word part as one English word all of the letters capitalised, and the non-word part as one capital letter and three digits). The success rate in all cases was zero. The tested crackers were from Time-Memory Trade Off and Password Cracking Research [7] , AuthSecu [9] and Online MD5 cracking project [5].
- On May 10 2012, the blog readers were given link to the previous study [17] to gather more information how these nine passwords are generated, because obviously common rules set do not work against their passwords.
- On May 23 2012, information about the password association was added. This information can be used, in theory, to reduce the number of words on a cracking list.

Fig. 2. The documented process on the blog site [33]

presented in Figure 1 are not easily cracked by password-cracking methodologies that are currently in use. This is also the case for passwords that are classified as weak, according to the applied password quality tool [16].

5.3   Using John the Ripper, Part II

In a final experiment, we came back to John the Ripper, with same setup as in Section 5.1, in order to carry out a targeted attack on three-word-passwords from the open challenge, described in Section 5.2. This means that, in this run, the representative passwords were unsalted MD5-hash values. The three passwords had been designed for two different service sites and a wordlist including all association words and all personal factors relating to these services was generated. In addition, the wordlist contained possible verbs, pronouns, and prepositions so that meaningful sentences could be created. The list originally contained 156 words. Furthermore, each word was written with the first letter as a capital letter, and this doubled the number of words on the list. Here we note that the personal factors are not publicly available information and are only available to us because of our access to the plaintext passwords.

Because the passwords were 'Word' passwords, Equation 1 was used to crack passwords. In Section 5.1, one- and two-word, 'Word' passwords had already been tested, so in this trial, we ran cracking mode with three- and four-word, 'Word' passwords. The modification rules encoded in Section 5.1 were also applied in this trial. It took three hours, twenty-nine minutes and twenty-seven seconds, at a speed of 6326K c/s to crack the weakest password (score 363). This password contained four words, each with first letter as an uppercase letter. John the Ripper finished the run in ten hours and 37 minutes. The two remaining passwords were not found. One reason for this was that in both passwords, several different letters were modified simultaneously, something that the cracking mode was not able to handle.

6   Conclusions

It is often stated that rainbow tables can crack your password in no time. However, the tables only work if they contain your password. Currently available rainbow tables from the Free Rainbow Table project contain only passwords which have a maximum length of nine characters for MD5 hashes [27]. These tables do not include special characters with length of nine among the passwords. Our guidelines recommend a minimum length of thirteen, eleven and nine characters for 'Word', 'Mixture' and 'Non-word', respectively. In addition, in the case of 'Word' passwords, it is recommended to use several short words, short being not longer than half of the whole password. Therefore, 'Word' passwords should, in general, contain three or more words with modifications. This is also the recommendation for 'Mixture' passwords. None of the good passwords were cracked in this study.

The passwords included in the cracking challenge were between twelve and twenty-four characters long. There are several ways to explain the failure of the hybrid attacks applied in the cracking challenge. One reason can be that the applied wordlists did not contain the correct words. Secondly, the hashcat wordlist included passwords from previously hacked sites [2]. These passwords are "well known", and the participants who had generated the passwords were educated to avoid such constructions. Thirdly, the passwords were rather long, which implies an increase in the computational complexity for cracking them. Uncommon capitalisation and several modifications have a particularly significant effect on the strength of a password.

Passwords based on primary associations were assumed to be easiest to crack, since, in theory, one can generate a list containing "all" associations of a service site. However, it is not enough to have a list of "all" associations. Passwords become memorable when the associated words are linked to each other logically, meaning that sentences are used. As a consequence, other words, such as verbs and pronouns have to be added to the dictionary. This leads to a larger set of words and increased complexity.

Based on our findings, we recommend the use of associative passwords combined with guidelines for categorized passwords. Using the associations and the guidelines, a password will be memorable and will also be strong. One weakness of this type of passwords arises if memorability is increased by applying similar primary associations, e.g., adding the same personal factor and the same structure to each password. This leads to a higher risk of revealing all of the passwords when one password has been revealed. However, this can be avoided if secondary and tertiary associations are used. Furthermore, users should always be encouraged to use both a personal factor and an association element. By doing so, adversaries are forced to use a large word set, which makes the cracking task more difficult.

It is important to keep in mind the way in which passwords are cracked. Computational power and storage capabilities are getting better and larger, so more complex wordlists and pre-computed hash value tables can be produced and used. There are easy countermeasures, such as using uncommon words, dialects, and misspellings. Sentences are easy for us to remember. Using sentences, the complexity of a password grows easily. In addition, the complexity can be increased by adding uncommon and/or uneven modifications and capitalisations.

Remembering a large number of good passwords is a challenge for users. Through our experiments in this study, and in previous work, we have shown that detailed approaches for designing passwords, partially based on publicly available information, can result in good passwords. In the series of attacks presented in this paper, only the weak passwords were cracked, a result that leaves us with a fair bit of optimism for the security of passwords that are based authentication systems.

Acknowledgements. We are grateful to all who voluntarily took part in password cracking.

References

1. Aspell dictionnaries (May 15, 2012),
   `ftp://ftp.gnu.org/gnu/aspell/dict/0index.html`
2. best64.rule (May 13, 2012), `http://beeeer.org/best64/`
3. findmyhash.py (May 13, 2012), `http://code.google.com/p/findmyhash/`
4. hashcat (May 13, 2012), `http://hashcat.net/oclhashcat-plus/`
5. Online md5 cracker (May 18, 2012), `http://www.cmd5.org/`
6. Rule based attacks (May 13, 2012), `http://hashcat.net/wiki/rule_based_attack`
7. Time-memory trade off and password cracking research (May 18, 2012),
   `http://www.tmto.org/pages/passwordtools/hashcracker/`
8. Adams, A., Sasse, M.A.: Users are not the enemy. Commun. ACM 42, 40–46 (1999)
9. AuthSecu. Décryptez votre hash md5par sébastien fontaine (May 18, 2012),
   `http://authsecu.com/decrypter-dechiffrer-cracker-hash-md5/decrypter-dechiffrer-cracker-hash-md5.php`
10. Bishop, M., Klein, D.V.: Improving system security via proactive password checking. Computers & Security Journal 14(3), 233–249 (1995)
11. Bonneau, J., Herley, C., van Oorschot, P.C., Stajano, F.: The quest to replace passwords: A framework for comparative evaluation of web authentication schemes. In: 2012 IEEE Symposium on Security and Privacy (May 2012)
12. Bonneau, J., Preibusch, S.: The password thicket: technical and market failures in human authentication on the web. In: WEIS 2010: Proc. of the Ninth Workshop on the Economics of Information Security, Boston, USA (June 2010)
13. Burr, W., Dodson, D., Perlner, R., Polk, W., Gupta, S., Nabbus, E.: NIST Special Publication 800-63-1 Electronic Authentication Guideline. Technical report, National Institute of Standards and Technology (2008)
14. Helkala, K., Snekkenes, E.: Password Generation and Search Space Reduction. Journal of Computers 4(7), 663–669 (2009)
15. Helkala, K.: An Educational Tool for Password Quality Measurements. In: Proc. of NISK, pp. 69–80. Tapir Akademisk Forlag (2008)
16. Helkala, K.: Password Education Based on Guidelines Tailored to Different Password Categories. Journal of Computers 6(5) (2011)
17. Helkala, K., Svendsen, N.K.: The Security and Memorability of Passwords Generated by Using an Association Element and a Personal Factor. In: Laud, P. (ed.) NordSec 2011. LNCS, vol. 7161, pp. 114–130. Springer, Heidelberg (2012)
18. Hellman, M.: A cryptanalytic time-memory trade-off. IEEE Transactions on Information Theory 26(4), 401–406 (1980)
19. Hopper, N.J., Blum, M.: Secure Human Identification Protocols. In: Proc. of the 7th International Conference on the Theory and Application of Cryptology and Information Security: Advances in Cryptology, pp. 52–66. Springer, London (2001)
20. Ives, B., Walsh, K.R., Schneider, H.: The domino effect of password reuse. Commun. ACM 47, 75–78 (2004)
21. Kuhn, B.T., Garrison, C.: A survey of passwords from 2007 to 2009. In: 2009 Information Security Curriculum Development Conference, InfoSecCD 2009, pp. 91–94. ACM, New York (2009)
22. Kuo, C., Romanosky, S., Cranor, L.F.: Human Selection of Mnemonic Phrase-Based Passwords. In: Proc. of 2nd Symposium on Usable Privacy and Security, pp. 67–78. ACM Press (2006)
23. Li, X.-Y., Teng, S.-H.: Practical Human-Machine Identification over Insecure Channels. Journal of Combinatorial Optimization 3(4), 347–361 (1999)

24. Matsumoto, T.: Human-Computer Cryptography: An Attempt. In: Proc. of the 3rd ACM Conference on Computer and Communications Security, pp. 68–75 (1996)
25. McCumber, J.: Information Systems Security: A Comprehensive Model. In: Proc. Ninth International Computer Security Symposium (1993)
26. Oechslin, P.: Making a Faster Cryptanalytic Time-Memory Trade-Off. In: Boneh, D. (ed.) CRYPTO 2003. LNCS, vol. 2729, pp. 617–630. Springer, Heidelberg (2003)
27. Openwall. Free rainbow tables (May 18, 2012), http://www.freerainbowtables.com/en/tables2/
28. Openwall. John the Ripper password cracker (May 18, 2012), http://www.openwall.com/john/
29. Ragan, S.: Report: Analysis of the Stratfor Password List (May 31, 2012), http://www.thetechherald.com/articles/Report-Analysis-of-the-Stratfor-Password-List
30. Sasse, M.A., Brostoff, S., Weirich, D.: Transforming the "Weakest Link" - Human/Computer Interaction Approach to Usable and Effective Security. BT Technol. 19, 122–131 (2001)
31. Smith, R.E.: The Strong Password Dilemma. Addison-Wesley (2002)
32. Stottmeister, C.: How to crack md5 passwords online (May 18, 2012), http://www.stottmeister.com/blog/2009/04/14/how-to-crack-md5-passwords/
33. Thorsheim, P.: Security nirvana blog: Challenge recieved (May 2012), http://securitynirvana.blogspot.com/2012/05/challenge-received.html
34. Verheul, E.R.: Selecting Secure Passwords. In: Abe, M. (ed.) CT-RSA 2007. LNCS, vol. 4377, pp. 49–66. Springer, Heidelberg (2006)
35. Villarrubia, C., Fernandez-Medina, E., Piattini, M.: Quality of Password Management Policy. In: The First International Conference on Availability, Reliability and Security, ARES 2006, p. 7 (April 2006)
36. Weinshall, D.: Cognitive Authentication Schemes Safe Against Spyware (Short Paper). In: Proc. of the 2006 IEEE Symposium on Security and Privacy (S&P 2006), pp. 295–300 (2006)
37. Weir, C.M.: Using Probabilistic Techniques to Aid in Password Cracking Attacks. PhD thesis, Florida State University (2010)
38. Wikipedia. Leet (May 20, 2012), http://en.wikipedia.org/wiki/Leet
39. Yan, J., Blackwell, A., Anderson, R., Grant, A.: Password Memorability and Security: Empirical Results. IEEE Security & Privacy 2(5), 25–31 (2004)

A Hybrid Approach for Highly Available and Secure Storage of Pseudo-SSO Credentials

Jan Zibuschka[1] and Lothar Fritsch[2]

[1] Fraunhofer IAO, Stuttgart, Germany
[2] Norsk Regnesentral, Oslo, Norway
jan.zibuschka@iao.fraunhofer.de, lothar.fritsch@nr.no

Abstract. We present a novel approach for password/credential storage in Pseudo-SSO scenarios based on a hybrid password hashing/password syncing approach that is directly applicable to the contemporary Web. The approach supports passwords without requiring modification of the server side and thus is immediately useful; however, it may still prove useful for storing more advanced credentials in future SSO and identity management scenarios, and offers a high password security, high availability and integration of secure elements while providing familiar interaction paradigms at a low cost.

Keywords: Single sign-on, authentication, syncing, hashing.

1   Introduction

One of pseudo-SSO systems' biggest problems is the synchronization of credentials between different devices, especially as the credentials should also be available on devices the user has never used before. There are several approaches addressing this problem, specifically *password syncing*, where stored password are copied from one system to another, and possibly also to a storage in the Cloud [1], and *password hashing*, where service-specific passwords are generated from a service identifier and a *master password* (MPW) using a *pseudorandom function* (PRF) [2]. This contribution presents a hybrid approach combining current password hashing and password syncing techniques, and building on readily available services on the Web to offer a solution combining the ubiquity of password hashing and the flexibility of password syncing. Our approach leverages cryptographic mechanisms such as encryption and threshold cryptography which can enable a secure management of passwords and other credentials without cooperation from service providers, and without putting an undue burden on users with regard to complexity of the system. We designed the present system to meet several key requirements, namely:

- *Improve password security*: In spite of many efforts to find a superior replacement, passwords are more widely used than ever [3]. Thus, it is crucial to supply tools improving passwords' security, especially since passwords for many scenarios offer a high degree of task-technology-fit, and will probably not be replaced for a

A. Jøsang and B. Carlsson (Eds.): NordSec 2012, LNCS 7617, pp. 169–183, 2012.
© Springer-Verlag Berlin Heidelberg 2012

significant amount of time [3]. To improve password security, we target the following objectives:

- — Offer a pervasive synchronization of passwords between arbitrary devices (supporting web browsers), enabling universal usage of the tool, and supporting very strong password policies with minimal burden on the user.
- — Offer single sign-on, enabling users to manage strong authentication secrets without password fatigue [4].
- — Securing the password storage process using compartmentalization and encryption, hiding sensitive user information from third parties during transmission to services and between devices, without requiring esoteric interactions from the user.

- *High availability of credential storage*: a system improving password security, or authentication security on the web in general, needs to ensure a high availability, as users of our system otherwise might become stranded without access to their accounts. To address this issue, we leverage redundancy:
  - — The system may cache information (in encrypted form) on several devices.
  - — Similarly, building on the compartmentalization aspect, the system also offers a secure, redundant storage.

- *Low cost*: When introducing measures protecting the confidentiality of users' sensitive information, cost is a critical factor that needs to be considered [5]. Our system minimizes standardization, operation and deployment costs:
  - — The system builds on password interfaces and therefore evades the standardization problem that requires a significant diffusion for non-password-based SSO systems before they become useful [6].
  - — The system can use arbitrary cloud storage services, even cases where the stored information is public, similarly to the Eternity Service [7].

- *High user acceptance*: User acceptance is often a problem for single sign on systems [8]. Our system addresses this on several fronts:
  - — It supports passwords, meeting user expectations by not introducing new interaction paradigms [8], and making it immediately useful [6].
  - — It offers single sign-on, supporting users' password management, which is perceived as cumbersome by many [9].

- *Potential integration of advanced secure elements*: To make our system future-proof while building mainly on existing technologies to ensure usefulness, we made sure to include hot spots for the integration of more advanced security technologies, for example:
  - — Smart cards may be added to our SSO system following the approach from [6].
  - — The storage facility of our system may also be used for storing more advanced credentials instead of passwords, such that our system can then transmit those credentials (or credentials derived from them) in place of passwords.

The rest of this article is structured as follows: we give an overview of our approach in the following section, and then walk through the protocol in more detail in the section after this. We discuss merits and limitations of our approach, give some related works and then conclude the article with a discussion of benefits, design options and future work.

2   Approach

The basic approach described in this contribution is summarized rather concisely: we build a Pseudo-SSO solution [10] on a password hashing layer; however, instead of configuring password policies for the entire Web, we only configure policies for a relatively small number of (public) services that have the capability to store information on behalf of the user. Those services can then be used, via automated logins using the pre-configured password policies and password hashing approaches, as a Cloud storage, which may be used to sync stored passwords for any number of sites. By supporting password interfaces and policies already in place at services, we minimize standardization costs and avoid the problem of network effects requiring us to build a critical mass of users [6].

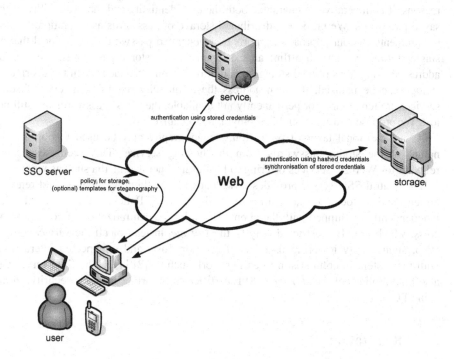

Fig. 1. Involved entities and their interactions

A system realizing the approach described above introduces two new entities into the Pseudo-SSO scenario (see Figure 1). First, storage services are used for storage of the users' passwords ($storage_i$). They represent only a fraction of the potential services supported by the Pseudo-SSO ($service_i$). The final component of the system is the SSO server distributing the SSO client component, and offering password policies for the *storage$_i$*, as part of the client component or on its own, as well as additional optional services which are elaborated later in this contribution. Similar servers have been used by related work such as PasswordSitter [11] or SXIPPER [12], however our server significantly differs in functionality.

The *service$_i$* may include Cloud storage services such as Dropbox[1], file hosting services such as RapidShare[2], hosting services for arbitrary file types such as PasteBin[3], and Web 2.0 services hosting user-created content, e.g. YouTube[4].
While we, throughout the discussion in this contribution, mostly assume a password-based Pseudo-SSO scenario (as implemented by e.g. [2] [11] [13]), implying that the information stored is passwords, the system can support any type of credential, as long as a (client-based) Pseudo-SSO interface to the authentication protocol can be realized. It handles pre-generated passwords, PINs and credentials without difficulty, a clear advantage over pure password hashing approaches. In principle, the storage services may be used to store any type of information, though the general case is not in the focus of this contribution.

Several storage services *storage$_i$* are used over one single storage service for security reasons: it is imperative to guarantee both the confidentiality and the availability of the saved passwords. We propose a distributed storage of passwords as a solution to those requirements. As our approach supports user-generated passwords, it is critical that no single *storage$_i$* can launch offline attacks against users' stored passwords. This can be addressed using a distributed storage. In addition, if some redundancy in the distributed storage can be realized, this can address the availability requirement: even if some services are temporarily or permanently not available, the users' passwords are still not lost. We propose to use threshold cryptography to realize this.

As an additional layer of protection, steganography may be used to obscure the nature of the stored passwords from the hosting service. This seems especially relevant for Web 2.0 services offering to host user-generated media such as video.

The central SSO server provides downloads of the client application and relevant policies and protocols for authentication at the *storage$_i$*. Policies may be downloaded independently or shipped with the client. This allows a centralization of configuration costs, which are also restricted only to the *storage$_i$* instead of all the *service$_i$* on the Web, significantly lowering users' configuration costs and unexpected interactions with the system in comparison to earlier work such as [2] [11]. The SSO server can also hold replicas of the *storage$_i$*'s SSL certificates to further increase security, in the vein of Convergence [14].

3   Realization

This hybrid approach combining password hashing and syncing has the potential to offer the best properties of both methods. Password hashing is used, in combination

---

with *direct login* and *lazy registration* [15], to realize an automatic single sign-on to a number of web sites accepting user-generated content. Those *storage_i* are used to store the actual data used in the user-facing pseudo-SSO system to authenticate to the services the user has accounts at (*service_i*). So, there is an upper password syncing layer built on the password hashing used to authenticate to the storage services. To make this immediately accessible to users, we envision it being built on current browser password/credential stores and syncing facilities.

3.1   On-the-Fly Generation of Passwords for Storage_i

Whenever synchronization is necessary, the master password is used to generate individual passwords for the *storage_i* (see Figure 2) using password hashing. The password hashing process is given in more detail in [13]. The generated user name and password are then used to authenticate to *storage_i*. The protocol used for this will typically be HTTP(S), in [13] a proxy server is used, while we envision a component that integrates into the browser. In our case, this amounts to:

$$genPassword(storage_i)=PRF(ID(storage_i),MPW,tweak(``password"))$$
$$genUser(storage_i)=PRF(ID(storage_i),MPW,tweak(``user"))$$
$$ID(storage)=encode(URL(storage_i))$$

PRF is a pseudorandom function, e.g. a password-based key derivation function based on a keyed hash function. For example, there are efficient JavaScript implementations of HMAC based on SHA-256/-512 [16]. Such constructions have been shown to hold security properties appropriate for our scenario in [17]. We will not reiterate the proof here.

3.2   Split/Merge of Data for Compartmentalized Storage at Storage_i

To realize a distributed storage, we use threshold cryptography. For the purpose of this paper, we will assume Shamir's secret sharing (using polynomial coefficients) for *split()* [18]; as it is fast enough to be run in the browser, implementations are readily available [19] [20], and it works as intended, as illustrated by its common usage in contemporary SSO systems. In this case, we would derive Lagrange polynomials from the points stored in the *storage_i* to reconstruct the original *PWList*, a database storing *service_i* and their corresponding passwords, giving us the *merge()* operation.

3.3   Setup

To implement this approach, our SSO system needs to provide an automated way of generating the needed login information – typically user name and password -for access to the storage services (*storage_i*). This is done using a pseudo-SSO component that the user installs on any local devices (e.g. as a browser plugin or simply by accessing a web page) (1), which uses a password hashing approach to generate user names and passwords, as described by Gabber et al. [13]. Those credentials are then used to create accounts at the *storage$_i$* (2), which are retrieved from the central SSO server as part of the client component or separately. Interactive parts of the registration process, e.g. CAPTCHAs required for authentication at many services to sort out bots, are passed to the user, and only have to be performed once when the user initially starts to use our proposed SSO solution (or alternatively once per master password if the user chooses to have several, see below).

The information is then written to the *storage$_i$* (2); authentication at the *storage$_i$* to perform password syncing is performed automatically by an underlying password hashing component that is mostly transparent to the user, which uses the password policies for the *storage$_i$* available from the central SSO server, or as part of the Pseudo-SSO client component. The specific steps are given in Fig. 2:

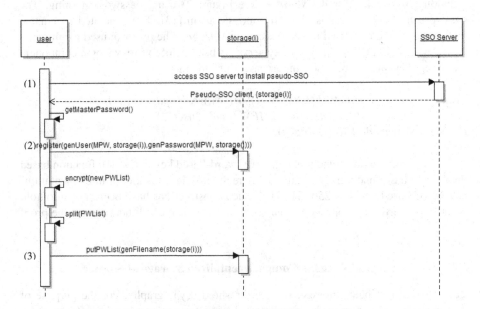

Fig. 2. Involved entities and their interactions

To avoid a single point of failure, the user can - using the system presented here - choose several passwords, or username/password combinations, as MPW, which will simply create additional accounts at the *storage$_i$* transparently, repeating the set-up phase.

3.4   Registration at Service$_i$

After this, the system can, using the underlying transparent password hashing SSO to the *storage$_i$*, provide a distributed storage infrastructure that serves as a basis for the storage of the actual *service$_i$*-facing user identities and credentials. The credential retrieval (2) can be triggered when the user starts the browser, while the storage will be triggered when the user changes passwords, adds or deletes an account (which can be detected using the authentication protocol details stored for the *storage$_i$* at the central SSO server). Also triggered at start up, the client will ask for the user's master password (MPW) (1), which (as with all SSO systems) serves as central secret.

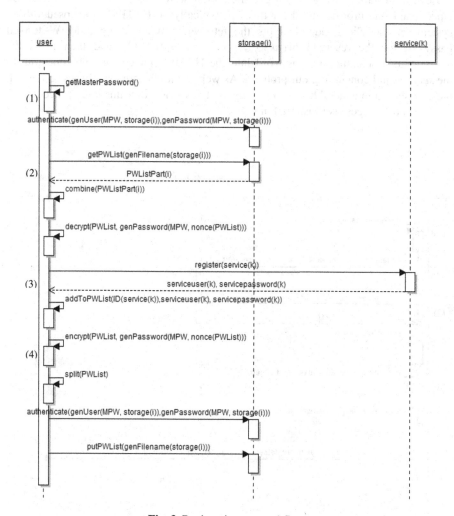

Fig. 3. Registration protocol flow

Similarly, to store information, we construct a polynomial (see section 3.2) hiding the original password store information (4), and pick points to distribute to the *storage$_i$*, uploading via HTTP(S). The whole sequence is given in Fig. 3. The same sequence is executed to update a password for a specific service, replacing (or deleting if that is requested) the old entry in step (3). Note that in step (3), the password is not necessarily provided by the service, but is determined in interaction between user, client, and service so it meets the user's preferences as well as the service's password policy.

3.5   Login at Service$_i$

Authentication is performed directly from the user's client (1). In case we want to retrieve information, we now retrieve the partial stores *store$_i$* from the *storage$_i$* (2). Once again, the protocol used for this will typically be HTTP(S). Our pseudo-SSO system on the client side decrypts the retrieved *PWList* using a MPW-derived password for the reserved *tweak$_{PWList}$* service identifier (3), and then feeds the appropriate user name and password into the HTTPS connection, authenticating to the *service$_i$* and concluding our protocol. As web site logins are usually session based, the user should in general be able to freely use the service after this login procedure.

The whole process is illustrated in Fig. 4.

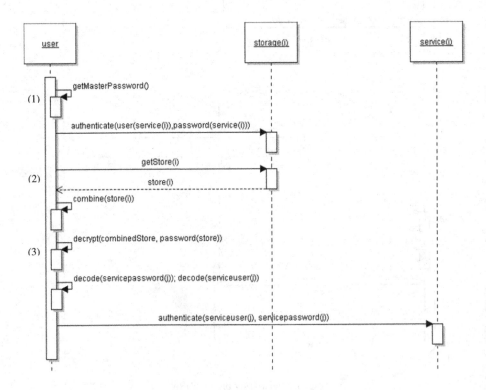

Fig. 4. Authentication protocol flow

4   Related Work

The *strong password dilemma* [9] has been known to security researchers for a long time, but has become more and more critical with the spread of the Web: it is impossible for users to have, for every web site they use today, an independent, random password of appropriate length, without writing it down or taking the risk of not being able to remember it when using the service again later [21], leading to password fatigue [4]. Cognitive psychology suggests that users may not be able to remember significantly more than 7 passwords [22]. Current studies of password usage on the Web reinforce this assumption [23], and at the same time show that users use those passwords to authenticate to 25 services on average.

One approach to solving this problem is to offer a *Reduced Sign-on* [24] or even *Single Sign-on* (SSO) to the users, allowing them to authenticate to several systems using a small number of credentials, without facing attacks resulting from cross-site reuse of passwords [25], and with minimal user interaction. There are a variety of approaches to implementing single sign-on, including browser plug-ins like LastPass [1] or PasswordMaker [26], as well as federated identity management systems (FIM) like OpenID [27] or CardSpace [28], and classical solutions like Kerberos [29] based on PKI or even symmetric cryptography with a trusted third party.

However, many of those systems have not been as successful as originally anticipated, and a meaningful reduction of sign-on on the web has not been reached. To the contrary, studies on password habits show an increase in the number of services users have to authenticate to [23]. As global, cross-domain SSO protocols entail significant standardization costs, some researchers have expressed doubts, whether SSO should be considered a realistic aim [24]. Similarly, there are many indications that passwords will be around for a long time, and may even be the superior solution to more elaborate SSO systems in many cases [3]. Thus, it is imperative to supply security-aware users with tools supporting their password management [3]

However, a new generation of FIM protocols has recently reached a significant level of adoption on the Web; specifically Facebook Connect [30] has been implemented by a wide range of services [31]. Yet, from a privacy perspective, it is unsettling to observe that the most successful contemporary SSO solution is operated by Facebook, which has been referred to as a „privacy train wreck"[32]. In general, FIM systems seem to be more successful with regard to diffusion if they do not provide elaborate privacy functionalities [31]. If we postulate that there is a niche for more secure and privacy-friendly SSO solutions, it seems prudent to investigate solutions that avoid the standardization problem, as a niche market will hardly push the broad diffusion necessary for a meaningful reduced sign-on.

One solution that has the potential to both support passwords and avoid the standardization costs are *Pseudo-SSO* systems [33], where credentials are provided by the client, as they can support multiple authentication protocols, and can be made to interoperate with the interfaces currently available on the web, even password-based systems [6]. In addition, they avoid the tracking of transactions and users made possible by some non-privacy-aware implementations of identity management [34]. Password-based pseudo-SSO may be realized using password hashing or syncing. Both approaches have their own advantages and disadvantages.

Password hashing approaches have problems customizing the generated credentials to service-specific restrictions such as password policies [35]. The password policies employed by web services are heterogeneous, and their restrictions are often arbitrary [36]. Service-specific passwords generated from hash values, for example, will run the risk of (randomly) not matching services' password policies [35]. This may be addressed by requiring manual user intervention [35], or by providing a central server storing policies for various web sites [37] (policies may be stored for each user individually [11], or users may collaborate to shape a public policy repository [37]).

Password syncing has its own issues, specifically that the service provider can – at least in a naive implementation – gain knowledge of all user passwords. To address this, such systems are usually combined with *host-proof hosting* [15] approaches, where the data is encrypted on the client using a passphrase entered by the user before transmission to the server. This may be executed as part of the client application (e.g. the password manager in Mozilla Firefox does it), part of a plug-in, or in e.g. JavaScript as part of a Web site. However, the user has to choose two independent passwords, one to encrypt the credential information on the client side, and one to authenticate to the server, to make this work. This may be hard to grasp for users. Failure to actively configure an encryption password, or usage of related passwords for both authentication and encryption, may lead to loss of the host-proof hosting property, and a sense of false security against breaches at the synchronisation cloud. This weakness has just recently led to significant security issues after a breach of the servers operated by the LastPass password manager [38].

We are – as already stated – not the first to use password hashing or syncing, nor are we the first to use threshold cryptography in the context of single sign-on.

There have been several implementations of SSO systems using threshold cryptography [39] [40] [41] [42], mostly with the aim of ensuring the availability of identity providers and similar trusted third parties; or mitigate the effect that an attack on one of those parties may have on the overall security of the system. However, as far as we know, the concept has not yet been applied to pseudo-SSO systems, which have the advantage of holding credentials on the client-side, and offering interoperability with a large number of authentication protocols, including the currently predominant password systems.

There have also been several implementations of password hashing-based pseudo-SSO systems, including [2] [11] [13]. PasswordSitter [11] is notable for providing a server where individual users can configure and store their password policies, which has some similarity to what we are proposing here.

There are also a large number of password managers supporting syncing of passwords. Most modern browsers support this out-of-the-box, in addition to the dedicated solutions available such as [43] [1] [12]. The host-proof hosting functionality to encrypt the information before upload is also implemented e.g. by LastPass [1]. SXIPPER [12] is notable for having offered a centralized configuration of service password policies by the user community to offer a highly interoperable SSO with a high reduction of user interactions, which has some similarity to the lower password hashing layer enabling a limitation of configuration costs in our approach. At the same time, those existing systems may serve as an illustration of possible user interfaces for Pseudo SSO.

With regard to the redundant storage of information in freely available online services, our approach is very similar to Anderson's Eternity Service [7], however, the Eternity Service lacks the relation to authentication or SSO, both in storing credential information, and in authenticating at the storage servers. In addition, Eternity Service does not support real-time fetch of storages, as it uses Usenet as a storage medium.

5   Conclusion

We presented a novel approach for password/credential storage in Pseudo-SSO scenarios based on a hybrid password hashing/password syncing approach that is directly applicable to the contemporary Web. The approach supports passwords without requiring modification of the server side and thus is immediately useful; however, it may still prove useful for storing more advanced credentials in future SSO and identity management scenarios. The system meets several clearly defined business requirements:

- *Improve password security*: The proposed system offers a secure solution for distributed password management.
- *High availability of credential storage:* In addition to being hardened against attackers and the hosting services, the system also supports redundant storage for availability.
- *Low cost:* The system minimizes configuration costs and does not require adjustment of service authentication interfaces.
- *High user acceptance:* The system supports passwords, which is desirable to users, as they are widely used, often appropriate, and meet user expectations.
- *Potential integration of advanced secure elements:* The underlying password hashing accommodates for integration of e.g. smartcards, typically using other pseudo-random functions, such as signatures, instead of hashing.

There are several additional pertinent design options with regard to the system. An additional possibility to increase offline attack resistance would be to obfuscate the nature of the stored information from the hosting server. For example, the central SSO server could provide additional protocol information enabling the client to interact with service interfaces at the $storage_i$ for managing user generated content. The client could then upload a number of media, only one of them holding the encrypted password storage, hidden using steganography, offering obfuscation and additional strengthening of the host-proof property and thus resistance to offline attacks. While JavaScript implementations of image-based steganography exist [44] [45], handling larger media files, e.g. videos, may require quite a lot of computational power and may not be feasible to implement in contemporary browsers. However, for most SSO scenarios, images should be sufficient.

Our approach minimizes configuration costs for the Pseudo-SSO system, as password policies only need to be preconfigured for a limited number of storage services. An alternative approach might be to have servers declare their password policies in a machine readable fashion, e.g. as parameter of the HTML INPUT field as suggested by [46], however, this would require changes on the server side, and a standardization initiative. Similar initiatives, such as P3P, have met limited success, and declared policies are often erroneous, even for the limited number of sites implementing policies [47].

The system minimizes the exposure of users to novel interaction paradigms, which are often a barrier to acceptance of identity management systems [48]. Instead, it employs familiar systems like password authentication, AJAX patterns like lazy login [15] and the internal logic of classical synced credential storages as realized by most modern browsers.

Our approach can also be used to securely synchronize additional information between devices in this scenario, such as bookmarks and partial identities (name, email address). The underlying protocol employs a distributed storage approach to guard against offline attacks, and its security should also be accessible to users, as it does not require separate passwords for authentication at the syncing server and encryption of content, as is common with host-proof hosting [15] approaches – it will generate those using password hashing approaches. Additional obfuscation versus the hosting server is possible by uploading several (plausible) decoy files or using steganography. Should this approach prove to be too low-performance to be implemented into browsers e.g. on mobile phones, it is also possible to apply the secret sharing to a randomly generated encryption key, and use this to encrypt a file for storage at one $storage_i$. However, offline attack resistance against this $storage_i$ will be lost using this method, so a very long key and strong/slow encryption algorithm should be chosen, as suggested by [2], as the system may fall to attacks leveraging known or easy-to-guess passwords otherwise.

However, the present results are preliminary in several regards. We are in the process of implementing the solution, and thus cannot offer a final evaluation, neither with regards to performance, nor with regards to usability of our solution. Thus, we cannot back up some of the claims made empirically yet. However, the size of the information to be synchronized is not especially large, and thus it should be possible to find methods offering sufficient performance both with regard to the threshold cryptography, and with regards to the steganography approaches. For example, there are several high-performance implementations of Shamir's secret sharing in JavaScript [19] [20], as well as steganography [44] [45].

We still need to validate the usefulness of our approach in practice; specifically we plan to implement the system, design a user interface meeting user expectations, and survey its perceived usefulness, specifically comparing it to other contemporary identity management and Web SSO solutions. However, we still feel we can make a contribution at this point. Passwords are often neglected in the research of strong security solutions, however, there are many indications that they will be around for a long time, and may even be the superior solution to more elaborate SSO systems in many cases [3]. Thus, it is imperative to supply users with tools supporting their password management [3] without putting too much of a burden on them, e.g. requiring them to learn entirely new interaction paradigms [48].

Acknowledgements. This work was partially funded by the Research Council of Norway through the VERDIKT PETweb II project under contract #193030.

References

1. LastPass: LastPass - Password Manager, Formular ausfüller, Password Management, http://lastpass.com/
2. Halderman, J.A., Waters, B., Felten, E.W.: A convenient method for securely managing passwords. In: Proceedings of the 14th International Conference on World Wide Web, pp. 471–479. ACM, Chiba (2005)
3. Herley, C., Van Oorschot, P.: A Research Agenda Acknowledging the Persistence of Passwords. IEEE Security & Privacy (forthcoming, 2012)
4. Jøsang, A., Zomai, M.A., Suriadi, S.: Usability and privacy in identity management architectures. In: Proceedings of the Fifth Australasian Symposium on ACSW Frontiers, vol. 68, pp. 143–152. Australian Computer Society, Inc., Ballarat (2007)
5. Jøsang, A., Fritsch, L., Mahler, T.: Privacy Policy Referencing. In: Katsikas, S., Lopez, J., Soriano, M. (eds.) TrustBus 2010. LNCS, vol. 6264, pp. 129–140. Springer, Heidelberg (2010)
6. Zibuschka, J., Roßnagel, H.: Implementing Strong Authentication Interoperability with Legacy Systems. In: Policies and Research in Identity Management (IDMAN 2007), pp. 149–160. Springer (2008)
7. Anderson, R.: The eternity service. In: Pragocrypt 1996, pp. 242–252 (1996)
8. Dhamija, R., Dusseault, L.: The Seven Flaws of Identity Management: Usability and Security Challenges. IEEE Secur. Privacy Mag. 6, 24–29 (2008)
9. Smith, R.E.: The Strong Password Dilemma. Computer 18 (2002)
10. Pashalidis, A., Mitchell, C.: A Taxonomy of Single Sign-On Systems. Information Security and Privacy, 249–264 (2003)
11. Password Sitter: Home, http://www.passwordsitter.de/
12. Putting Sxipper Down – Dick Hardt dot org, http://dickhardt.org/2011/03/putting-sxipper-down/
13. Gabber, E., Gibbons, P.B., Matias, Y., Mayer, A.J.: How to Make Personalized Web Browsing Simple, Secure, and Anonymous. In: Proceedings of the First International Conference on Financial Cryptography, pp. 17–32. Springer (1997)
14. Convergence | Beta, http://convergence.io/
15. Mahemoff, M.: Ajax Design Patterns. O'Reilly Media, Inc. (2006)
16. jsSHA - SHA Hashes in JavaScript, http://jssha.sourceforge.net/
17. Yao, F.F., Yin, Y.L.: Design and Analysis of Password-Based Key Derivation Functions. In: Menezes, A. (ed.) CT-RSA 2005. LNCS, vol. 3376, pp. 245–261. Springer, Heidelberg (2005)
18. Shamir, A.: How to share a secret. Commun. ACM 22, 612–613 (1979)
19. RLR UK Ltd.: Secure Secret Sharing, https://www.rlr-uk.com/tools/SecSplit/SecureSplit.aspx
20. Feild, H.: Shamir's Secret Sharing Scheme, http://ciir.cs.umass.edu/~hfeild/ssss/index.html
21. Brown, A.S., Bracken, E., Zoccoli, S., Douglas, K.: Generating and remembering passwords. Applied Cognitive Psychology 18, 641–651 (2004)
22. Miller, G.A.: The Magical Number Seven, Plus or Minus Two: Some Limits on Our Capacity for Processing Information. Psychological Review 63, 81–97 (1956)
23. Florencio, D., Herley, C.: A large-scale study of web password habits. Proceedings of the 16th International Conference on World Wide Web, New York, NY, USA, pp. 657–666 (2007)

24. Chinitz, J.: Single Sign-On: Is It Really Possible? Information Security Journal: A Global Perspective 9, 1 (2000)
25. Ives, B., Walsh, K.R., Schneider, H.: The domino effect of password reuse. Commun. ACM 47, 75–78 (2004)
26. LeahScape: PasswordMaker, http://passwordmaker.org/
27. Recordon, D., Reed, D.: OpenID 2.0: a platform for user-centric identity management. In: Proceedings of the Second ACM Workshop on Digital Identity Management, pp. 11–16. ACM, Alexandria (2006)
28. Cameron, K., Jones, M.B.: Design Rationale behind the Identity Metasystem Architecture. ISSE/SECURE 2007 Securing Electronic Business Processes, 117–129 (2007)
29. Neuman, B.C., Ts'o, T.: Kerberos: an authentication service for computer networks. IEEE Communications Magazine 32, 33–38 (1994)
30. Facebook's OpenID Goes Live, http://www.allfacebook.com/2009/05/facebooks-openid-live/
31. Hühnlein, D., Roßnagel, H., Zibuschka, J.: Diffusion of Federated Identity Management. In: SICHERHEIT 2010. GI, Berlin (2010)
32. Boyd, D.: Facebook's Privacy Trainwreck. Convergence: The International Journal of Research into New Media Technologies 14, 13–20 (2008)
33. de Clerq, J.: Single Sign-on Architectures. In: Proceedings of Infrastructure Security, International Conference, Bristol, UK, pp. 40–58 (2002)
34. Dimitriadis, C.K., Polemi, D.: Application of Multi-criteria Analysis for the Creation of a Risk Assessment Knowledgebase for Biometric Systems. In: Zhang, D., Jain, A.K. (eds.) ICBA 2004. LNCS, vol. 3072, pp. 724–730. Springer, Heidelberg (2004)
35. Karp, A.H.: Site-Specific Passwords (2003), http://www.hpl.hp.com/techreports/2002/HPL-2002-39R1.html
36. Summers, W.C., Bosworth, E.: Password policy: the good, the bad, and the ugly. In: Proceedings of the Winter International Symposium on Information and Communication Technologies, Cancun, Mexico, pp. 1–6 (2004)
37. Kolter, J., Kernchen, T., Pernul, G.: Collaborative Privacy – A Community-Based Privacy Infrastructure. In: Gritzalis, D., Lopez, J. (eds.) SEC 2009. IFIP AICT, vol. 297, pp. 226–236. Springer, Heidelberg (2009)
38. LastPass: LastPass Security Notification, http://blog.lastpass.com/2011/05/lastpass-security-notification.html
39. Josephson, W.K., Sirer, E.G., Schneider, F.B.: Peer-to-Peer Authentication with a Distributed Single Sign-On Service. In: Voelker, G.M., Shenker, S. (eds.) IPTPS 2004. LNCS, vol. 3279, pp. 250–258. Springer, Heidelberg (2005)
40. Chen, T., Zhu, B.B., Li, S., Cheng, X.: ThresPassport – A Distributed Single Sign-On Service. In: Huang, D.-S., Zhang, X.-P., Huang, G.-B. (eds.) ICIC 2005. LNCS, vol. 3645, pp. 771–780. Springer, Heidelberg (2005)
41. Brasee, K., Kami Makki, S., Zeadally, S.: A Novel Distributed Authentication Framework for Single Sign-On Services. In: IEEE International Conference on Sensor Networks, Ubiquitous and Trustworthy Computing, SUTC 2008. pp. 52–58. IEEE (2008)
42. Zhong, S., Liao, X., Zhang, X., Lin, J.: A Novel Distributed Single Sign-On Scheme with Dynamically Changed Threshold Value. In: Fifth International Conference on Information Assurance and Security, IAS 2009. pp. 563–566. IEEE (2009)
43. Password Manager, Form Filler, Password Management | RoboForm Password Manager, http://www.roboform.com/

44. vecna/Rabbisteg - GitHub, `https://github.com/vecna/Rabbisteg`
45. Steganography in Javascript – Blog, `http://antimatter15.com/wp/2010/06/steganography-in-javascript/`
46. Sandler, D., Wallach, D.S.: <input type="password"> must die! W2SP 2008: Web 2.0 Security and Privacy 2008. IEEE Computer Society, Oakland (2008)
47. Leon, P.G., Cranor, L.F., McDonald, A.M., McGuire, R.: Token attempt: the misrepresentation of website privacy policies through the misuse of p3p compact policy tokens. In: Proceedings of the 9th Annual ACM Workshop on Privacy in the Electronic Society, pp. 93–104. ACM Press, New York (2010)
48. Maler, E., Reed, D.: The Venn of Identity: Options and Issues in Federated Identity Management. IEEE Secur. Privacy Mag. 6, 16–23 (2008)

Assessing the Quality of Packet-Level Traces Collected on Internet Backbone Links

Behrooz Sangchoolie[1], Mazdak Rajabi Nasab[1],
Tomas Olovsson[1], and Wolfgang John[2]

[1] Chalmers University of Technology, Department of Computer Science and Engineering,
SE-412 96 Gothenburg, Sweden
`behrooz.sangchoolie@chalmers.se`, `mazdak@student.chalmers.se`,
`tomas.olovsson@chalmers.se`
[2] Ericsson Research, Kista, Sweden
`wolfgang.john@ericsson.com`

Abstract. The quality of captured traffic plays an important role for decisions made by systems like intrusion detection/prevention systems (IDS/IPS) and firewalls. As these systems monitor network traffic to find malicious activities, a missing packet might lead to an incorrect decision. In this paper, we analyze the quality of packet-level traces collected on Internet backbone links using different generations of DAG cards[1]. This is accomplished by inferring dropped packets introduced by the data collection system with help of the intrinsic structural properties inherently provided by TCP traffic flows. We employ two metrics which we believe can detect all kinds of missing packets: i) packets with ACK numbers greater than the expected ACK, indicating that the communicating parties acknowledge a packet not present in the trace; and ii) packets with data beyond the receiver's window size, which with a high probability, indicates that the packet advertising the correct window size was not recorded. These heuristics have been applied to three large datasets collected with different hardware and in different environments.

We also introduce *flowstat*, a tool developed for this purpose which is capable of analyzing both captured traces and real-time traffic. After assessing more than 400 traces (75M bidirectional flows), we conclude that at least 0.08% of the flows have missing packets, a surprisingly large number that can affect the quality of analysis performed by firewalls and intrusion detection/prevention systems. The paper concludes with an investigation and discussion of the spatial and temporal aspects of the experienced packet losses and possible reasons behind missing data in traces.

Keywords: Traffic measurement, measurement errors, packet drop, intrusion detection/prevention system, firewall.

1 Introduction

Firewalls and intrusion detection/prevention systems monitor network traffic for malicious activities. These systems make decisions based on the observed traffic. For

---

[1] This work was supported in part by Swedish University Computer Network (SUNET).

A. Jøsang and B. Carlsson (Eds.): NordSec 2012, LNCS 7617, pp. 184–198, 2012.
© Springer-Verlag Berlin Heidelberg 2012

instance if an attack's signature is a sequence of two packets, with the first one containing pattern X followed by the second one containing pattern Y, missing either of these packets by intrusion detection/prevention systems might result in a false negative decision. For this reason, it is vital that they have the ability to capture all packets on network. This is one of the motivations for network traffic analysis.

Even though simulating the behavior of different Internet protocols is possible using well-known simulators, it is mostly believed that genuine Internet traffic analysis is more advantageous. Plenty of traffic measurement research has been performed so far; some focused on backbone traffic [1] [2] [3] while others aimed more at edge links [4] [5]. In spite the advantages of analyzing genuine Internet traffic, operational limitations always create challenges. As an example, special purpose hardware and software are required in order to capture traffic from high speed backbone links. Manufacturers of high speed measurement cards claim that these cards can capture Internet traffic with 100% accuracy [6].

The community generally relies on the manufacturer's claim; therefore not much research has been done to verify trace quality. Plenty of literature focuses on statistical properties of Internet traffic where missing a couple of packets do not have any consequences. Others aim at systems that require all transmitted packets to be present, such as intrusion detection systems. In order to detect all kinds of malicious traffic, an intrusion detection/prevention system should be able to capture all the transmitted packets.

In this paper we have analyzed the quality of packet-level traces with respect to missing packets. The data has been collected on 10Gbit/s Internet backbone links within the MonNet[2] project [1]. The result of our work can be used to find out whether systems such as firewalls and intrusion detection/prevention systems are able to capture all transmitted packets for malicious traffic detection. This can then be used to verify the correctness of their behavior.

1.1   Related Work and Contributions

To the best of our knowledge, there have been very little investigations showing that measurement cards are capable of capturing all the ongoing packets of their capturing link. Even NSS labs' *Attack Leakage* test [7] only evaluates deep packet inspection capability of *EndaceProbes*, a server hardware product capable of running high speed packet analysis using DAG cards. In this test the accuracy and performance of IPS/IDS devices are evaluated. Devices are tested against a test traffic that contains known number of attack vectors. The load is increased to a point where the device under the test starts to miss detection of attack vectors. They also show that *EndaceProbes* can capture 100% of packets at 10 Gbit/s although they have not tested DAG cards on other server solutions to see if they drop any packets for example as a result of resource limitations.

---

[2] MonNet project aimed to provide better understanding of Internet traffic characteristics based on passive measurement of backbone links.

Among the available tools, *tcpanaly* [8] is one of the oldest. Given a trace file, *tcpanaly* verifies whether the observed TCP implementations follow the TCP standard. It can also produce detailed statistics for TCP connections. One weakness of *tcpanaly* is that it performs a two-pass analysis on the trace file. The two-pass analysis results in a more time-consuming assessment and is not suitable for real-time analysis. *Tcpanaly* also assumes that an ACK will always be sent back on the arrival of any out-of-sequence data [8] which is a big limitation since not all end systems follow this behavior. *Tstat* [5] is another relevant tool developed especially for statistical analysis of TCP/IP traffic. *Tstat* uses the libpcap library and is capable of calculating more than 80 different performance statistics. However *tstat* does not take missing packets into account within its comprehensive TCP logs; therefore it cannot be used to analyze packet drops.

The main goal of this paper is to analyze the quality (in term of completeness) of collected traffic traces. In this way, we can investigate whether systems such as firewalls have access to all the transmitted packets to detect suspicious activities. Specifically, this paper contributes with the following:

- The development and implementation of a method to analyze the quality of data with respect to missing packets in data captured in traffic measurement campaigns.
- An investigation of the spatial and temporal aspects of the experienced missing packets in traces and plausible reasons behind missing data.
- A tool called *flowstat*, designed for this purpose, which can operate on saved traces and on real-time traffic. *Flowstat* is written in standard C and is open to the research community for further development[3].

The remainder of this paper is organized as follows. In section 2, we describe the data collection hardware and data sets which we used in our analysis. In section 3 we present the reasons for missing packets in collected data. Section 4 describes our methodology to detect missing packets. We present the overview of *flowstat* in section 5 and in section 6 we present the results of our analysis. We conclude with a summary of major findings and suggestions for further research in section 7.

2   Data Collection Hardware and Data Sets

Three different data collection campaigns of PoS HDLC traffic have been performed. The first campaign was conducted during 2006 on an OC192 link inside the GigaSUNET [9] network. The second campaign was conducted with the same hardware but at a new physical location in the updated OptoSUNET [10] network. In the third campaign, the physical location remained unchanged while the infrastructure was slightly altered. Moreover, new system hardware including a new generation of DAG cards was used. The hardware used consisted of high-end systems at the time of purchase. For simplification, we name campaign (2) and (3) OptoSUNET1 and OptoSUNET2, respectively. In GigaSUNET and OptoSUNET1, two measurement nodes were used, one

---

[3] The tool is available at http://sourceforge.net/projects/flowstat/

for each traffic direction and each equipped with one DAG card. In OptoSUNET2, one system was used with two data collection cards (Table 1).

The DAG cards were configured with a buffer reserved from the system's main memory in order to deal with traffic bursts. For the hardware used in GigaSUNET and OptoSUNET1, Endace recommends a buffer size of at least 32MB for OC-12 links, thus we conservatively chose a large buffer of 512 MB for our OC-192 links. In OptoSUNET2 we used DAG Tools ver. 4.2.0 without changing the default configuration which used a buffer of 256 MB. The optical splitters were changed between GigaSUNET and OptoSUNET1, but remained the same between OptoSUNET1 and OptoSUNET2. Since the signal strength was quite high, splitters with a 90/10 ratio turned out to be sufficient for the sensitivity of the measurement cards in all campaigns [11].

All traces have a duration of 20 minutes or longer. Packets with IP checksum errors are preserved in our traces although packets with link-level CRC errors were automatically discarded by the cards. In GigaSUNET, the DAG cards were configured to capture only the first 120 bytes, and in OptoSUNET1 and OptoSUNET2, only 160 bytes. Given that the average packet size on the links was 687 bytes and that 44% of all frames were smaller than 120 bytes and 160 bytes, respectively (and thus not truncated by the DAG card), we calculated the average packet size to be stored on disk to 88 and 110 bytes, respectively.

This means that even at a maximum link utilization of 10 Gbps, only about 200 MByte/s had to be transferred to disk. However, due to heavy over-provisioning of the links, in reality the nodes rarely needed to store more than 35 MByte/s (280 Mbps) on disk during the measurement campaigns. Disk and processor performance should therefore never have been an issue.

Table 1. Collection systems technical specifications

	GigaSUNET and OptoSUNET1	OptoSUNET2
Motherboard	Tyan K8SR	Dell PowerEdge R710
CPU	Two 2 GHz 64-bit AMD Opteron	Two Intel Xeon E5620 2.4 GHz Quad-core Hyper-Threaded
Memory	2 GB (1 GB per CPU)	16 GB DDR3 (shared among CPUs)
Bus dedicated to DAG cards	133 MHz 64-bit PCI-X	Dual PCIe x8
Disk controller	Dual-channel Ultra-320 SCSI	PERC 6/I RAID controller
Disks	Six SCSI RAID-0 (software)	Six SATA RAID-0 (hardware)
Tested sustained disk write throughput	410 MByte/s (for each DAG card)	520 Mbyte/s (shared between DAG cards)
Measurement card (DAG)	DAG6.2SE	DAG8.1SX
Number of cards per system	1	2

A longer discussion of possible limitations in data collection campaigns can be found in [11]. After frame truncation, traces were *de-sensitized* and *sanitized* [11] [12]. The de-sensitization consisted of two phases; first the payload of each packet was removed using CAIDA's coralReef [13] crl_to_dag utility and then IP addresses were anonymized using prefix-preserving Crypto-Pan [14]. Also as a result of the prefix preserving nature of the anonymization, neighbor addresses will also be neighboring after anonymization. Sanitization checks were also applied before and after each de-sensitization step to verify the correctness of trace pre-processing.

3   Reasons for Missing Packets in Collected Network Data

According to Paxson [8], there are four types of measurement errors that affect the quality of data; drops, additions, resequencing and timing. In this paper, our main focus is to investigate and quantify the amount of packets dropped by the measurement nodes or missed before being captured. Based on the mentioned measurement errors and the data collection hardware used, we identify four sources of measurement errors:

- Errors that are introduced by the DAG card, possibly as a result of frame truncation, insufficient buffer space, PCI bus limitations and losses between the DAG card and memory.
- Errors that occur if the measurement nodes do not accept all packets communicated by the end nodes, like packets with link-level CRC errors.
- Errors introduced in trace pre-processing, e.g. de-sensitization.
- Missing packets that did not appear on the measured link due to alternative routes between the communicating nodes. These packets might be missed due to routing policies along the end-to-end path, such as load balancing.

Any packet drop due to insufficient buffer space, PCI bus limitations and losses between the DAG card and memory is supposed to be reported by DAG cards. [11] Moreover, however unlikely, it is possible that buggy or faulty sanitization tools introduce errors like packet drops into the traces.

All SUNET generations follow a per-flow routing policy. For this reason when a flow's packet is observed on the link we expect to observe all of that flow's packets on the same link. However, there is no guarantee for this assumption. As routing happens on a packet-per-packet basis, it is possible that a flow's packets are routed through different links.

Since TCP packets account for more than 90% of our captured packets, we made the decision to apply two TCP based metrics on the traces in order to discover missing packets. In the first metric, described in sub-section 4.1, we keep track of packets to see if any packet that is not recorded by the measurement node is acknowledged by the end systems. The second metric, explained at sub-section 4.2, assesses whether any end-points transmit data beyond the allowed TCP window size, which is a possible indication of missing packets.

4   Methodology

We have focused on two metrics that we believe are sufficient for detecting all types of missing packets in TCP flows. Only bidirectional flows that have finished their three-way handshake are evaluated. For simplicity throughout the remaining of this paper, we use the term "bidirectional flows" instead of "bidirectional flows with observed three-way handshake". In this section the used metrics are explained.

4.1 Metric One[M1]: End Systems Acknowledge a Packet Not Present in the Trace

In this metric, *flowstat* keeps track of the next expected ACK number, *expack*, in each direction (Fig. 1). After a successful three-way handshake, *flowstat* keeps track of the packets and compares each ACK with the data it has observed up to that point. *Flowstat* compares each packet's ACK number with its corresponding *expack*. A packet with an ACK number greater than *expack* denotes one or more missing packets (Fig. 2). *Flowstat* is able to deal with out of order packets.

As soon as a measurement error is detected, the erroneous flow will no longer be analyzed by *flowstat*, i.e. *flowstat* currently counts the number of flows with at least one missing packets and not the total number of missing packets in the flow. We decided on this approach because it is not possible to know exactly how many packets were actually missed when there is an ACK greater than *expack*. Moreover an M1 measurement error will also most probably lead to more M1 measurement errors. If desired, it is easy to modify *flowstat* to update *expack* with the value found in the packet raising the error in order to approximate the amount of erroneous packets.

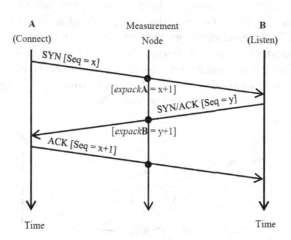

Fig. 1. The initial *expack* for each direction (measurement node's view of the traffic)

Despite the fact that M1 is a powerful metric, it is unable to detect missing zero-length packets such as ACK packets carrying no data, keep alive packets, etc. Since TCP is using a cumulative ACK system, keeping track of the packet lengths, as explained in M1, will not assist us in discovering missing zero-length packets. In our next proposed metric, the *TCP window* field will be used to equip *flowstat* with yet another way of detecting missing packets including zero-length packets.

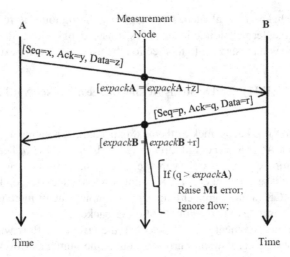

Fig. 2. When to raise an M1 measurement error (measurement node's view of the traffic)

4.2   Metric Two[M2]: Data Beyond the Advertised Window

Inspired by Vern Paxson [8], we also implement another powerful check that can be used to detect missing packets. M2 evaluates whether a sender has sent data beyond the receiver's earlier advertised window size. Nonstandard or faulty TCP implementations may cause this behavior. Feng Qian et al. [15] believe that apart from erroneous TCP implementations, the underutilization of the congestion window is another reason for observing data beyond the receiver's window size.

However, if both communicating parties are following the TCP standard, it can be assumed with a high probability that the packet advertising the correct window size has not been observed by the measurement node (Fig. 3).

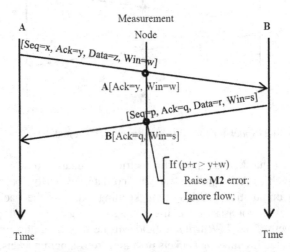

Fig. 3. When to raise an M2 measurement error (measurement node's view of the traffic)

Since there are other reasons apart from packet drops involved in observing data beyond the advertised window size such as different implementation problems of TCP/IP stacks, M2 is not as accurate as M1. On the other hand, unlike M1, M2 can detect missing zero-length packets. Since we used different TCP properties to detect missing packets corresponding to M1 and M2, none of them are necessarily a superset of the other. Therefore *flowstat* reports both these metrics in order to detect missing packets in TCP flows.

5   Flowstat Overview

In this section, an overview of *flowstat* is given. *Flowstat* keeps a connection table for all active TCP connections and stores necessary information for sessions in each direction. Only flows with an observed 3-way handshake are evaluated. *Flowstat* also recognizes the value of TCP window scale option from the first two packets of each flow's three-way handshake and uses it to calculate the correct advertised window size for each direction to be used in M2.

In our traces, we found packets with TCP set in the IP protocol field but without enough data to build a TCP header [16]. *Flowstat* recognizes these malformed packets and reports them as *packet size errors*, see Table 2. For all other TCP packets, *flowstat* looks up the corresponding active flow from its connection table. If a SYN packet is captured and no associated entry in the connection table is found, a new entry will be created; whereas a non-SYN packet with no corresponding active flow will be ignored. If there is an entry in the connection table that corresponds to a newly captured packet, *flowstat* will update the entry's necessary fields.

Each time an entry is updated, M1 and M2 checks are performed and in case an error is detected, the erroneous flow counter is incremented and the flow's entry is removed from the connection table. Apart from M1 and M2 errors which can lead to the removal of an entry from the connection table, RST and FIN packets also result in removing the corresponding entry. These policies make sure that the size of the connection table does not grow infinitely.

Flowstat also takes advantage of two timers to detect inactive flows and remove them from the connection table. Choosing a proper value for these timers is a tradeoff between longer execution time and the ability to evaluate more flows. The first timer waits for the completion of the uncompleted three-way handshakes for 30 seconds before removing these entries from the connection table. We also used 60 and 120 seconds as the value for this timer, but number of newly added bidirectional flows was negligible. The second timer triggers the removal of entries for which no related packet has been observed in a 120-second period. Claffy et al. in [17] show that 64 seconds is a good flow timeout. However, we choose a conservative large timeout in order to make sure that *flowstat* detects all possible missing packets.

In order to validate the correctness of *flowstat* and the proposed metrics, two types of tests have been performed on *flowstat* to test its ability to detect missing packets. In the first test, errors were injected manually into random captured files i.e. a number of packets were intentionally removed from these files. *Flowstat* could correctly detect all these missing packets. In the second test, five sample trace files including around one million bidirectional flows were examined by *flowstat* for missing packets. We then randomly selected 10% of the flows with missing packets and manually verified that they correctly were detected as being erroneous.

6   Data Analysis

In this section, we analyze the results of running *flowstat* on the captured traces. After evaluating more than 400 captured traces, the total number of detected measurement errors is shown in Table 2. As Table 2 illustrates, there are a great number of unidirectional flows. This might to some degree be due to the fact that SYN attacks and SYN scans are counted as unidirectional flows. SUNETs network layout and routing policies also introduce a fair amount of asymmetrical routing [18] (e.g. hot-potato routing), and many flows are indeed unidirectional.

Table 2 also shows that the total number of M2 measurement errors is almost three times as large as M1. This might be due to the fact that not just missing packets, but also nonstandard and faulty TCP implementations as well as underutilization of the congestion window and implementation problems of TCP/IP stacks cause us to observe data beyond the receiver's window size, which in turn result in M2 measurement errors.

Table 2. Total number of M1 and M2 measurement errors in different SUNET generations. The values inside parenthesis refer to the number of analyzed traces.

SUNET generation	Total number of packets	Unidirectional flows	Bidirectional flows	Flows with M1 errors	Flows with M2 errors	Packet size error
GigaSUNET(240)	21,136,187,688	62,808,014	54,724,892	44,549	118,177	66,122
OptoSUNET1 (163)	28,446,722,927	192,709,261	19,488,316	9,335	39,102	887,384
OptoSUNET2 (4)	1,838,475,707	495,312,512	1,127,806	4,324	1,235	31,675
Total(407)	51,421,386,322	750,829,787	75,341,014	58,208	158,514	985,181

Fig. 4 shows the percentage of M1 and M2 measurement errors in bidirectional flows. It can be seen that there is only a small difference in the detected percentage of measurement errors between GigaSUNET and OptoSUNET1, while OptoSUNET2 is considerably different. However, only four trace files have been analyzed from OptoSUNET2 and these traces have been captured on the same day and during a three-hour time period which makes it difficult to draw any accurate conclusions. Moreover, the dissimilar behavior of OptoSUENT2 might be due to new routing policies or the new hardware, which could be faulty or, more likely, not able to cope with the load.

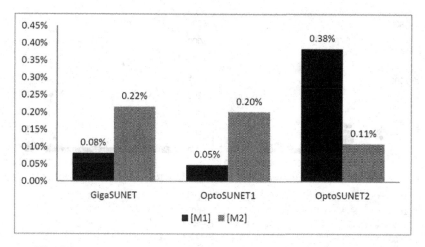

Fig. 4. Percentage of M1 and M2 measurement errors in bidirectional flows

The IP addresses were anonymized in the trace files using the same key, so each IP address consistently shows up as the same IP address after anonymization. Therefore it is possible to check if there are specific erroneous IP addresses which are more represented than the others. Fig. 5 shows the erroneous IP addresses and number of times they occur in each SUNET generation.

In the first two SUNET generations, in Fig. 5, the IP addresses have been scattered more for M2 than for M1, and there are some IP addresses that are overrepresented in the erroneous flows, especially in M2. A possible reason can be that there are nodes that either do not follow the proper TCP implementation or that they send packets with link-level CRC errors which are considered as erroneous by the measurement node and are dropped. Moreover, Fig. 5 shows that a lot of overrepresented erroneous IP addresses are adjacent which might indicate that they belong to the same subnets. It is noticeable that the systems responsible for many of the M1 errors are also responsible for M2 errors in both the GigaSUNET and OptoSUNET1 generations. And as mentioned before, the limited number of OptoSUNET2 traces makes it difficult to draw any accurate conclusions about this SUNET generation.

Table 3, shows the percentage of erroneous IP addresses which were detected more than 10 times along with the percentage of erroneous flows containing these IP addresses. The selected value, 10, is good enough to show that a small group of IP addresses were observed in a lot of erroneous flows. This is also another indication that there might be systems that are not following proper TCP implementations and are responsible for most of the errors. It can also be seen that these small groups of IP addresses are seen in all (100%) of the erroneous flows detected by M2 and M1 in GigaSUNET and OptoSUNET2 respectively. There are several possible explanations for this behavior:

- The overrepresented end systems send large bursts of traffic and the measurement node's hardware cannot cope with the load.

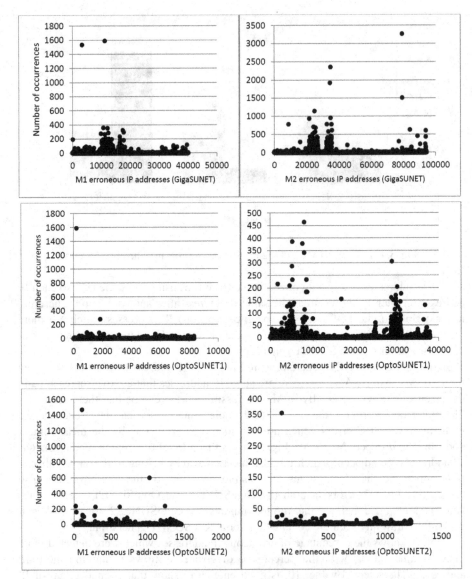

Fig. 5. Number of times an IP address has been seen in erroneous flows. The smallest and the largest values on the x-axis correspond to the smallest and the largest IP addresses respectively.

- The overrepresented end systems send lots of data which leads to more M1 and M2 errors.
- Some packets of the overrepresented end systems are routed a different way.

As mentioned before, all traces have a duration of 20 minutes or longer and have been captured at different times during the day. We have also classified the traces according to the time that they have been captured. The percentage of measurement

Table 3. Percentage of erroneous IP addresses detected more than 10 times and the percentage of erroneous bidirectional flows containing these IP addresses

	M1 error		M2 error	
	IP addresses	Flows	IP addresses	Flows
GigaSUNET	2.7%	85%	2.6%	100%
OptoSUNET1	2.6%	64%	2.8%	75%
OptoSUNET2	8.3%	100%	1.5%	51%

errors in different time periods is shown in Table 4. The different time periods roughly experienced the same percentages of measurement errors, even though traces which were captured between 12pm and 12am hold slightly more erroneous flows. It is notable that the percentage of measurement errors is larger during the working hours (6am to 6pm) compared to the other periods and grows even more during the evening. This might be due to the fact that traffic patterns and services differ during night time.

Table 4. Percentage of M1 and M2 measurement errors in bidirectional flows captured in different time periods. N/A indicates that no trace file has been analyzed in this time period.

	[12am – 6am)		[6am – 12pm)		[12pm – 18pm)		[18pm – 12am)	
	M1	M2	M1	M2	M1	M2	M1	M2
GigaSUNET	0.02%	0.04%	0.01%	0.04%	0.01%	0.05%	0.03%	0.06%
OptoSUNET1	0.007%	0.02%	0.006%	0.03%	0.018%	0.07%	0.015%	0.07%
OptoSUNET2	N/A	N/A	N/A	N/A	0.38%	0.1%	N/A	N/A

7   Conclusions

In this study more than 400 traces were analyzed in order to evaluate the quality of packet-level traces collected from Internet backbone traffic using Endace DAG cards. The quality of captured traffic is important for systems such as firewalls and intrusion detection/prevention systems which make decisions based on the captured network traffic. Missing an attack's signature packet by these systems might result in an incorrect or false negative decision.

We have proposed two TCP-based metrics, M1 and M2 which detect missing packets in TCP flows in the collected traces, and we believe that these metrics are good indicators of the quality of the collected data.

The first metric, M1, detects packets with an ACK number greater than the expected ACK number, something that indicates that the end-nodes have acknowledged packets that are not present in the traces. The reasons for this behavior is either that the measurement system has dropped the packet, or that the packet was actually not present on this link due to routing decisions along the end-to-end route. Even though M1 is a powerful metric, it cannot detect missing zero-length packets i.e. packets containing no data such as keep-alive packets, since ACKs are cumulative in their nature, see subsection 4.1.

The second metric, M2, deals with observing data beyond the receiver's advertised window size, which corresponds to the situation where the packet advertising the receiver's correct window size has been dropped by the measurement node. M2 measurement errors may also be triggered by implementation problems of TCP/IP stacks or nonstandard TCP implementations sending packets outside the advertised window, possibly with the hope of gaining better performance. As opposed to M1, M2 can also detect missing zero-length packets.

Nearly 0.08 and 0.2 percent of the bidirectional flows were considered as erroneous by M1 and M2, respectively. While there was only minor differences between the results of the GigaSUNET and OptoSUNET1 campaigns, OptoSUNET2 showed slightly different results. After evaluating the erroneous IP addresses, we realized that a small percentage of IP addresses have been observed in many, sometimes even in all, of the erroneous flows. We also showed that the numbers of measurement errors are rather similar regardless of at what time the traces were collected.

The result of our study showed that a considerable number of flows had missing packets. Even though the source of missing packets is not clear, they can affect the correctness of the decisions made by firewalls or intrusion detection/prevention systems. This is especially valid for Internet backbone links where huge amount of network traffic is transmitted in a second.

In order to do the analysis of the traces, we have developed a tool called *flowstat* which is capable of analyzing captured trace files. Depending on the specifications of the computer system and link speed, *flowstat* is also capable of analyzing real-time traffic.

Limitation. There are some limitations which influence our methodology. First, the possibility of asymmetrical routing may cause different packets of a flow to be routed through different links. Second, due to the possible improper implementations of TCP/IP stack from end points, the second metric is not as accurate as the first one.

Future Work. In this paper we have shown that packet losses are present in all our collected traces, regardless of when, where and with what hardware they have been collected. We have also given some reasons for packet loss, but more work is needed to investigate the sources for errors and to find out why and to what degree they contribute. The systems we have used may or may not be representative for many other data collection campaigns, but the overall conclusion must be that it is worth investigating the quality of the traces using the *flowstat* tool if 100% accuracy is desired. We would also like to encourage the community to use *flowstat* to check other traces taken in other environments (e.g. using a single link to ensure 100% visibility of inbound and outbound traffic) and compare the results with ours.

As discussed in section 6, a small percentage of IP addresses/hosts experienced a large number of packet drops. It would be interesting to investigate these hosts in more detail, for example to use packet headers to find out what operating system they have. These erroneous flows might as well have other common characteristics which can be checked to find yet other reasons behind the missing packets. *Flowstat* can be improved in a number of ways. *Flowstat*'s default behavior is to remove erroneous flows from the connection table as soon as they are detected by any of the metrics. This prevents the metrics from being applied multiple times on the observed flow.

References

1. John, W.: Characterization and Classification of Internet Backbone Traffic, Chalmers University of Technology, gothenburg, Sweden. PhD Thesis 0346-718X (2010)
2. Brauckhoff, D., Dimitropoulos, X., Wagner, A., Salamatian, K.: Anomaly extraction in backbone networks using association rules. In: Proceedings of the 9th ACM SIGCOMM Conference on Internet Measurement Conference, IMC 2009, New York, NY, USA, pp. 28–34 (2009)
3. Fraleigh, C., et al.: Packet-Level Traffic Measurements from the Sprint IP Backbone. IEEE Network 17(6), 6–16 (2003)
4. Shang, F.: Research on the Link Traffic Measurement System Based on Edge Measurement. In: International Conference on Communications, Circuits and Systems, Guilin, Guangzi, China, pp. 1791–1795 (2006)
5. Mellia, M., Cigno, R.L., Neri, F.: Measuring IP and TCP behavior on edge nodes with Tstat. Computer Networks 47(1), 1–21 (2005)
6. Endace. Enterprise Network Monitoring Tools, Network Security System, Application Performance Monitoring (September 2011), http://www.endace.com/the-endace-platform.html
7. NSS lab, Network Intrusion Detection System individual product test result, NSS Labs, Auckland, New Zealand (2010)
8. Paxson, V.: Automated packet trace analysis of TCP implementations. In: Proceedings of the ACM SIGCOMM Conference on Applications, Technologies, Architectures, and Protocols for Computer Communication, Cannes, France, pp. 167–179 (1997)
9. SUNET, History of the Swedish University Computer Network (Online) (September 2011), http://basun.sunet.se/karta/
10. SUNET. The Swedish University Computer Network OptoSUNET (Online) (September 2011), http://basun.sunet.se/aktuellt/optosunetbroschyr_eng.pdf
11. John, W., Tafvelin, S., Olovsson, T.: Passive Internet Measurement Overview and Guidelines Based on Experiences. Computer Communications 33(5) (March 2010)
12. John, W., Tafvelin, S.: Analysis of Internet Backbone Traffic and Header Anomalies Observed. In: IMC 2007: Proceedings of the 7th ACM SIGCOMM conference on Internet measurement, San Diego, pp. 111–116 (2007)
13. Keys, K., et al.: The Architecture of CoralReef:An Internet Traffic Monitoring Software Suite. In: A Workshop in Passive and Active Measurement, Amsterdam, The Netherlands (2001)
14. Fan, J., Xu, J.J., Ammar, M.H., Moon, S.B.: Prefix-preserving IP address anonymization: measurement-based security evaluation and a new cryptography-based scheme. In: ICNP: Proceedings of the 10th IEEE International Conference on Network Protocols, Washington, DC, USA, pp. 280–289 (2002)
15. Qian, F., et al.: TCP revisited: a fresh look at TCP in the wild. In: Proceeding of the 9th ACM SIGCOMM Conference on Internet Measurement Conference, Chicago, Illinois, pp. 76–89 (2009)

16. Olovsson, T., John, W.: Detection of malicious traffic on backbone links via packet header analysis. Campus-Wide Information Systems 25(5), 342–358 (2008)
17. Claffy, K.C., Braun, H.W., Polyzos, G.C.: A parameterizable methodology for Internet traffic flow profiling. Selected Areas in Communications 13(8), 1481–1494 (1995)
18. John, W., Dusi, M., Claffy, K.C.: Estimating routing symmetry on single links by passive flow measurements. In: IWCMC 2010 Proceedings of the 6th International Wireless Communications and Mobile Computing Conference, Caen, France, pp. 473–478 (2010)

Everything But the Kitchen Sink:
Determining the Effect of Multiple Attacks
on Privacy Preserving Technology Users

Jason W. Clark

George Mason University Fairfax, VA, USA
jclarks@masonlive.gmu.edu

Abstract. We investigate the degree to which privacy preserving technologies (PPT) are able to protect an organization against a variety of attacks aimed at undermining their privacy. We studied a PPT at a United States based organization and executed multiple attacks associated with network monitoring, phishing, and online social networks (OSNs). To begin, we received written authorization to conduct this study from the General Counsel of the case study organization and completed a formal application with the George Mason University Human Subject Review Board. Next, we surveyed 160 of the PPT users to get an idea of their background and security knowledge when it comes to privacy and anonymization on the Internet. We incorporated a network monitoring solution to monitor the websites and the actions performed by the users while on the PPT. The point of the phishing attack was to determine what additional information the users were willing to give up. We found that 92 of the 160 (58 percent) participants fell victim to our phishing campaign. The last attack phase shows the extent to which information made freely available on an online social network can negatively impact the anonymization offered by the PPT. We were able to determine the (Facebook) profiles of 34 of the 160 participants (21 percent). Upon completion of the attacks, we compiled the information and presented it to the users as security awareness training.

1 Introduction

Organizations and their employees often have a need to remain anonymous while on the Internet. This need is typically predicated on the fact that undermining of the organization or its employees privacy and anonymity would have a severe negative impact on the mission of such an organization. These privacy concerns include identity and financial theft, biased and tailored website content delivery, and compromised true geographic location. To this end, organizations often implement and configure privacy preserving technologies (PPT) to help protect their identity and that of their users while traversing the Internet. We[1] define a PPT as a privacy service or technique that attempts to hide the users' IP address, location, and additional information including but not limited to their research tasks as they access websites on the Internet.

---

[1] We is used to recognize all of the different people who wished to remain anonymous that assisted with the experiment.

A. Jøsang and B. Carlsson (Eds.): NordSec 2012, LNCS 7617, pp. 199–214, 2012.
© Springer-Verlag Berlin Heidelberg 2012

It is worth differentiating between two closely related concepts: privacy and secrecy. According to Warren et al. privacy and secrecy both involve boundaries and the denial of access to others; however, they differ in the moral content of the behavior that is concealed [22]. While we use the term privacy throughout the paper, one could argue that we are really dealing with a problem of secrecy because an organization is already by the definition of privacy not concerned about its privacy as it is not an individual. As we will show later, the organization is concerned about secrecy (e.g. research tasks).

The privacy implications of data gathered when users access websites on the Internet especially under the supposed "protection" of a PPT need to be examined and addressed more closely. The exposure of information on the Internet poses a genuine threat to the privacy of users. There are numerous ways in which an online entity can profile and track a website visitor. We propose to investigate how an adversary can collect information from website visitors through the actions of the user, the website itself, or programs that are transmitted through the Internet.

In this paper, we configured a network monitoring application to monitor network traffic coming from the case-study privacy preserving technology organization's (CSPPTO) users. The network monitoring application is set to create a daily report showing network activity going to websites including online social networks (OSNs), personal email, and other attributable websites. We define attributable as search queries that can yield the website visitors true origin such as the address and phone number of a local pizza place in the visitors true geographic location. The categorization of the network traffic was entirely based on DNS names/IP addresses as opposed to intercepting network traffic in a manner that would allow the authors to examine the content of a participants email or social network profile.

Meanwhile, we created an initial 20 question survey[2] that gathers answers to questions associated with demographic information, Internet behavior, and overall feelings toward privacy and security on the Internet. The objective of the survey is to determine the privacy awareness of users who utilize a real-world implementation of a PPT. The first phase of the experiment is to compare the results of the survey with the true network traffic captured by the network monitoring application. The rationale for collecting demographic information is to determine if gender, age, education, and Internet experience play a role when it comes to privacy and anonymity best practices. We compared the results of the survey with real network traffic that was collected on the PPT.

Next, we transition to the second phase of the experiment namely phishing. The objectives of the phishing campaign phase included crafting a phishing email based on previously completed tradecraft and reconnaissance of the target organization. Furthermore, we included a link within the phishing email to a Facebook application that has profiling and tracking enabled. We leveraged the Facebook application design from our previous research study [3]. We offered security awareness training and discussed defense mechanisms to help prevent against the attacks we discuss in our threat model.

In summary we make the following contributions: 1) Introduce a threat model that describes the motivation, goals, methodology, resources, and tactics of an adversary. 2) Examine how real users behave while on a real-world implementation of an PPT.

---

[2] The specific survey questions and answers can be found at
http://www.jamigen.com/uploads

3) Discuss the role of the adversary and their goal when it comes to discerning the identity of a user behind a PPT. 4) Evaluate experimentally the impact that identified threats can have on profiling and tracking website visitors using actual human subjects. 5) Discuss the need for security awareness training by gauging the current level of awareness within the CSPPTO.

The remainder of this paper is organized as follows. Section 2 describes the privacy preserving techology used by the participants. Section 3 describes the threat model. The experimental design and methodology is described in Section 4, while Section 5 discusses the experimental evaluation and the unleashing of our "Kitchen Sink"[3] attack. The results of the experiment are stated and analyzed in Section 6. Section 7 provides defense mechanisms to help against the profiling and tracking threats outlined in our threat model. Section 8 discusses related work. Finally, Section 9 presents our conclusions, including the direction for future research.

2   Privacy Preserving Technology (PPT)

The PPT used in this experiment is a variation of Anonymizer which acts as a service that submits HTTP requests to websites on behalf of its users. Because the request is submitted by the Anonymizer rather than the user, the only IP address revealed to the website is that of the Anonymizer [5]. The PPT used in the experiment is designed to prevent an open Internet connection from being exploited and all network traffic is routed through dedicated hardware housed in a secure facility [4]. The PPT incorporates a "IP Rotator" scheme which utilizes a large pool of IP addresses maintained by the vendor. In the IP Rotator scheme, anonymized users are mixed with "regular" worldwide consumers to help prevent behavioral patterns from being noticed [4]. The regular users are essentially diverting attention from the Anonymizer users by virtue of the search queries and network traffic that they are generating.

3   Threat Model

The network monitoring capability could leverage the network monitoring already implemented at the enterprise. The adversary may also use open source tools such as Wireshark and periodically capture the packets from the CSPPTO [18]. Wireshark has the ability to capture and interactively browse the network traffic running on a computer network [13]. It includes a rich feature set that allows for live capture and offline analysis, multi-platform support, graphical user interface, filtering capabilities, reporting, etc [18]. Moreover, this can be considered a subset of the more popular global passive adversary threat model discussed in the context of anonymity [19]. In the global passive adversary threat model, the adversary logs network traffic both to and from all of the CSPPTO users. The adversary's goal with respect to this particular threat model is to link the connections to outgoing connections [19].

---

[3] The idiom "Everything but the Kitchen Sink" is meant to humorously show all of the different attack vectors at the disposal of the adversary.

In order to emulate a true phishing attack, one of the authors acted as an adversary trying to infiltrate the CSPPTO network using only public knowledge and resources. The next major aspect of the threat model is to coerce the target organization's user into clicking on a Facebook application that might allow a connection back to a rogue server or website with tracking enabled. This would have consequences as a user might unknowingly put the privacy and anonymity of the target organizations mission in jeopardy.

3.1 Goal of the Adversary

Now we state the goal of the adversary associated with our threat model. The adversary seeks to invade the privacy and determine the true identity of the CSPPTO and its users. For example, the adversary is likely an outsider who is interested in the type of research being conducted at the CSPPTO. A successful adversary will use real names, numbers, and email addresses and include a topic that is relevant and noteworthy to the unsuspecting recipient of the phishing email. Phishing attacks are usually the foundation for more advanced attacks on unsuspecting organizations and its employees. We assume that the adversary has been able to target an organization that might be conducting research which falls in line with the objective of the adversary. For example, the adversary may perform search criteria such as "terrorism, "nuclear bomb", "missiles", etc. This search would yield results that the adversary could explore in greater detail.

We incorporated a set of questions that would be of interest to the adversary based on their objective. The questions of interest include: 1) What type of PPT is being used? 2) Who are the users? 3) What kind of PII is shared? 4) What is the users real IP address? 5) Are there sensitive documents? 6) Do the users have an OSN profile? 7) What tasks are the users working on? 8) What websites do the users access?

Our threat model provides value in the sense that it includes realistic attacks that can be performed by a single adversary or a small group of adversaries. Our threat model assumes that the adversary would have time and budget constraints. Section 5 describes the attack vectors unleashed by the adversary as part of the experiment we conducted.

4 Experimental Design and Methodology

Our experiments aim at understanding the behavior and motivations of users when they are accessing the Internet where protecting privacy and anonymity is crucial. There was a team consisting of the research manager, security manager, and several authors who conducted and implemented the attacks. We administered an initial survey to the CSPPTO users to gain an understanding of how they valued their anonymity and privacy. Furthermore, the survey allowed us to gauge whether or not the CSPPTO users were aware of best practices in protecting their anonymity and privacy. The survey was complemented by analysis of data captured from the CSPPTO users. All of the data from the survey, captured network traffic, phishing emails, questionnaire, and Facebook application was collected, analyzed, and written into a final report that was briefed to the CSPPTO managers. Based on the results, tailored security awareness training was provided to all CSPPTO users. However, we still continued to monitor the network traffic to attributable websites to determine if it has been reduced or stopped by virtue of the (successful) security awareness training.

Initially, we captured network traffic and generated a report showing the websites accessed by the users via the PPT. As a necessary prerequisite for luring the CSPPTO users we devised a phishing campaign targeted at the CSPPTO users. We investigated the frequency and type of information the CSPPTO users placed on increasingly popular OSNs, such as Facebook. It should be pointed out that these attacks were very much interconnected and did not run in sequence but rather in parallel.

The adversary (e.g., one of the authors) viewed OSNs, such as LinkedIn and Facebook, to find employees of the targeted organization. To add to the legitimacy of the email, we also scoured the Internet looking for a sample of writing of the sender. Upon completion of the survey and subsequent attacks, we provided security awareness training that discussed possible defenses against the attacks outlined in our threat model. At the conclusion of the training, we continued to monitor the network traffic in an effort to see if the CSPPTO users refrained from accessing websites that would allow an adversary to discern their true identity, location, and/or relevant task work.

4.1 Ethics

Given the potential ethical issues associated with this type of experiment, some organizations and their users may feel that purposely trying to collect and discover system data is a violation. The entire survey and subsequent experiments were authorized by the general counsel of the organization and the managers of the CSPPTO users. However, the employees/users themselves were unaware that this was an experiment. We feel this is a necessary pre-condition to have an effective experiment that shows the true ramifications of the privacy and anonymization concerns we are discussing. Additionally, we gained authorization from the George Mason University (GMU) Human Subjects Review Board (HSRB). The process required both of the authors to take an online ethics training course.

We tried to follow the best practices for computer research and human subjects according to Ayock et al. [2]. These best practices begin by stating that ethics oversight is needed in computer security research. Additionally, the HSRB should be in a position to understand technological issues and provide appropriate guidance [2]. To this end, we submitted our application in a manner that included all relevant technology and techniques used during the course of the experiment [2]. We continuously revised our application and experiment based on the feedback from the GMU HSRB.

4.2 Participants

The participants were all employees of the case study organization and were users of the PPT offered by the organization. We used a confidence interval of 95 percent to make an inference of the CSPPTO population, along with a deviation of 5 percent, and a sample proportion of 50 percent we arrived at a required sample size of 385. Using an estimated population of 400 CSPPTO users, the 385 participants in the sample size was adjusted to 196 based on our statistical assumptions. However, for various reasons some participants were unauthorized to participate in the experiment and so this gave us a true sample size of 160 individuals, which would reduce confidence slightly. The 160 participants were essentially recruited by the CSPPTO and provided to one of the authors since they were the users that would most likely be impacted by the threats defined in our threat model. The adversary would most likely only acquire a subset of this particular group of users following the tactics explained in the earlier threat model. Table 1 displays the demographics of the survey participants including gender, age range, field of study, education, and Internet usage. The purpose of this table is to determine whether or not we can draw any conclusions about the likelihood of the user falling victim to our attacks based on demographics.

Table 1. This table shows the demographics of the survey respondents

Survey Results Demographics		
Gender	Male	89 (56%)
	Female	71 (44%)
Age Range	18 to 30	92 (58%)
	31 to 40	51 (32%)
	41 to 50	11 (7%)
	51 to 60	3 (2%)
	61 to 70	2 (1%)
	71 and older	1 (1%)
Field	Computer Related	118 (74%)
	Non-Computer Related	42 (26%)
Education	Doctorate (PHD)	38 (24%)
	Masters	41 (26%)
	Bachelors	81 (50%)
Internet Usage Per Week	0 to 40	121 (76%)
	41 to 80	29(18%)
	81 to 120	9 (6%)
	121 and higher	1 (less than 1%)

4.3 Survey Design

The survey questionnaire contained 20 questions: a consent section, demographic section, usage questions, privacy questions, anonymizer-related questions, and Facebook-related questions. We asked the participants to answer all questions as truthfully as possible. Only participants affiliated with the CSPPTO were allowed to take the survey and it was anonymous. We used a non-technical approach by way of using a locked drop box that the participants could drop the survey into. Upon completion of the survey, we compared the survey responses with the results of our attacks. Specifically, we compared the networking monitoring that we collected to determine if the responses of the survey were accurate as to what the users were truly doing on the PPT.

5   Unleashing the Kitchen Sink Attack

5.1   Phase 1: Network Monitoring

In order to invoke this attack we used a commercial network monitoring tool. The network monitoring tool we selected provides real-time situational awareness, security event correlation, and vulnerability assessments. Using this tool one of the authors created a daily report showing the network monitoring access of the CSPPTO users. We could have easily used an open source monitoring tool such as the aforementioned Wireshark, but the commercial tool gave us the ability to capture different types of network traffic and generate reports. With the assistance of the CSPPTO system administrators we configured the commercial tool to monitor network traffic coming from the PPT. The network monitoring tool is set to create a monthly report showing network monitoring activity to online social networks.

As an adversary might do, we utilized the tool to capture all of the network activity. Thus, we tried to determine what websites' users were accessing and whether they might yield interesting data from an adversaries point of view. Additionally, we took the results of the network monitoring we captured and determined whether it conformed to the results of the initial survey. The rationale for doing that was to see if users were honest about their behavior and even more so whether or not they were aware that they might be giving up information so easily. We captured the initial network traffic prior to the training. After that, we gave the security awareness training and re-monitored the network traffic. We only analyzed the network traffic that was captured on the weekdays since that is when the CSPPTO users were expected to be working on their research tasks. In Figure 3 we show the amount of weekdays that we saw at least one user accessing a given website category before and after the training.

5.2   Phase 2: Phishing

Phishing is a common first step used by an adversary trying to penetrate and acquire sensitive information from a targeted organization. Essentially, phishing is a form of social engineering in which an adversary attempts to fraudulently acquire sensitive information from a victim [11]. This practice is usually done by directing or luring users to fraudulent websites and/or tricking them into clicking on attachments. Therefore, we decided to conduct an experiment in which we designed an internal phishing attack on the CSPPTO users. The purpose was to study whether CSPTTO users would be coerced into revealing information via a well-crafted phishing attack. Additionally, we also wanted to assess the level of awareness of the CSPPTO research staff when it comes to protecting their privacy.

To assist with our phishing campaign, we utilized an open source tool called the "Simple Phishing Toolkit" (SPT) [10]. To create a phishing campaign, we modified an existing SPT template and systematically selected an individual target for the attack. The SPT allows us to embed links directing to the website of our choosing. Figure 1 shows both the initial phishing email and the follow-up email sent to the CSPPTO users. Where applicable, the notation of "intentionally left blank" was not present in the original email sent to the users and is only used here to help protect the identity of the CSPPTO.

As part of the initial phishing email, we attached a document that provided an overview of the anonymity and privacy firm and a brief questionnaire for the CSPPTO researchers to complete and return. The objective of the questionnaire is determine the rate of success of the phishing campaign. Presumably, any CSPPTO users who will-ingly provide answers to the questionnaire would likely provide information about the research task. We waited for the questionnaire to be sent back to us. Upon receiving the questionnaire we collected the results of the number of people that responded to the questions. After a period of 3 days we sent a follow-up phishing email from the SPT.

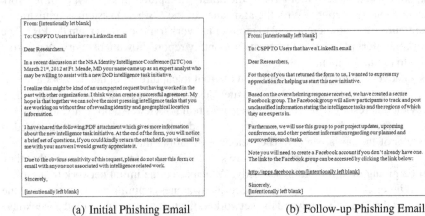

(a) Initial Phishing Email   (b) Follow-up Phishing Email

Fig. 1. Phishing Emails

5.3 Phase 3: Online Social Networks

The OSN attack phase had two goals from the adversaries point of view. First, to deter-mine whether the CSPPTO users have OSN accounts. Second, to determine if those that do access their OSN account while on a PPT attempt to protect their PII. We tested the hypothesis that the majority of visitors can be led to reveal their identity by an adver-sary mostly due to the actions the visitor performs on the Internet and the information they display on their Facebook profiles [3]. We leveraged the previous phishing emails and the link to the Facebook application. The application, if allowed, can track which Facebook profiles accessed it, from what location, and when.

6 Results

In the initial survey, we asked about users' knowledge of phishing, and feelings toward organizational, and individual privacy concerns. Additionally, we asked whether users have a Facebook account and if they regularly post PII to their profile. Finally, we asked whether or not users alter their privacy and geographical settings, allow Facebook appli-cations, and are aware that Facebook can reveal PII. The survey responses were either Yes / No or based on a 5-point Likert scale, which included the following acceptable responses: Extremely Important (5), Very Important (4), Neutral (3), Somewhat Important (2), and Not Important at All (1). The number of users who answered with a given response and the corresponding percentages are shown in Table 2.

Table 3 displays the responses associated with the participants use of a PPT to search various categories of websites. We asked the users to state how often they access Facebook, Twitter, personal email, and search for local restaurants/sports while under the protection of a PPT. The survey responses were based on a 5-point Likert scale, which included the following responses: All the time (5), Almost Always (4), Often (3), Sometimes (2), and Never (1).

In regards to the phishing phase of the "Kitchen Sink" attack, 92 of the 160 participants (58 percent) sent back the questionnaire with validated information. We found no correlation between gender, age, field of study or Internet usage when it came to falling victim to our phishing experiment. This correlation validated what was found in other phishing experiments such as the work completed by Acquisti et al. [1] and Dhamija et al. [8].

Additionally, 6 victims replied to the sender of the initial phishing email (e.g., one of the authors of this paper) asking if the content of the email was valid. We of course responded to this inquiry, assuring them that everything was legitimate and safe. Another 31 participants, sent the email directly to the CSPPTO internal phishing monitoring email inbox. Of the 160 participants, we were able to determine the Facebook profile name of 34 participants for a success rate of 21 percent which we later confirmed to be real employees at the CSPPTO. This was a much lower success rate compared to the results of our previous study [3]. This may be due to the smaller participant pool initially used. The remaining 126 participants did not click on the Facebook application. One interesting result is that there was 1 person who did not send back the questionnaire but did click on the Facebook application.

In Section 7 we will discuss the details of the security awareness training; however, we wanted to share the results of the post training survey here in the results section of the paper. After the training on phishing awareness was given, a survey was provided to all the participants to help determine the effectiveness of education as it relates to defending against phishing attacks. Of the 160 participants, 96 responded to the post training survey. For a variety of reasons not all of the participants either attended the training or wished to fill out the post survey.

Figure 2 shows the responses to the question of "What was your understanding of phishing **before** the security awareness training? and "What was your understanding of phishing **after** the security awareness training? In conclusion, the phishing experiment was successful and by the number of responses showed that our phishing email was quite convincing and/or that people are just replying to emails without attempting to analyze their authenticity.

7   Security Awareness Training and Other Defenses

In this section, we discuss the security awareness training that we offered to all of the CSPPTO participants along with other defense mechanisms. First, the training began by explaining the "Kitchen Sink" experiment that we conducted. Specifically, we discussed the results of the experiment and the importance of attending and participating

Table 2. Survey results associated with phishing knowledge and privacy on the Internet

Survey Results Privacy		
Individual Privacy	5	60 (38%)
	4	69 (43%)
	3	16 (10%)
	2	11 (7%)
	1	4 (3%)
Organization's Privacy	5	55 (34%)
	4	65 (40%)
	3	20 (13%)
	2	9 (6%)
	1	11 (7%)
Facebook Account	Yes	157 (98%)
	No	3 (2%)
Purposely Post Inaccurate PII	Yes	42 (26%)
	No	118 (74%)
Change Privacy Settings	Yes	43 (27%)
	No	117(73%)
Change Geographical Settings	Yes	63 (39%)
	No	97 (61%)
Allow Applications	Yes	50 (31%)
	No	110 (69%)

Table 3. Survey results associated with PPT usage

PPT Usage		
Local Restaurant	5	5 (3%)
	4	19 (12%)
	3	43 (27%)
	2	42 (27%)
	1	51 (32%)
Local Sports	5	6 (4%)
	4	19 (12%)
	3	30 (19%)
	2	38 (24%)
	1	67 (42%)
Facebook on PPT	5	7 (4%)
	4	19 (12%)
	3	32 (20%)
	2	38 (24%)
	1	64 (40%)
Twitter on PPT	5	4 (3%)
	4	9 (6%)
	3	15 (9%)
	2	38 (24%)
	1	94 (59%)
Personal Email on PPT	5	21 (13%)
	4	39 (24%)
	3	14 (9%)
	2	20(13%)
	1	66 (41%)

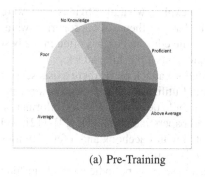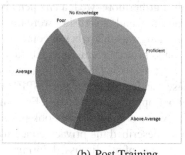

(a) Pre-Training   (b) Post Training

Fig. 2. Security Awareness Training

in the security awareness training that we developed. We began the security awareness training by explaining to the CSPPTO users the dangers and drawbacks of performing personal and attributable search websites on the Internet. In this part of the security awareness training, we covered the fact that search engines such as Google are often able to correlate search queries with a user's true location. We provided a list of attributable search queries and websites that were verboten. This included the previously discussed categories, such as personal email, personal banking, and online social networks, etc. In Figure 3 we see a noticeable decrease in the amount of network traffic to attributable websites.

Next, we shifted our attention to the phishing aspect of our experiment. We explained the importance of recognizing a phishing attempt as the first layer of defense in defending against a phishing attack. Given the significant number of users that still clicked on the phishing link, this suggested to us that greater awareness and educational seminars are indeed warranted. To this end, we introduced the Simple Phishing Toolkit and demonstrated the ease with which adversaries can create legitimate looking phishing

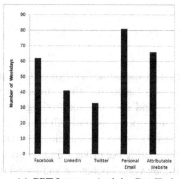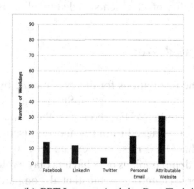

(a) PPT Internet Activity Pre-Training   (b) PPT Internet Activity Post Training

Fig. 3. Security Awareness Training

emails. Furthermore, we led an open discussion to explain what the obvious signs were that the email and/or websites were forged. The underlying theme of our security awareness training was that when it comes to phishing, the educated user is often in the best position to protect against an adversary who implements a phishing attack.

In regards to the OSN (e.g., Facebook Application) attack phase there exists several defense mechanisms that the CSPPTO user could utilize to help prevent against the Facebook application attack [3]. First, the visitor should be cognizant of the information that they place on their Facebook profile. Several papers including [1], [14], [12], and [7] have described the privacy concerns associated with Facebook and a few defenses we are aware of are discussed during the rest of this section.

We defended our phishing exercise by suggesting sending periodic internal phishing emails is a good way to increase awareness from employees and to improve the overall security posture of the CSPPTO. We predict that if enough phishing campaigns are sent over a long period of time, the users will eventually learn to combat phishing attacks. The security awareness training devoted to improving susceptibility to phishing attacks was beneficial for the participants. At the conclusion of the training, we polled the attendees and they claimed a definite increase in understanding and awareness of phishing. However, we wanted to confirm whether our training was truly a success. To accomplish this, we continued to monitor the network traffic of the CSPPTO users.

Aside from the previously described security awareness training, there exists several defense mechanisms that the CSPPTO users could implement. The users should be vigilant enough not to access and allow the unfamiliar Facebook application in the first place. Luo et al. present an architecture known as "FaceCloak" that enforces user privacy on OSN by shielding a users personal information from the site and from other users that were not explicitly authorized by the user [15]. Another defense mechanism to consider is "SafeBook" [6]. "SafeBook" was specifically designed to prevent privacy violations by intruders, malicious users, and OSN providers [6]. Essentially, "SafeBook" is mainly characterized by a decentralized architecture relaying on cooperation among peers in order to prevent potential privacy violations due to a centralized architecture [6]. Sirivianos et al., created a system called "FaceTrust" that verifies online personas in an efficient manner [21]. This particular system was designed to assess the credibility of statements made by online users.

8   Related Work

One of the inspirations for this paper came by virtue of the paper,"Imagined Communities: Awareness, Information Sharing, and Privacy on Facebook" the authors survey a sample number of Facebook members at a college and compare the findings to the information retrieved from the network itself [1]. The hypothesis set forth by Acquisti et al. is that OSNs raise privacy and security concerns. However, it is unclear as to how different demographics or behaviors play a role in impacting the privacy and security of OSN users. Therefore, Acquisti et al. compare attitudes versus behavior and found that individual privacy concerns are a weak predictor of membership.

Similarly, it was determined that so-called privacy concerned individuals join the OSN and reveal great amounts of personal information that they may not even be aware of [1]. The results of the research performed by Acquisti et al. showed that the Facebook privacy concerns stated in the survey were actually quite high; however, the privacy concerns that were actually captured were mixed but were on the low scale [1]. The reasons as stated by Acquisti et al. were due to peer pressure and unawareness of the true visibility of their profiles.

Dhamija et al. provides the first empirical evidence about which malicious strategies are successful in deceiving general users [8]. To this end, Dhamija et al. developed a large set of phishing attacks and hypothesized why these attacks might work [8]. Most phishing attacks focus on either a fake email or a fake website to lure unsuspecting users to. Dhamija et al. primarily focused on answering the question of what makes a website credible? However, they added an interesting twist and researched what made a bogus site credible? [8]. The key findings of this paper were that good phishing websites fooled 90 percent of the participants and that existing anti-phishing browsing cues are ineffective [8]. They found that participants proved vulnerable across the board to phishing attacks and that neither age, sex, experience, nor hours of computer used mattered when it came to likelihood of falling victim for a spoofed website.

The study performed by Jagatic et al. points out the need for extensive education campaigns about phishing and other security threats [11]. The training allows people to become less vulnerable due to a heightened awareness of the dangers of phishing [11].

Third-party applications further escalate the privacy concerns as OSN user data are shared with these applications [20]. When considering Facebook applications, there is typically minimal control over what user information these applications are allowed to access. Even more concerning is the fact that these applications are not hosted on the actual OSN (e.g., Facebook). This makes it difficult to police the data being leaked from the application after the data are shared with the application [20]. This usually occurs due to user error such as the user inadvertently allowing the application or in other cases it is due to vulnerabilities in the application itself. Sing et al. are concerned with protecting users' private information from leaks by third-party applications and as a result present a mechanism called "XBook" to control not only what the third-party application can access but also what these applications can do with the data they are allowed to access [20].

Given the amount of available PII, OSNs have the ideal properties to become attack platforms. Makridakis et al. define the term "Antisocial Networks" that refer to distributed systems based on social networking websites which can be exploited to carry out network attacks [16]. Jagatic et al. completed an experiment to quantify, in an ethical manner, how reliable social context would increase the success rate of a phishing attack [11]. This was accomplished by mining information about relationships and common interests provided on a growing number of OSN such as Facebook. This allowed the phisher to harvest large amounts of reliable social network information.

Moody et al. point out the use of the Internet and networking technologies continues to rise. Alongside the benefits that are derived from the use of these technologies, numerous threats continue to emerge. The study performed by Moody et al. examines several variables within the message characteristics, personality traits, and Internet-related experience to determine an individual's susceptibility for phishing attacks [17]. The results of an ethical phishing experiment show that message characteristics and

Internet-related variables are better predictors of whether an individual will be more susceptible to phishing attacks [17].

Dodge et al. performed an experiment that considers the benefits of training as it relates to phishing susceptibility. The authors report on a recent phishing experiment where the effects of training were evaluated [9]. Additionally, Dodge et al. gathered demographics data to explore the susceptibility of given groups. The results indicated that over a very short periods of time (e.g., 10 days), there is no significant difference in susceptibility based on training. However, over longer periods of time (e.g., 63 days), training does contribute significantly to the reduction in susceptibility. These findings are in-line with what we concluded based on our training exercises. Therefore, it is recommended that the CSPPTO and other organizations balance the importance of reducing susceptibility of security threats with the increased time and organization efforts involved with providing mandatory training resources [9].

In summary, our paper contributes to the related work in several different ways. First, it combines a few different attack vectors (e.g., networking monitoring, phishing, and (malicious) Facebook applications) into a single experiment. We are unaware of any other papers that frame these attack vectors into one experiment. Next, our experiment was conducted using real employees at an organization which gives more credibility to our results. By completing the experiment in the manner that we did, we were able to verify many of the same findings that were presented in other papers contained within our literature review. For example, we confirmed that demographics had little to no impact when it came to a user falling victim to a phishing attack.

Lastly, we extended our study to include the effectiveness of our custom security awareness training. In general, our paper takes many well-known ideas (e.g., networking monitoring, phishing, malicious applications, and training) and combines them into one experiment with real users at an organization where protecting PII is of paramount importance.

9   Conclusions and Future Work

In this paper, we learned that users can fall victim to an adversary who can monitor network traffic, develop a phishing campaign based on reconnaissance, and utilize a (potentially malicious) Facebook application that has tracking enabled. By virtue of using these different attack phases, we show that we can determine the answers to a variety of questions of interest to an adversary.

Our results show that given 160 users we are able to determine and validate answers to the questions of interest for 92 users (58 percent). Furthermore, we are able to identity the Facebook profile of 34 participants for a 21 percent success rate from the adversary's point of view. We learned that users are not aware of quite prevalent attacks to their privacy and secrecy. While this is not surprising, this experiment did help convince the CSPPTO upper management to implement further monitoring of certain attributable websites that were outlined in this experiment.

The major limitation of our work is the low number of participants that we had. We had a difficult time gathering participants for this experiment since we were restricted to one single organization. Our critics might argue that we simply just created a "new" problem if the participants utilized fake or fictitious profiles and claimed them to be their own [3]. The OSN phase of the experiment was limited to Facebook and given more time and resources, we would have considered extending this experiment to reach other OSNs.

The public, and specifically those users on OSNs, has to be aware that their personal information provided in their profile is of interest to a wide variety of adversaries. These adversaries will use all available means to acquire private information. Therefore, we conducted security awareness training that yielded a dramatic decrease in the network traffic we were seeing to personal and attributable websites.

Additionally, as part of future research we plan to send out a very similar phishing email in a few months to see if the CSPPTO users "learned their lesson" of protecting their privacy and anonymity. Lastly, we hope to interview each of the participants to ask why they acted as they did and why they considered (or not considered) the email to be a phishing attempt. We believe valuable lessons could be learned as a result of a post-training interview and the findings can be generalized to a larger population for future training seminars.

References

1. Acquisti, A., Gross, R.: Imagined Communities: Awareness, Information Sharing, and Privacy on the Facebook. In: Danezis, G., Golle, P. (eds.) PET 2006. LNCS, vol. 4258, pp. 36–58. Springer, Heidelberg (2006)
2. Aycock, J., Buchanan, E., Dexter, S., Dittrich, D.: Human subjects, agents, or bots: Current issues in ethics and computer security research. In: Proceedings from 2nd Workshop on Ethics in Computer Security Research, St. Lucia (2011)
3. Clark, J.: Correlating a persona to a person. To appear in the 3rd International Workshop on Security and Privacy in Social Networks (2012)
4. Clark, J., Stavrou, A.: Breaching & protecting an anonymizing network system. In: 6th Annual Symposium on Information Assurance (ASIA 2011), p. 32 (2011)
5. Cranor, L.F.: Internet privacy. Communications of the ACM 42(2), 28–38 (1999)
6. Cutillo, L.A., Molva, R., Strufe, T.: Safebook: A privacy-preserving online social network leveraging on real-life trust. IEEE Communications Magazine 47(12), 94–101 (2009)
7. Debatin, B., Lovejoy, J.P., Horn, A.K., Hughes, B.N.: Facebook and online privacy: Attitudes, behaviors, and unintended consequences. Journal of Computer-Mediated Communication 15(1), 83–108 (2009)
8. Dhamija, R., Tygar, J.D., Hearst, M.: Why phishing works. In: Proceedings of the SIGCHI Conference on Human Factors in Computing Systems, pp. 581–590. ACM (2006)
9. Dodge, R., Coronges, K., Rovira, E.: Empirical benefits of training to phishing susceptibility. In: Information Security and Privacy Research, pp. 457–464 (2012)
10. http://www.sptoolkit.com
11. Jagatic, T.N., Johnson, N.A., Jakobsson, M., Menczer, F.: Social phishing. Communications of the ACM 50(10), 94–100 (2007)
12. Jones, H., Soltren, J.: Facebook: Threats to privacy. In: Project MAC: MIT Project on Mathematics and Computing (2005)
13. Lamping, U., Warnicke, E.: Wireshark user's guide. Interface 4, 6 (2004)
14. Lipford, H.R., Besmer, A., Watson, J.: Understanding privacy settings in facebook with an audience view. In: Proceedings of the 1st Conference on Usability, Psychology, and Security, pp. 1–8 (2008)

15. Luo, W., Xie, Q., Hengartner, U.: Facecloak: An architecture for user privacy on social networking sites. In: International Conference on Computational Science and Engineering, CSE 2009, vol. 3, pp. 26–33 (2009)
16. Makridakis, A., Athanasopoulos, E., Antonatos, S., Antoniades, D., Ioannidis, S., Markatos, E.P.: Designing malicious applications in social networks. In: IEEE Network Special Issue on Online Social Networks (2010)
17. Moody, G., Galletta, D., Walker, J., Dunn, B.: Which phish get caught? an exploratory study of individual susceptibility to phishing (2011)
18. Orebaugh, A., Ramirez, G., Burke, J.: Wireshark & Ethereal network protocol analyzer toolkit. Syngress Media Inc. (2007)
19. Serjantov, A., Murdoch, S.J.: Message Splitting Against the Partial Adversary. In: Danezis, G., Martin, D. (eds.) PET 2005. LNCS, vol. 3856, pp. 26–39. Springer, Heidelberg (2006)
20. Singh, K., Bhola, S., Lee, W.: xbook: Redesigning privacy control in social networking platforms. In: Proceedings of the 18th Conference on USENIX Security Symposium, pp. 249–266. USENIX Association (2009)
21. Sirivianos, M., Kim, K., Yang, X.: Facetrust: Assessing the credibility of online personas via social networks. In: Proceedings of the 4th USENIX Conference on Hot Topics in Security, p. 2. USENIX Association (2009)
22. Warren, C., Laslett, B.: Privacy and secrecy: A conceptual comparison. Journal of Social Issues 33(3), 43–51 (1977)

Can We Identify Manipulative Behavior and the Corresponding Suspects on Review Websites Using Supervised Learning?

Huiying Duan[1] and Cäcilia Zirn[2]

[1] Heidelberg Institute for Theoretical Studies gGmbH
Heidelberg, Germany
Huiying.Duan@h-its.org
[2] KR & KM Research Group, University of Mannheim
Mannheim, Germany
caecilia@informatik.uni-mannheim.de

Abstract. Identification of manipulative behavior and the corresponding suspects is an essential task for maintaining robustness of reputation systems integrated by review websites. However, this task constitutes a great challenge. In this paper, we present an approach based on supervised learning to automatically detect suspicious behavior on travel websites. We distinguish between two types of manipulation, treating them as separate tasks: promoting manipulation, which is performed in order to push the reputation of a hotel, and demoting manipulation, which is used to demote competitors. Both tasks consist of three separate levels: detecting suspicious reviews (review level), suspicious reviewers (reviewer level) and suspicious objects of the reviews, i.e. hotels (object level). A separate classifier for each of the levels is trained on various sets of textual and non-textual features. We apply state-of-the-art machine learning algorithms like Support Vector Machines. The performance of our approach is evaluated on a new dataset that we created based on reviews taken from the platform TripAdvisor and which was carefully annotated by human judges. The results show that it is possible to identify manipulating reviewers and objects of manipulation with over 90% accuracy. Identifying suspicious reviews, however, seems to be a much harder task, for which our classifier achieves an accuracy of 68% detecting promoting manipulation and 84% detecting demoting manipulation. We argue that there is the need to identify more efficient features for the classification on review level. Finally, we analyze and discuss statistical characteristics of manipulative behavior based on the predictions of the reviewer and object level classifiers.

Keywords: reputation system, trust management, manipulative behavior identification and analysis, opinion mining, supervised learning, TripAdvisor.

A. Jøsang and B. Carlsson (Eds.): NordSec 2012, LNCS 7617, pp. 215–230, 2012.
© Springer-Verlag Berlin Heidelberg 2012

1   Introduction

Recently, a large number of review websites like TripAdvisor[1] or Yelp[2] have gained great success by integrating reputation into their systems. Reputation refers to public opinions regarding trust on a certain object, e.g. a restaurant or a hotel. Trust is defined as a subjective probability by which an individual A expects that another individual B performs a given action on which its welfare depends [3]. The reason behind the magnificent achievement of these websites is that reputation acts as a social catalyst which aids travelers to decrease the degree of uncertainty and the risk of decision making in virtual environments, where much information of concern is missing. For instance, via a review website, a traveler can check the reputation of hotels which are around his travel location before booking.

Usually, once these websites become popular, manipulative behavior emerges[3,4,5]. In this paper, manipulative behavior is defined as an operation of injecting fraudulent reviews. A service provider (e.g. a hotelier or a restaurateur) "hires" people either to give fraudulent positive reviews or to give negative ones on the service provider's competitors. We call the former one promoting manipulation and the latter one demoting manipulation. Generally, a review refers to a personal and subjective evaluation in terms of quality of service. Its content consists of both a numerical and a textual value. For instance, a hotel review on TripAdvisor contains a total score, sub-scores on particular aspects of a hotel (such as the room, value, cleanliness etc.) and a piece of text describing the experience of the service consumption. In the perspective of trust and reputation management, the robustness of reputation systems is largely threatened by these "attacks". For instance, the reputation value of a hotel could be miscalculated by considering fraudulent reviews, and this miscalculation indirectly influences the ranking of hotels in terms of their reputation value.

The research on the robustness of reputation systems [5–13] can be categorized in terms of different criteria. Regarding the choice of the dataset, [5–8] study Amazon[6] product reviews; [9–13] use TripAdvisor as a case study. There is a large difference between the two datasets. On Amazon, reviews are about products, while on TripAdvisor, most of the reviews are related to hotel or restaurant services. Service is a more complicated concept for trust management than products due to the subjectivity and the variation of quality. Hence, manipulative behavior detection on TripAdvisor is supposed to be more difficult than on Amazon. For instance, the quality of a product usually does not

---

[1] www.tripadvisor.com

[2] www.yelp.com

[3] http://www.dailymail.co.uk/travel/article-2013391/Tripadvisor-Hotel-owners-bribe-guests-return-good-reviews.html

[4] http://www.rhinocarhire.com/Car-Hire-Blog/May-2012/Hotel-Reviews-Faulty-Towers-or-The-Ritz.aspx

[5] http://www.sfgate.com/technology/article/Yelp-s-trust-at-risk-from-phony-reviews-3708962.php

[6] http://www.amazon.com/

change, whereas the quality of hotel service might vary over time. Regarding types of features for machine learning, textual features are used in [5, 7, 9–12]; non-textual features in [5, 6, 8, 9, 12, 13]. Considering detection as a supervised learning approach, [9] labels reviews by the proportion of positive feedback given to a review. We adopt some of the representative features in our work, e.g. the proportion of "Positive Singletons", which refers to positive reviews written by users who wrote only this one review, and "Reactive Positive Singletons", which refer to positive reviews written by a hotel as reaction to negative reviews [12]. Textual features such as unigrams and bigrams are commonly used in suspicious review identification [7, 10, 11] to capture the textual content of a review.

The main contribution of this paper is to identify manipulative behavior - both promoting and demoting - on three different levels: the object level, the reviewer level and the review level. Considering all types of information, i.e. non-textual and textual features, six classifiers (three levels, for each two types of manipulative behavior) are trained using Support Vector Machines. Second, we annotate a corpus of hotel reviews. Considering one of the main results in [11], which shows that human performance is low for annotating fake reviews[7], we create the gold-standard annotation for our dataset in a careful manner. Experienced annotators are selected and trained to perform the annotation task using the relation of information between reviews, reviewers and hotels, and we finally only choose those reviews on which all annotators reach a consensus. We evaluate the performance of the classifiers on the newly created gold standard.

The rest of this paper is organized as follows. The next section introduces the dataset. In section 3, the basic idea of suspect identification is represented and features for learning are proposed. Section 4 introduces the process of annotation generation. Section 5 shows the main results about learned classifiers and the corresponding discussion.

2   Dataset Review

We selected 167,909 reviews about New York City's hotels from TripAdvisor for our dataset. New York City (NYC) is considered as one of the most ideal cities for traveling all around the world, and there are a large number of hotels. We assume it is more likely to find manipulative behavior in NYC than in any other region due to keen competition. A basic statistics of the dataset is listed in Table 1. We collect hotel information, reviewers who provide reviews about the hotels and the corresponding reviews. Note that the amount of reviews which have the singleton feature in [12] is only 3.24%. The fact indicates that the most representative features might be different from one dataset to another. Therefore, it is necessary to specify the most representative features in terms of a concrete dataset.

---

[7] In their work, only textual information is considered by human annotators to make a decision whether it is fraudulent or not.

Table 1. Basic Statistics of TripAdvisor's Dataset

Dataset Statistics	New York City (NYC)
Duration	January 1999 - June 2011
Hotels	404
Reviewers	110,128
Reviews	167,909
Singletons	5,446 (3.24%)

3   Suspect Detection

Obviously, there are three types of objects that are involved in manipulative behavior: the review, the reviewer and the hotel. A service provider (e.g. the hotelier) "hires" reviewers either to give positive fraudulent reviews, or to give negative ones on the service provider's competitors. We call the former one promoting manipulation and the latter one demoting manipulation. For each level and each type of manipulation we build a separate classifier. In the following, we introduce the features we use for classification.

Advanced Positive Singleton (AdvPositiveSingleton), formalized by formula (1), is the improved version of Positive Singleton [12,13]. It is defined on the review level for promoting manipulation. In [12,13], a positive rating[8] is one assigned 4 or 5 points, and a rating with less than 4 points is negative. This definition could be inaccurate. For instance, a newly posted 4-point rating should be considered as negative, if the previous 100 ratings are all 5-point. Therefore, we improve the feature by adding a new condition which estimates the distance between a new rating and the current reputation of the hotel, i.e. the reputation evaluated at the moment when the rating is created. If the distance is larger than a threshold TH_p, we then consider the rating as positive. In the experiment, we empirically set the threshold to 1. Likewise, **Advanced Negative Singleton (AdvNegativeSingleton)** is specified for demoting manipulation.

$$AdvPositiveSingleton(r_i^t) = \begin{cases} 1 & \text{if } r_i^t \text{ is PS and } (r_i^t - TV^t) > TH_p \\ 0 & \text{Otherwise} \end{cases} \quad (1)$$

Time Interval between Posted Date and Stayed Date (TimePosted-Stayed) refers to the difference between the date a review is posted and the date the reviewer stayed in this hotel. It is defined on the review level for both promoting and demoting cases.

Time Interval between Consecutive Contributions (TimeConsec-Contributions). Contributions of a reviewer are ordered by the time a review is posted. Then the time interval between two consecutive reviews can be regarded as a random variable. This feature contains two subfeatures, mean (TimeConsecContributions_MEAN) and variance (TimeConsecContributions_VAR) of the

---

[8] In this section, "rating" refers to the numerical value and "review" refers to the textual value.

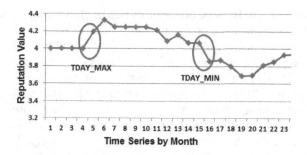

Fig. 1. An example for TurningDay

time interval variable. They are defined on the review level for both promoting and demoting cases.

Rating Preference (RatingPreference), formalized by formula (2), is an indicator for describing a reviewer's attitude towards rating provision. In formula (2), $SUBR()$ denotes a function whose inputs are the overall rating and the index of the sub-rating, and the output is the value of the corresponding sub-rating. When writing a review, a reviewer does not only give an overall rating r_i^t, but sub-ratings $SUBR(r_i^t, k)$ for value, rooms, location, cleanliness, service, etc. It is defined on the review level for both promoting and demoting cases.

$$RatingPreference(r_i^t) = r_i^t - \frac{\sum_{k=1}^{N} SUBR(r_i^t, k)}{N} \tag{2}$$

Turning Day (TurningDay), demonstrated by Fig. 1, indicates the maximal reputation variation of a hotel. Each point represents an evaluation of reputation on a certain time stamp. The circle of evaluation is one month. Then we develop a simple algorithm to identify the intervals which have the largest and smallest slopes TurningDay_MAX and TurningDay_MIN. These are the places where the reputation value has the largest variation during a hotel's life time. We specify TurningDay_MAX as a feature for promoting manipulation, and TurningDay_MIN for demoting manipulation. Furthermore, the logical relationship among a hotel, a reviewer and a review is also taken into consideration, since the variation results from reviews and reviewers who provide them. Therefore, the corresponding reviews and reviewers are also covered by this feature. TurningDay is defined on all levels for both promoting and demoting cases.

Inactive Duration (InactiveDuration) refers to the duration from the last post to the time when data is collected. It is defined on the reviewer level for both promoting and demoting cases.

Contribution Statistics (ContributionStatistics) contains the number of contributions (ContributionNum), mean (Contribution_MEAN) and variance (Contribution_VAR) of contributions which are generated by a reviewer. A unit of contribution refers to a review. All the three subfeatures are defined on the reviewer level for both promoting and demoting cases.

Consistency of Ratings (ConsistencyRating), contains variance of mode (VAR_ MODE) and variance of mean (VAR_MEAN) with respect to different types of ratings for a hotel. First, we categorize ratings of a hotel by the type of traveler, such as "business", "couples" etc., then we calculate mode and mean of these variables respectively. Finally, variance of each mode and mean are calculated. Formula (3) shows the calculation of (VAR_MEAN), (VAR_ MODE) is calculated respectively. R_j denotes the set of ratings for a hotel. $SUBS()$ is a function which returns the subset of ratings in terms of type index k. $MEAN$ and VAR are defined to evaluate mean and variance respectively. The idea behind this feature is to measure to what degree different types of ratings are consistent with each other, and it is defined on the hotel level for both promoting and demoting cases.

$$VAR\_MEAN(R_j) = VAR(MEAN(SUBS(R_j, k))) \tag{3}$$

Average Number of Reviews per Month (AverageNumPerMonth) refers to the mean of the amount of reviews posted on a hotel in one month. It is defined on the hotel level for both promoting and demoting cases.

Proportion of Advanced Positive Singleton (PropAdvPositive-Singleton) refers to the proportion of AdvPositiveSingleton and it is defined on the hotel level for promoting manipulation. The feature is adopted from [12]. We only replace Positive Singleton by AdvPositiveSingleton. Parallel to this, **Proportion of Advanced Negative Singleton (PropAdvNegativeSingleton)** is defined for demoting manipulation.

Reactive Advanced Positive Singletons (ReactiveAdvPositiveSingleton), is also adopted from Reactive Positive Singletons [12]. In order to recover from negative ratings, the management may react by posting some positive shill reviews. The strength of evidence can be quantified as $\frac{T-t_i}{T}$ where T is the length of the entire time period, and t_i is the reaction time associated with shill i. It is formalized by formula (5), where T_h is a normalization factor for hotel h. It is defined on the hotel level for promoting manipulation.

$$ReactiveAdvPositiveSingleton(h) = \frac{1}{|T_h|}(1 - \prod_{i=1}^{n}(1 - \frac{T-t_i}{T})) \tag{4}$$

Truncated Positive Rating (TruncPositiveRating) is adopted from [12], in which it is called Truncated Rating. The idea is to remove a portion of the most positive ratings for a hotel and recalculate the average to see if it deviates much from the original value. It is formalized by formula (4), where R_h^{tr} is the truncated rating set. It is defined on the hotel level for promoting manipulation. Parallel to this, **Truncated Negative Rating (TruncNegativeRating)** is defined for demoting manipulation.

$$TruncPositiveRating(h) = \frac{1}{|R_h|}\sum_{r \in R_h} r - \frac{1}{|R_h^{tr}|}\sum_{r \in R_h^{tr}} r \tag{5}$$

Rating Mean (Rating_MEAN) refers to the mean of the overall ratings on a hotel. It is defined on the hotel level for both promoting and demoting cases.

Rating Variance (Rating_VAR) refers to the variance of the overall ratings on a hotel. It is defined on the hotel level for both promoting and demoting cases.

Ratio of Room Number to Review Number (RatioRoomReview) refers to the ratio of the amount of rooms a hotel owns to the amount of reviews for it. The intuition is that it is suspicious for a hotel who owns only few rooms to have a large number of reviews. It is defined on the hotel level for promoting behavior.

Hotel Reviews Contradiction Degree (ContradictionDegree), formalized by formula (6), refers to the maximum variance of sub-ratings for a hotel. There are N sub-ratings for items as value, rooms, location, cleanliness, service, etc.. MAX is a function to find the maximum of the ratings. It is defined on the hotel level for both promoting and demoting cases.

$$ContradictionDegree(h) = MAX(\{VAR(SUBS(r_i^h, k)), \text{where } i = 1...N\}) \tag{6}$$

Textual Features (UniBigram) refer to the textual features extracted from the review content. Like in [7,10,11], we use unigrams and bigrams, representing the review text by the amount of its words and consecutive word pairs.

4   Gold Standard Annotation

Since we are going to apply classic supervised learning approaches, having properly labeled data is the most significant part in our work. Before describing the annotation process, we have some comments on the experiment in [11], who used Amazon Mechanical Turk[9] to purposely create fake reviews. They mix them with real reviews from TripAdvisor which they consider to be written by honest reviewers, and they ask human annotators to spot the malicious ones. One of the main findings of their experiment is that humans are bad at identifying fraudulent reviews. We agree with that, yet we argue that generating fraudulent reviews using Amazon Mechanical Turk is a valid way which has its own limits. It is still unclear whether the character of fraudulent reviews written by virtual workers is matchable to that in TripAdvisor[10]. Furthermore, the annotators in [11] make their decision based on the review text only. In our opinion, a better solution is to identify fraudulent reviews which are extracted from a dataset using all complimentary information given, i.e. checking various reviews of the same reviewer or the date they were posted. We therefore assume that if the annotation process is carefully handled, an appropriate gold standard can be manually generated.

---

[9] https://www.mturk.com/mturk/welcome

[10] http://tripadvisorwatch.wordpress.com/2010/10/10/tripadvisor-pay-review-fake/

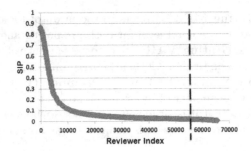

Fig. 2. Distribution of Suspicious Index for Promoting Manipulation

We select three well-trained and independent annotators. Well-trained means every annotator has at least a basic notion of manipulative behavior. They are encouraged to evaluate each review by identifying logical inconsistency within the information related to a review. The information does not only refer to the numerical and textual value of a review per se, but all types of information of the corresponding reviewer, such as uploaded pictures, reviewer profile etc. Interestingly, the annotators based their decisions on facts like one of the uploaded pictures was the only one looking quite different from the pictures uploaded by other reviewers. We randomly pick 1000 reviews from the dataset whose total rating score is either 1 or 5, and let all of the annotators evaluate the same 1000 reviews separately. We believe that a review with a score of 1 or 5 is most likely to be suspicious. Like we expected, the annotation process is a very time-consuming procedure, since an annotator has to check a lot of information in order to make a decision. In addition, we calculate the inter-annotation agreement using Fleiss Kappa, which is $\kappa = 0.18$. This indicates only slight agreement, which is consistent with the findings in [11]. To provide a reliability of the labels, we chose only those reviews for our final gold standard that were unanimously labeled by all three annotators. Thus having a complete agreement level and considering the fact that our annotators made use of all information provided about the review, the reviewer and the hotel, we assume the labels in the gold standard to constitute the truth.

So far, only reviews are labeled, but we still need suspiciousness labels for the reviewer and the hotel level. Considering logical relations among different levels, a set of labeled suspicious reviewers and hotels can be generated from labeled reviews. There are two logical implications we use. If a review is suspicious, the corresponding reviewer is also suspicious; if a number of reviews posted on a hotel are all suspicious, the hotel is also suspicious. Following this idea, the sets of suspicious reviewers and hotels are generated. In addition, in our previous work [1], we succeeded in assigning a Suspicious Index (SI) to the objects on different levels. Fig. 2 demonstrates the distribution of the SI on the reviewer level with respect to promoting manipulation. The data can be fitted by an exponential function. In this case, we simply set a threshold for SI (e.g. 0.01) to choose a set of genuine reviewers with respect to promoting manipulation. Parallel to that, we are able to find a set of least suspicious reviewers and hotels by choosing the set of objects which have the lowest SI. The statistics of annotated objects is listed in Table 2.

Table 2. Annotations Statistics

Annotated Object	Number
Number of Genuine Reviews	180
Number of Promoting Reviews	139
Number of Demoting Reviews	24
Number of Genuine Reviewers	390
Number of Promoting Reviewers	131
Number of Demoting Reviewers	20
Number of Genuine Hotels	43
Number of Promoting Hotels	26
Number of Demoting Hotels	2

5   Experimental Results and Discussion

In this section, in order to evaluate the effectiveness of the proposed features, we compare the feature value distribution of the different groups (i.e. genuine, promoting manipulation and demoting manipulation) with respect to the annotations. We list the classification results and present a ranking of the most effective features based on the training data. Using the predictions of the classifiers for hotels and reviewers, we explore statistical characteristics of the suspects.

5.1   Feature Evaluation

To illustrate the effectiveness of the proposed features, we plot the distribution of feature values with respect to genuine and suspicious objects considering the gold standard annotations. In this section, we sample the most representative features only due to the paper limitation.

Average number of reviews per month (AverageNumPerMonth) is one of the key features specified on the hotel level. The value distribution of AverageNumPerMonth is plotted in Fig. 3(a). All the hotels are ordered by their AverageNumPerMonth value, which is represented on the y-axis. The x-axis corresponds to the indexes of the hotels. There are three groups of hotels: those with genuine reviews (genuine group), those with promoting reviews (promoting group) and those with demoting reviews (demoting group). The values of the demoting group clearly differ from those of the genuine group. Comparing the promoting group to the genuine group, all of the hotels whose AverageNumPerMonth is larger than 15 are suspicious. This numerical difference can be captured by machine learning approaches.

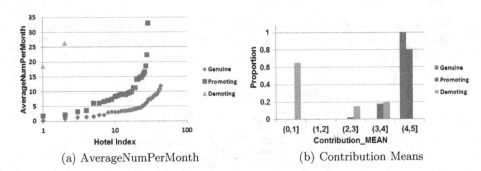

(a) AverageNumPerMonth   (b) Contribution Means

Fig. 3. Some Results for Feature Evaluation

Contribution Mean (Contribution_MEAN) is a feature specified on the reviewer level. Its value distribution is plotted in Fig. 3(b). On the x-axis, there are 5 points and each represents a range of values. The y-axis denotes the percentage of reviewers whose feature value falls into this range. Fig. 3(b) shows that the range of Contribution_MEAN of the genuine group is between 4 and 5[11]. Contribution_MEAN of the promoting group is mostly distributed between 4 and 5, whereas Contribution_MEAN of the demoting group is distributed between 0 and 4. Again, boundaries among the different groups can be learned.

5.2   Learning Results

The main learning results are shown in Table 3. For machine learning, we use the toolkit Weka[12]. Due to the experience of previous work [5,11], several classic supervised learning approaches are applied, such as linear logistic regression, SVMs and Naive Bayes. Since SVMs clearly outperform other classifiers, we only show those classification results. Achieving accuracies above 90%, identifying manipulative behavior on hotel and reviewer level seems to work quite well. Especially demoting manipulation could be detected correctly in all cases. However, the classification results on review level are not what we had expected. All the scores are much lower than those on the reviewer and hotel level. Although the accuracies ranging between 65% and 84% do not seem to be that low, the actual performance for detecting fraudulent reviews has an f-measure as low as 13% for detecting demoting behavior. Comparing non-textual features and textual features, the latter ones clearly outperform non-textual features. We draw the conclusion that it is extremely difficult to identify fraudulent reviews. More representative features for identifying suspicious reviews need to be developed. In the following part, we will focus on the results for reviewer and hotel level only.

---

[11] This is determined by the way we generate the labels for genuine reviewers within the annotation process.

[12] www.cs.waikato.ac.nz/ml/weka/

Table 3. Classification Results, where A for Accuracy, P for Precision, R for Recall and F for F-Score [2] in %. UniBigram denotes that both Unigrams and Bigrams are considered during learning process. Non-textual denotes all the corresponding features described in section 3.

			Genuine			Fraudulent		
Types	**Features**	**A**	**P**	**R**	**F**	**P**	**R**	**F**
Hotel$_{promoting}$	Non-Textual	**91.3**	100.0	87.8	93.5	76.9	100	87.0
Hotel$_{demoting}$	Non-Textual	**100.0**	100.0	100.0	100.0	100.0	100.0	100.0
Reviewer$_{promoting}$	Non-Textual	**96.4**	100	95.4	97.6	85.5	100	92.2
Reviewer$_{demoting}$	Non-Textual	**100.0**	100.0	100.0	100.0	100.0	100.0	100.0
Review$_{promoting}$	Non-Textual	65.2	71.1	68.4	69.8	57.6	60.6	59.0
Review$_{promoting}$	UniBigram	68.3	76.7	70.1	73.2	57.6	65.6	61.3
Review$_{demoting}$	Non-Textual	80.4	89.4	88.5	89	14.3	13.6	13.0
Review$_{demoting}$	UniBigram	84.3	90.0	92.0	91.0	41.7	35.7	38.5

5.3   Feature Selection

In this section, we explore the performance of the single features. Given the human annotations, features are ranked by the weight assigned by the SVMs [4]. Table 4 shows the top five features for suspicious hotel classification. As we expected, Average Number of Reviews per Month (AverageNumPerMonth) is the best feature for detecting promoting manipulation, and second best for detecting demoting manipulation. A hotel suffering from demoting manipulation usually has a large value for AverageNumPerMonth, since in order to recover from slander, the hotels "hire" reviewers to give fraudulent positive reviews. The singleton related feature is shown in the list as well.

Table 4. Top 5 Features in the Hotel Level

Ranking	Features$_{PM}$	Features$_{DM}$
1	AverageNumPerMonth	Rating_VAR
2	Rating_VAR	AverageNumPerMonth
3	RatioRoomReview	PropAdvNegativeSingleton
4	TurningDay	Rating_MEAN
5	PropAdvPositiveSingleton	VAR_MODE

Table 5 shows the top five features for suspicious reviewer classification. As we expected, Contribution Mean (Contribution_MEAN) is the top one for both promoting and demoting manipulation detection. Interestingly, Inactive Duration (InactiveDuration) is ranked second for promoting manipulation detection, since providing a singleton review usually implies a large value of InactiveDuration. Contribution Variation (ContributionVAR) is ranked third for promotion detection and second for demoting detection.

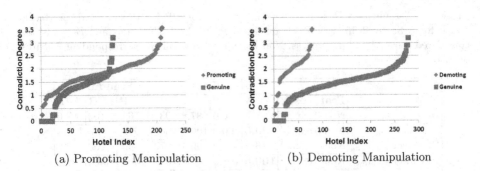

(a) Promoting Manipulation   (b) Demoting Manipulation

Fig. 4. ContradictionDegree Evaluation Results

Table 5. Top 5 Features on the Reviewer Level

Ranking	Features$_{PM}$	Features$_{DM}$
1	Contribution_MEAN	Contribution_MEAN
2	InactiveDuration	ContributionVAR
3	ContributionVAR	ContributionNum
4	TurningDay	InactiveDuration
5	ContributionNum	TimeConsecContributions_MEAN

5.4 Statistical Characteristics of Suspects

In this section, we investigate uncertain assumptions and explore statistical characteristics of suspects by considering the predictions made by our trained classifiers.

In section 3, we specify Hotel Reviews Contradiction Degree (Contradiction-Degree) with the expectation that the larger the ContradictionDegree of a hotel is, the more suspicious is the hotel. Applying the same technology for feature evaluation, we plot the ContradictionDegree value distribution for both promoting and demoting cases in Fig. 4. Hotels are ranked by their ContradictionDegree value. Both cases show that the ContradictionDegree ranges of the suspicious and the genuine group completely overlap. This result completely rejects the validity of ContradictionDegree, which is not very useful for suspect identification.

[9] considers the helpfulness of a review as a representative feature for evaluating the trustworthiness of a review. We can not evaluate this hypothesis on the review level since we do not have a good classifier. However, we can still learn some similar notion on the reviewer level where we have qualified classifiers. The helpfulness of a reviewer is equal to the sum of helpfulness of all the reviews which are provided by the reviewer. Fig. 5 shows the distribution of helpfulness of reviewers with respect to the different groups. In the dotted circle area, the value for the promoting group is much larger than that for the genuine group. It is an indirect evidence to reject the hypothesis of [9] that the more helpfulness, the less suspicious.

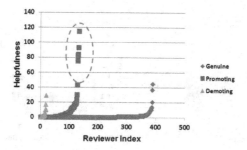

Fig. 5. Distribution of Reviewer's Helpfulness

It is not enough to restrict the observations to the human annotations, we would like to explore the statistical character of the whole dataset. One of the most important questions is what the rating distribution looks like with respect to different groups of reviewers. Do reviewers who try to promote a hotel always give 5 points? Similarly, do reviewers who try to demote a hotel always give the lowest rating? The prediction for the whole population is done using the trained classifiers. The results are shown in Fig. 6. In Fig. 6(a) we can see, regarding the predictions made by the classifier for promoting manipulation detection, that genuine reviewers provide mostly 4 or 5 points, whereas suspicious reviewers provide all from 1 to 5 points. This is a surprising insight. The proportion of 1 or 2 points given by suspicious reviewers is much larger than that given by genuine reviewers. It is shown that suspects who intend to promote a hotel provide more negative ratings than honest reviewers, which is a very counterintuitive result. A reasonable explanation for that is that it is a strategy to avoid being identified by TripAdvisor's detection algorithm. An alternative explanation is that in order to maximize the profit per account, a reviewer provides both positive and negative fraudulent reviews. For the case of demoting, which is plotted in Fig. 6(b), suspicious reviewers do not only provide negative fraudulent reviews but positive ones as well. The reason for that is similar than before. Another result we can derive is that most of the negative reviews are fraudulent. Note that, as we mentioned before, the results are subject to the particular dataset. We might draw quite different conclusions in different areas.

Regarding the ranking of hotels in terms of their reputation value, the ranking distribution of different groups is shown in Fig. 7. Three groups are extracted from the prediction which is generated by the classifiers. Promotion group refers to the set of suspicious hotels which are predicted to be related to promoting manipulative behavior; demotion group refers to the set of suspicious hotels which are predicted to be related to demoting manipulative behavior; BOTH group is the intersection of the first two groups. The x-axis represents 10 intervals that hotels fall into in terms of their ranking. For instance, the top 10% ranked hotels fall into the first interval and so on. The y-axis denotes the number of suspicious hotels which fall into an interval. Fig. 7 shows that manipulation appears in all intervals and promotion is much more popular than demotion.

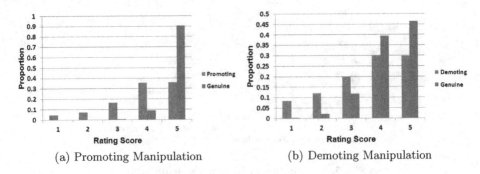

(a) Promoting Manipulation   (b) Demoting Manipulation

Fig. 6. Rating Distribution of Subpopulations

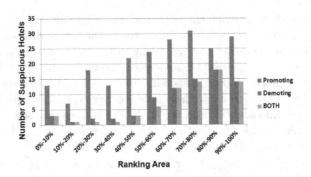

Fig. 7. Reputation Ranking Distribution of Subpopulations

Note that this result is derived from TripAdvisor, which probably already applies detection mechanisms. Even considering TripAdvisor applies manipulation prevention, there is still a number of suspects existing in the system. Another fact is that most suspicious hotels suffering from demotion are also related to promotion. It seems that promotion behavior is triggered by demotion behavior, since in order to recover from slander, the hotels "hire" reviewers to provide fraudulent positive reviews.

6   Conclusion

This paper shows the results for learning classifiers to identify manipulative behavior on the levels of reviewers and hotels, and explores the statistical characteristics of manipulative groups. The experiments are conducted on review data from TripAdvisor about NYC's hotel scene. Manipulative behavior annotations regarding the review, reviewer and hotel level are generated by taking the unanimous votes of three human annotators considering the logical relationship among the levels. Annotations for genuine behaviour are generated by the clustering approach presented in [1]. Sets of features are specified regarding different levels and types of manipulative behavior, promoting and demoting manipulation. Using the annotations and SVMs, several classifiers are learned. The results show that it is possible to learn highly accurate classifiers on the levels of reviewers and hotels, but not on the level of reviews, even considering both non-textual and textual features. Regarding the levels of reviewer and hotel, the specified features are ranked using the weight assigned by the SVMs, such as the Average Number of Reviews per Month (AverageNumPerMonth), the Contribution Mean (Contribution_MEAN) and the Hotel Reviews Contradiction Degree (ContradictionDegree). The value distributions show that different groups of suspects can be distinguished using features such as AverageNumPerMonth and Contribution_MEAN, but not using ContradictionDegree. Characteristics of the data based on the predictions of the classifiers are shown as well. The rating distribution with respect to the different groups (genuine, promoting and demoting) indicates that suspicious reviewers provide reviews with a large variation. The reason could be either that a suspicious reviewer provides both fraudulent positive and negative reviews in order to maximize the profit, or that he does this to avoid being detected by TripAdvisor's manipulation detection mechanism. Even though TripAdvisor applies prevention of manipulative behavior, there is still manipulative behavior going on attempting to take advantage of the reputation system.

The practical significance of the methodology proposed in this paper deserves to be discussed here. Supervised learning is an expensive methodology to apply in general, if the labels for the training have to be created first. However, considering the current situation of review websites like e.g. TripAdvisor and Yelp, some of them already possess labeled data regarding different levels (i.e., review, reviewer and hotel) from earlier manual manipulation detection approaches. As far as we know, some of the websites filter reviews manually. They can make accurate judgments based on the complete information they have, such as the IP address attached to a review, previous reviews written by the user, etc.. It is not as difficult to generate the annotations as we encounter in this work. A problem is that the character of manipulation might differ from region to region, e.g. it might be different in NYS compared to big cities in China due to cultural and social factors. Once obtained sufficient labeled data, there are two ways of applying supervised learning. Either different local classifiers capturing the characteristics of manipulation in a certain region could be learned, or a general classifier capturing universal characteristics could be applied. It is the freedom of analysts to make a choice depending on the dataset and the particular goal.

Regarding future work, there are several ways to improve the learning quality with respect to fraudulent review identification. The logical relationship among the different levels is not explored enough yet. This type of relationship could be used as an advanced feature for identifying fraudulent reviews. Whether a reviewer or a hotel is suspicious can be treated as a new feature for learning on the review level. Furthermore, since we have two different types of features, textual and non-textual ones, semi-supervised learning might be suitable in this case. Using semi-supervised learning we can learn from both types of information and combine them in order to achieve a better result.

References

1. Duan, H., Yang, P.: Building robust reputation systems for travel-related services. In: Proceedings of the 10th Annual Conference on Privacy, Security and Trust (PST 2012), Paris, France (2012), http://sites.google.com/site/duanhuiying/publications
2. Forman, G., Scholz, M.: Apples-to-apples in cross-validation studies: pitfalls in classifier performance measurement. SIGKDD Explorations 12(1), 49–57 (2010)
3. Gambetta, D.: Can we trust trust? In: Trust: Making and Breaking Cooperative Relations, pp. 213–237. Basil Blackwell (1988)
4. Guyon, I., Weston, J., Barnhill, S., Vapnik, V.: Gene selection for cancer classification using support vector machines. Mach. Learn. 46(1-3), 389–422 (2002)
5. Jindal, N., Liu, B.: Opinion spam and analysis. In: Proceedings of the International Conference on Web Search and Web Data Mining, WSDM 2008, pp. 219–230. ACM, New York (2008)
6. Jindal, N., Liu, B., Lim, E.P.: Finding unusual review patterns using unexpected rules. In: Proceedings of the 19th ACM International Conference on Information and Knowledge Management, CIKM 2010, pp. 1549–1552. ACM, New York (2010)
7. Lau, R.Y.K., Liao, S.Y., Kwok, R.C.W., Xu, K., Xia, Y., Li, Y.: Text mining and probabilistic language modeling for online review spam detection. ACM Trans. Manage. Inf. Syst. 2, 25:1–25:30 (2012)
8. Lim, E.P., Nguyen, V.A., Jindal, N., Liu, B., Lauw, H.W.: Detecting product review spammers using rating behaviors. In: Proceedings of the 19th ACM International Conference on Information and Knowledge Management, CIKM 2010, pp. 939–948. ACM, New York (2010)
9. O'Mahony, M.P., Smyth, B.: Learning to recommend helpful hotel reviews. In: Proceedings of the Third ACM Conference on Recommender Systems, RecSys 2009, pp. 305–308. ACM, New York (2009)
10. Ott, M., Cardie, C., Hancock, J.: Estimating the prevalence of deception in online review communities. In: Proceedings of the 21st International Conference on World Wide Web, WWW 2012, pp. 201–210. ACM, New York (2012)
11. Ott, M., Choi, Y., Cardie, C., Hancock, J.T.: Finding deceptive opinion spam by any stretch of the imagination. In: Proceedings of the 49th Annual Meeting of the Association for Computational Linguistics: Human Language Technologies, HLT 2011, vol. 1, pp. 309–319. Association for Computational Linguistics, Stroudsburg (2011)
12. Wu, G., Greene, D., Cunningham, P.: Merging multiple criteria to identify suspicious reviews. In: Proc. 4th ACM Conference on Recommender Systems, RecSys 2010 (2010)
13. Wu, G., Greene, D., Smyth, B., Cunningham, P.: Distortion as a validation criterion in the identification of suspicious reviews. In: Proceedings of the First Workshop on Social Media Analytics, SOMA 2010, pp. 10–13. ACM, New York (2010)

Privacy-Friendly Cloud Storage
for the Data Track
An Educational Transparency Tool

Tobias Pulls

Department of Computer Science
Karlstad University
Karlstad, Sweden
tobias.pulls@kau.se

Abstract. The Data Track is a transparency-enhancing tool that aims to educate users by providing them with an overview of all their data disclosures. In this paper, we describe a cryptographic scheme for storing all data disclosures tracked by the Data Track centrally in the cloud in a privacy-friendly way. Our scheme allows users to store their data anonymously, while keeping the cloud provider accountable with regard to the integrity of the data. Furthermore, we introduce a separation of concerns for the different components of the Data Track, well suited for tracking data disclosures from semi-trusted devices that may become compromised. We provide an informal evaluation of our scheme and briefly describe a proof of concept implementation.

Keywords: data track, privacy by design, anonymity, cloud storage, transparency, applied cryptography.

1 Introduction

The Data Track is a transparency-enhancing tool developed as part of the EU research projects PRIME and PrimeLife [9, 24]. It provides users with an overview of their data disclosures to service providers, allowing them to search through their history of data disclosures to see what personal data they have disclosed, to whom, and under which privacy policy. Furthermore, if supported by the service's side, the tool (even for anonymous users) facilitates remote access functionality to disclosed data. This enables users to directly assert their right to access and rectify the data concerning them, in accordance with the EU Data Protection Directive 95/46/EC [3]. Last, but not least, the Data Track allows users to request that their disclosed data should be deleted, in line with recent proposals for introducing "the right to be forgotten", as part of the proposed reform of the European data protection rules [2].

In this paper, we describe a cryptographic scheme for using cloud storage to store all of the data in the Data Track in a privacy-friendly way. The scheme

A. Jøsang and B. Carlsson (Eds.): NordSec 2012, LNCS 7617, pp. 231–246, 2012.
© Springer-Verlag Berlin Heidelberg 2012

constitutes our main contribution. While the scheme is tailored to the Data Track, parts of it may be of interest for making regular cloud storage services privacy-friendly and accountable. In particular, the way anonymous credentials are used to ensure the size of the anonymity set is a key observation in this setting. Using a history tree construct, in favour of hash chains, also provides a more efficient construct. The remainder of this section provides a motivation for the use of cloud storage and an overview of the setting. In Section 2, we explain our adversary model and derive the requirements for our scheme. The cryptographic primitives used to construct the scheme are described in Section 3. Section 4 presents the scheme, which is informally evaluated in Section 5. Section 6 describes related work. Finally, Section 7 concludes this paper.

1.1 Motivation

The Data Track, as designed in PRIME and PrimeLife [9, 24], depends on a middleware called the PRIME Core [17, 29]. The PRIME Core is a privacy-friendly identity management system consisting of user- and services-side software. The PRIME Core running at the user-side provides local storage and the ability to track data disclosures for the Data Track. On the services-side the PRIME Core enables remote access to disclosed data. One of the major drawbacks of this reliance on the PRIME Core, which also contains a lot of other functionality not needed by the Data Track[1], is the use of local storage. Today individuals use (and hence disclose data from) multiple devices, including but not limited to smartphones, tablets and laptops. There is a clear need to track data disclosures from all devices users use to provide a comprehensive overview. Instead of synchronising data disclosures from multiple instances of local storage, the natural solution is to introduce a central storage in the cloud.

With cloud storage, all tracked data disclosures would be written to a central location in the cloud. To display data disclosures they would be read from the cloud. This approach introduces the added benefit of *separation of concerns*. Software responsible for tracking, storing and displaying data disclosures can be distinct. This is especially beneficial for tracking data disclosures, since some devices might be resource constrained and only used to disclose data, not to view data disclosures. One reason for this might be that users only trust a few selected devices with the capability of viewing all their data disclosures, while they wish to track data disclosures from semi-trusted devices as well.

In essence, the Data Track scheme stores a copy of all data a user ever discloses to any service provider. It is apparent that such a scheme needs to be privacy-friendly. Without assuring users that it is safe to use the Data Track, the potential downside of using the tool far outweighs any potential benefits.

---

[1] The PRIME Core performs local and remote access control, issues and fetches credentials, supports access policies and provides several user interfaces. For a full list see [29].

1.2 Overview of the Setting

Figure 1 shows an overview of the setting for the Data Track using cloud storage. The cloud provider is a service provider that *issues* credentials to their users so that they can *claim* storage nodes run by the cloud provider. Each storage node offers an identical amount of storage. When a user claims a storage node, the cloud provider *verifies* that the credential the user presents was issued by the cloud provider and has not already been used. When a user has claimed a storage node the node belongs to the user until released by the user.

To track data disclosures, a user uses one or more *Data Track Agents*, which are extensions to applications used to disclose data. A prime example is a browser extension that tracks data disclosed by the user through web forms. When a user discloses data to remote services through an application that has a Data Track Agent running, the agent will detect the data disclosure and write it to the user's storage node at the cloud provider. As data is written, the agent assists in creating an index over the disclosed data. The index is used to enable searching over the content of a data disclosure.

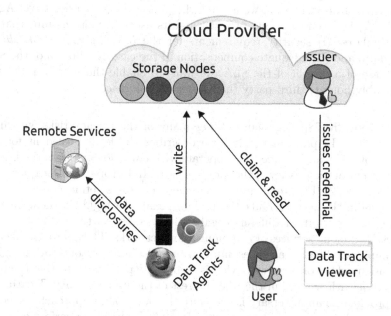

Fig. 1. Overview of the setting for the Data Track using cloud storage

To view all tracked data disclosures, a user uses the *Data Track Viewer*, which is an application that is running locally on one of the user's devices. With the user's credentials, the Data Track Viewer allows the user to read all the user's data disclosures stored in the user's storage node at the cloud provider. Also, it assists the user in communication with the remote services side, to for example access or rectify data, if the remote services allow it.

2   Adversary Model and Requirements

In this section we first define our adversary model, then define some requirements that our scheme should fulfil.

2.1   Adversary Model

Our main adversary is the cloud provider. Furthermore, we assume that Data Track Agents can become compromised, potentially in collusion with the malicious cloud provider. We only trust Data Track Agents at the time of data being disclosed[2]. The Data Track Viewer is fully trusted. For the sake of scope we consider the network benign and unobservable. We make the typical assumptions about the strength of the cryptographic primitives (as in the Dolev-Yao model), introduced in Section 3. Next, we briefly describe service level agreements, a key part of our adversary model, and then motivate our adversary model.

Service Level Agreements. Using a similar approach to that of CloudProof [23] (discussed in Section 6), we assume the presence of a Service Level Agreement (SLA) between the cloud provider and its users. We also assume that the SLA stipulates: (i) security requirements for the *integrity* and *availability* of stored data, and (ii) adequate compensation in the case of a breach of the SLA. In the case of a breach of the SLA, we want to enable the user to prove to a (presumably honest) third party that a breach took place.

Motivation. In [28], Soghoian outlines many of the privacy risks with using cloud services. In particular detail, he describes the legal precedent for how service providers can be forced to cooperate with law enforcement in the U.S., to the detriment of the privacy of the service's users. In Europe, the Data Retention Directive 2006/24/EC [16] requires that member states retain communication data (including location) for all citizens. These examples highlight the willingness of governments to grant different legal entities access to the data of users of services, be it cloud services or communication networks. The approach taken by, for example, intelligence agencies, military organisations, or totalitarian regimes can be assumed to converge with what is technically possible to further their own agenda, not with what is in the best interest of the users' privacy. Treating the cloud provider as an adversary is therefore the only sound approach, especially in our case where the provider stores all data disclosures ever performed by the user.

2.2   Requirements

Below, we define four key requirements for our scheme: confidentiality of disclosed data, ensuring that the cloud provider can be held accountable, minimally trusted agents, and anonymous storage. The definition of confidentiality

---

[2] This is the minimal amount of trust possible to assign in this setting, see [13, 14].

is given in Requirement 1. Confidentiality of disclosed data is a bare minimum for ensuring the privacy of the users of the Data Track.

Requirement 1 (Confidentiality of disclosed data). *The data disclosures stored at the cloud provider are considered confidential iff the user whom disclosed data is the only entity that can read the copy of the disclosed data, once it has been stored at the cloud provider.*

Ensuring that the cloud provider can be held accountable, as defined in Requirement 2, is our approach to indirectly ensure availability and integrity of the stored data. Due to the nature of our setting, the cloud provider can always deny service. The best we can strive for is to be able to prove that the provider is indeed denying service or has modified data, and hope for any compensation, as part of for example a SLA.

Requirement 2 (An accountable cloud provider). *The cloud provider is considered accountable iff a user of the service can prove to a third party that the provider (i) has agreed to offer the user service, (ii) has agreed to store specific data for the user, and (iii) cannot violate the integrity of the specific data without being detected.*

Minimally trusting Data Track Agents, defined in Requirement 3, enables users to track data disclosures made from semi-trusted devices. While having to trust a Data Track Agent at the time of data disclosure is not ideal, we believe it is unavoidable. According to [13, 14], this is to be considered the minimal trust model in this setting.

Requirement 3 (Minimally trusted agents). *A Data Track Agent is minimally trusted iff (i) all the information, except for the contents of data disclosures, known by the agent is also known by the cloud provider, and (ii) the agent only has to be trusted at the time of data disclosure.*

Requirements 1–3, if realised, greatly restricts a malicious cloud provider from invading the privacy of its users. However, the provider could still target a specific user and his or her (albeit confidential) data. This would allow the provider to profile a specific user, in essence performing traffic analysis [15] on the access to the stored data, or abusing other side-channels present in the service [18, 25]. Therefore, there is a need for anonymous storage, as defined in Requirement 4, to break the link between users and stored data.

Requirement 4 (Anonymous storage). *A user is considered anonymous iff he or she is not identifiable, by the cloud provider, within the set of potential users who may own a specific storage node.*[3]

With Requirement 4 in place, the cloud provider cannot target the storage of a specific user of its service. If, for example, the provider is ordered by a force majeure to profile or deny service for a particular user the provider would have to target every user in the anonymity set to ensure compliance with the order.

---

[3] This definition is based on the anonymity definition by Pfitzmann and Hansen [22].

3   Cryptographic Primitives

In this section, we describe the cryptographic primitives we use as part of our scheme. *Encryption* and *signatures* are used to provide confidentiality and play a role in providing accountability. *History trees* provide us with a way to ensure integrity of stored data and are another piece of the puzzle in providing accountability. *Anonymous credentials* are used to enable users to claim storage nodes anonymously.

3.1   Encryption and Signatures

To provide confidentiality of stored data, as defined in Requirement 1, we opt for using an asymmetric encryption algorithm. With asymmetric encryption, we can provide the Data Track Agents with a public key, while keeping the corresponding private key secret.

Furthermore, with regard to Requirement 4, there is a need for *probabilistic encryption* using an algorithm with the *key privacy* [4] property. Probabilistic encryption is needed to prevent the cloud provider from encrypting known plaintext with the public key of a user and successfully comparing it with ciphertext it has stored on the user's behalf. Similarly, the key privacy property prevents the provider from determining which public key (out of all the public keys it knows) was used to encrypt a given ciphertext.

Last, but not least, there is a need for the encryption algorithm to be indistinguishable under adaptive chosen-ciphertext attack (IND-CCA2) secure [5]. This is needed because, in our setting, the cloud provider could insert arbitrary ciphertext into a user's storage node which later on the user (after decrypting) may provide directly or indirectly to the cloud provider as part of a complaint.

Signatures are used as part of our scheme when the cloud provider attests[4] to some value. In the scheme, only the cloud provider performs signatures. This means that the signatures are only relevant with regard to Requirement 2. For this definition, the only required property for the signature algorithm is *non-repudiation*. Non-repudiation ensures that the cloud provider cannot later deny having signed anything they have in fact signed.

To summarise, for encryption we use an asymmetric probabilistic encryption algorithm with key privacy that is IND-CCA2 secure[5]. For encrypting a message with a public key and decrypting with a (secret) private key we use the following notation: $\mathtt{Dec}_{sk}(\mathtt{Enc}_{pk}(\text{message})) = \text{message}$. For signatures, our only requirement is that the signature algorithm provides non-repudiation. We denote signing a message using a (secret) private key as $\mathtt{Sig}_{sk}(\text{message})$.

---

[4] We use the term attestation in favour of commitment to avoid confusion with credentials in our notation.

[5] An adept reader will note that IND-CCA2 secure implies IND-CPA secure which in turn requires probabilistic encryption.

3.2   History Trees

To make sure that the cloud provider can be held accountable, as defined in Requirement 2, a key building block is a *history tree* as described by Crosby and Wallach [13, 14]. A history tree is a tamper-evident history data structure. In essence, it is a (not necessarily balanced) binary hash tree together with five algorithms. All entries in a history tree are leaf nodes, while intermediate nodes are hashes of their corresponding child nodes. The root node is the hash of its children, which value ultimately depends on all leaf nodes. We require that the underlying hash algorithm is collision and preimage free.

Crosby and Wallach define a tamper-evident history system as consisting of the following five algorithms, adjusted to our notation and setting:[6]

- $\texttt{Add}(H, E) \to A_i$. Given an entry E the system appends it to the history tree H as the i:th entry and then outputs an attestation[7] A_i.
- $\texttt{IncGen}(H, A_i, A_j) \to p$. Generates an incremental proof p between A_i and A_j, where $i \leq j$, from the history tree H. Outputs p.
- $\texttt{MembershipGen}(H, i, A_j) \to (p, E_i)$. Generates a membership proof p for the i:th entry from attestation A_j, where $i \leq j$, from the history tree H. The algorithm outputs p and the entry E_i.
- $\texttt{IncVerify}(p, A'_i, A_j) \to \{\top, \bot\}$. Verifies that p proves that A_j fixes every entry fixed by A'_i (where $i \leq j$). Outputs $\top$ if true, otherwise $\bot$.
- $\texttt{MembershipVerify}(p, i, A_j, E'_i) \to \{\top, \bot\}$. Verifies that p proves that E'_i is the i:th entry in the history defined by A_j (where $i \leq j$). Outputs $\top$ if true, otherwise $\bot$.

The first three algorithms are run by the cloud provider, who maintains a history tree for each storage node. The outputs of the first three algorithms are signed by the provider when given to the user. The user can then use the two last algorithms to verify the integrity and consistency of his or her stored data.

3.3   Anonymous Credentials

For anonymity, defined in Requirement 4, we use the anonymous credential system *idemix* by Camenisch et al. [6, 8, 10, 11, 19]. The idemix system has a large number of of privacy-friendly features compared to regular (for example X.509) credentials, such as providing unlinkability between issuance and usage of a credential, allowing selective attribute disclosure, and the ability to prove properties of a credential without revealing any of its attributes. While privacy-friendly, idemix is also extendable to introduce limited spending, tracing of specific attributes on a credential, and revocation of credentials.

In our scheme, we rely on (i) the fact that issuing and usage of a credential is unlinkable, (ii) that it is possible to prove predicates over attributes using zero-knowledge proofs, and (iii) the ability to create *domain pseudonyms*. Without

---

[6] These definitions are in parts verbatim from Crosby and Wallach [13, 14].
[7] An attestation A_i is the root of the history tree for the i:th entry.

the property that the issuing and usage of credentials are unlinkable, idemix would be unsuited for our scheme because the cloud provider is both the issuer and verifier of the credentials. The possibility to prove predicates over attributes is used to define the anonymity set for the user, discussed later in Section 5.4. A domain pseudonym is a unique identifier generated for a particular credential for a particular domain. One credential can only be used to generate one valid domain pseudonym per domain[8], hence the name. This is used in our scheme to ensure that one credential can only be used to claim one storage node.

4   The Data Track Scheme

We assume that each participant has generated any necessary keying material in advance. Furthermore, we assume that all relevant public cryptographic parameters are known to all participants. This includes, but is not limited to, the public key of the cloud provider, the public keys of all users, and the keying material for issuing idemix credentials. We also assume that all cryptographic primitives reach a minimum security level of s bits (Shannon entropy).

For our scheme, there is one publicly known value that is of utmost importance: τ. τ is set by the cloud provider to a value representing a point in time in the future. For example, τ could be set to midnight the following day at the time of issuance. While the cloud provider sets the value, every participant in our scheme can verify that τ is set to the expected value. To enable this, we presume that all participants can agree on the current time in sufficient resolution (minutes would suffice). The role of τ is explained later in Section 5.4. Next, we present the Data Track scheme.

Protocol 1 describes the setup of the Data Track service between the cloud provider and a user. A credential is issued that later is used to claim a storage node at the provider. Note that it is not possible in (2) for the user to construct a valid proof until after the current time is past the attribute t in the credential.

Protocol 1. Service setup between the cloud provider P and user U

$$P \longrightarrow U : \text{idemix credential } C \text{ with attribute } t, \text{ where } t \leftarrow \tau \qquad (1)$$

$$U \longrightarrow P : \text{idemix proof } p \text{ that } C_t < c, \text{ where } c \text{ is the current time} \qquad (2)$$

$$P : \text{extracts domain pseudonym } d \text{ from } p, \text{ creates storage} \qquad (3)$$
$$\text{node } N_d \text{ and history tree } H_d$$

$$P \longrightarrow U : (\text{Sign}_{sk}(L_{N_d}, d), L_{N_d}), \text{ where } L_{N_d} \text{ is the location of} \qquad (4)$$
$$\text{storage node } N_d \text{ and } sk \text{ is the signing key of the provider}$$

---

[8] A domain is a value selected by the verifier as part of generating an idemix proof.

Protocol 2 describes how a user, after having claimed a storage node, can later authenticate themselves as the owner of that storage node by proving possession of the domain pseudonym used to claim the node in question. Once authenticated, we assume that the provider is convinced for the remainder of the session that the user is in possession the credential for domain pseudonym d.

Protocol 2. Authentication between the cloud provider P and user U, authenticating access to storage node N_d claimed as part of the service setup described in Protocol 1

$$U \longrightarrow P : \text{idemix proof } p \text{ of possession of domain pseudonym } d \quad (5)$$
$$U : \text{generates a random } r \leftarrow_R \{1,0\}^s \quad (6)$$
$$U \longrightarrow P : (\text{Enc}_{pk}(r), n, M_a) \rightarrow \text{entry, where } M_a \text{ is a marker} \quad (7)$$
$$\text{for the entry type and } n \text{ the current time now}$$
$$P : \text{Add}(H_d, \text{entry}) \rightarrow A_i \quad (8)$$
$$P \longrightarrow U : (\text{Sign}_{sk}(A_i, d), A_i), \text{ where } A_i \text{ is the attestation} \quad (9)$$

Protocol 3 describes the setup of a new Data Track Agent. The agent authenticates with the help of a password (shared secret) to the cloud provider when writing, see (20), in Protocol 4.

Protocol 3. Data Track Agent setup between the cloud provider P and user U, to setup the agent G

$$U \longleftrightarrow P : \text{authentication, see Protocol 2} \quad (10)$$
$$U : \text{generates a random } r \leftarrow_R \{1,0\}^s \quad (11)$$
$$U \longrightarrow P : r \quad (12)$$
$$P : \text{adds } r \text{ as a valid password to write to } N_d \quad (13)$$
$$P \longrightarrow U : \text{Sign}_{sk}(r, L_{N_d}, d) \rightarrow s \quad (14)$$
$$U \longrightarrow P : (\text{Enc}_{pk}(r, s), n, M_g) \rightarrow \text{entry} \quad (15)$$
$$P : \text{Add}(H_d, \text{entry}) \rightarrow A_i \quad (16)$$
$$P \longrightarrow U : \text{Sign}_{sk}(A_i, d), A_i \quad (17)$$
$$U \longrightarrow G : (L_{N_d}, r, pk, A_i) \quad (18)$$

Protocol 4 describes how a Data Track Agent writes to the cloud storage. In (19), the index is a Bloom filter with fixed (presumably globally known) parameters. In (24), we assume that (as noted in our adversary model in Section 2) the communication between G and U is unobservable by the provider.[9]

Protocol 4. Between agent G with (L_{N_d}, r, pk, A_i), belonging to U, who wishes to write *data* to N_d, and the cloud provider P:

$$G : \text{generates an } index \text{ for searching over } data \tag{19}$$
$$G \longrightarrow P : (r, L_{N_d}) \tag{20}$$
$$G \longrightarrow P : (\text{Enc}_{pk}(index), \text{Enc}_{pk}(data), n, M_d) \to \text{entry} \tag{21}$$
$$P : \text{Add}(H_d, \text{entry}) \to A_j \tag{22}$$
$$P \longrightarrow G : (\text{Sign}_{sk}(A_j, d), A_j) \to (s, A_j) \tag{23}$$
$$G \longrightarrow U : (s, A_j) \tag{24}$$

Protocol 5 describes how the user verifies the integrity and consistency of the data stored at the cloud provider. Similarly, as IncGen and IncVerify are used in (28) and (30), MembershipGen and MembershipVerify respectively (as described in Section 3.2) could be used to accomplish the same task.

Protocol 5. Between the provider P and user U, where U has a list of attestations $(A_0, A_1, .., A_{i-1}, A_i)$:

$$U \longleftrightarrow P : \text{authentication, see Protocol 2} \tag{25}$$
$$U : r_1, r_2 \leftarrow_R [0, i+1], \text{ where } r_1 < r_2 \tag{26}$$
$$U \longrightarrow P : (A_{r_1}, A_{r_2}) \tag{27}$$
$$P : \text{IncGen}(H_d, A_{r_1}, A_{r_2}) \to p \tag{28}$$
$$P \longrightarrow U : p \tag{29}$$
$$U : \text{IncVerify}(p, A_{r_1}, A_{r_2}) \to \{\top, \bot\} \tag{30}$$

For reading data from a storage node, the cloud provider requires that the user proves possession of the credential used to claim the node. This was described in Protocol 2. Once authenticated, the user can request entry by index, entry type, or time. As part of the authentication procedure, the user received an attestation A_i for the last entry stored in his or her history tree. From this, the user knows that the index range for entries are $[0, i]$. The entry type, specified

---

[9] This leads to an uncertainty for the provider if an agent has really sent the returned signed attestation or not, which may be exploited by the user to save space by simply skipping (24). When a user authenticates to the provider, as described in Protocol 2, the provider is forced to commit to a state of the entire history tree in (9). At this point, the provider has to decide if he wants to attempt to fork the history tree to discard any data written in (16) or not.

by its marker (M_a for authentication, M_g for agents, and M_d for disclosures) is known by the cloud provider. Similarly, the cloud provider knows the timestamp for when an entry was added. Naturally, the user needs to verify the integrity and completeness of the replies, using the integrity verification as described in Protocol 5 and further inspection of the proofs returned by the cloud provider, unspecified in this paper due to space constraints.

Protocol 6 describes how a user would use the index constructed by agents, in (19), to search for data without having to download the majority of the data stored at the cloud provider[10].

Protocol 6. Between the provider P and user U, where U has a list of attestations $(A_0, A_1, .., A_{i-1}, A_i)$:

$$U \longleftrightarrow P : \text{authentication, see Protocol 2} \tag{31}$$
$$U : \text{selects keyword } k \text{ to search for in timeframe } [t_x, t_{x+1}] \tag{32}$$
$$U \longleftrightarrow P : \text{get index part of all entries in timeframe } [t_x, t_{x+1}] \tag{33}$$
$$U : \text{decrypt and check each index for } k \tag{34}$$
$$U \longleftrightarrow P : \text{download matching entries} \tag{35}$$

What has just been presented is a bare-bones version of the Data Track scheme. Features left unspecified due to lack of space include (but are not limited to) (i) freeing a storage node and reclaiming a credential, (ii) integrity verification by agents, (iii) the procedure for requesting a range of entries either by time, index or type, (iv) deleting data, and (v) revoking agents.

5 Informal Evaluation

Section 2.2 defined four requirements for the Data Track scheme. In this section, we evaluate our scheme as it was described in Section 4 and argue as to why the proposed scheme fulfils the different requirements.

5.1 Confidentiality of Disclosed Data

Since (i) the encryption algorithm is IND-CCA2 secure, (ii) all data disclosures are encrypted before uploaded to the cloud provider (see (21)), and (iii) only the user knows the private key for decrypting the data, the data disclosures stored in our scheme are confidential with regard to Requirement 1.

---

[10] If the Bloom filters are configured to store up to 95 keywords with a false positive rate of 10^{-9}, using 30 different hash functions, then the size of one index is 4098 bits. If a user performs one data disclosure every hour for a non-leap year then the total size of all indexes for all the data disclosures made that year is 4382 KiB.

5.2 An Accountable Cloud Provider

Our definition of accountability, Requirement 2, requires that a user is able to prove to a third party that the cloud provider: **(i)** has agreed to offer the user service, **(ii)** has agreed to store specific data for the user, and **(iii)** cannot violate the integrity of the specific data without being detected.

For item (i), the credential issued by the cloud provider can ipso facto be attributed to being issued by the provider. Furthermore, as part of the service setup in (4), the provider signs that a given location for a storage node belongs to a particular domain pseudonym. The domain pseudonym in turn can only be generated with a particular credential. A user may cryptographically show their domain pseudonym for a particular domain to any party, simply because the domain is just a value selected by the verifying party [19].

For item (ii), the cloud provider provides a signed attestation for each piece of data stored in (9), (17), and (23). All signatures are non-repudiate, as defined in Section 3.1, and verifiable by a third party.

For item (iii), data is stored at the cloud provider in (8), (16), and (22). Integrity protection of data stored for authentication purposes, more precisely the domain pseudonym in (3) and password in (13), are considered out of scope since any modification by the cloud provider of these values are equivalent to denying service, which we consider out of scope of our scheme. So, all relevant data stored at the cloud provider is added to a history tree, and in the respective subsequent equations (9), (17), and (23) the data is signed by the provider to be part of the same history tree for the same domain pseudonym. We note that all signatures are non-reputable, as specified in Section 3.1. Therefore, the cloud provider cannot deny that all attestations returned in (9), (17), and (23) belong to the same history tree. With this in mind, making undetectable modifications to the stored data is reduced to either breaking the history tree or the underlying hash algorithm. The hash algorithm is, per definition in Section 3.2, collision and preimage free. This is a sufficient condition for the history tree to be provably consistent, see [14, p. 38–41]. Thus, in our proposed scheme the cloud provider can be held accountable with regard to Requirement 2.

5.3 Minimally Trusted Agents

Data Track Agents are minimally trusted, with regard to Requirement 3, since: (i) all the information given to agents, as specified in (18), are already known by the cloud provider, and (ii) agents only play a role in detecting and writing data disclosures (see Protocol 3), at which point in time they are trusted.

5.4 Anonymous Storage

To show that our proposed scheme offers anonymous storage, as defined in Requirement 4, we need to show that: **(i)** the anonymous credentials are indeed anonymous, **(ii)** that the way we use anonymous credentials create an anonymity set in which owners of storage nodes cannot be identified, and **(iii)** that no other part of the scheme leaks information that the cloud provider can use to identify a user.

For item (i), Camenisch and Lysyanskaya in [10, 11] show that their so called CL signatures (a building block of idemix) allows a holder to convince a verifier of possession of a valid signature on a message from an issuer without revealing neither the signature nor the message. This holds even if the issuer and verifier are the same entity or collude [10, 11, 19]. Proving an inequality, in our case the *lesser-than* inequality, is possible without revealing any value [19].

For item (ii), we use the issued credentials in two different ways: (i) to prove possession of a credential with a domain pseudonym, and (ii) to claim a storage node. Proving possession of a credential with a specific domain pseudonym, as done in (5), can be done without revealing any other information [19]. When a user claims a storage node in (2), an inequality proof is constructed that an attribute of the credential, t, is less than the current time c. The value of the attribute t is determined at the time of issuance in (1), and is set to a time in the future τ. The time Δ between issuance and the value of τ, which the attribute of all issued credentials depend on, is key in creating our anonymity set.

Figure 2 shows an example timeline of how our anonymity set is created. Between t_0 and t_1 the value of τ is set to t_1. After t_1, five users can construct the proof needed in (2). Between t_1 to t_2, the value of τ is set to t_2 and seven new users are issued credentials. After t_2 there are seven people, and all the people that did not yet claim a storage node from the period t_0 to t_1, that can perform (2). So, to generalise, the anonymity set at t_x is defined as all the people that got issued a credential in the time period t_{x-1} to t_x, plus any additional people that are yet to claim a storage node from previous time periods.

Fig. 2. An example timeline of how our anonymity set is created

For item (iii), beyond the interactions with the issued anonymous credential, the provider gets encrypted data, random values, indexes, or attestations. The encrypted data, in (7), (15), and (21), are encrypted with a IND-CCA2 secure probabilistic encryption algorithm that has key privacy. This prevents the cloud provider from deducing any useful information from the ciphertext. The random values, provided in (12) and (20), are randomly generated and therefore leak no information. The indexes, provided in (33), (35) and when reading data, are all already known by the provider. Last, but not least, the attestations provided in (27) are already known by the provider and give no further information. Thus, our proposed scheme provides anonymity with regard to Requirement 4.

5.5   Proof of Concept

To further evaluate the feasibility our scheme we have created a proof of concept implementation in Java. It uses the idemix [19] and Bouncy Castle [1] libraries for cryptographic operations. Crosby and Wallach's history tree had to be implemented from scratch. The source code is available upon request under any reasonably permissive and free license.

6   Related Work

Kamara et al. provide both a good overview of what is possible in the cloud storage setting in terms of cryptographically securing a service [20], and a provably secure cryptographic cloud storage system named CS2 [21]. Soghoian, as mentioned earlier in Section 2, highlights the potential dangers of trusting cloud providers [28]. Several other works investing potential problems with how cloud storage services are constructed can be found in the literature, such as [18, 25].

For anonymity and cloud storage, the scheme by Slamanig [27] is closely related to our approach. They focus on fine-grained resource usage (such as storage) in an anonymous way in the cloud setting, using CL signatures [11], which are also used in idemix. Beyond the difference in focus, where we see each storage node as equal in size and Slamanig deals exclusively with fine-grained resource usage, the settings differ due to our notion of separation of concerns. Our Data Track Agents are minimally trusted, and mapping the scheme by Slamanig to our setting would require the agents to have full access to the credential.

Popa et al., with their cloud storage system CloudProof [23], sets the precedence for enabling security properties for cloud storage through the use of SLAs. We use a similar setting for our adversary model, described in Section 2, where the cloud provider continuously attests to the state of the storage as part of the scheme. However, CloudProof uses hash chains for their storage, where we instead opt for the use of history trees. History trees, compared to hash chains, allow for more efficient proofs to be constructed ($O(\log_2 n)$ vs $O(n)$ [13]).

For searching, our approach is identical to that taken by Chang et al. for Bigtable [12], where Bloom filters are used to reduce the number of disk reads. We opt for not using searchable encryption schemes, for the sake of simplicity and due to issues highlighted by Shen et al. [26] and Bellare et al. [7].

7   Concluding Remarks

We have presented a scheme for the Data Track using cloud storage, where a user can *anonymously* claim some storage space by an untrusted cloud provider. The user can add Data Track Agents, small extensions to applications, that tracks the user's data disclosures and stores them at the cloud provider. These agents are *minimally trusted*. The user can read all of their data disclosures from the cloud provider using their Data Track Viewer. All the data stored at the cloud provider is *confidential*. Last, but not least, the cloud provider can be held *accountable* with regard to the data it stores and the service it is offering. Interesting future work would be to generalise the scheme for generic cloud storage services, and tackle the issue of how to manage payment in a privacy-friendly way.

Acknowledgements. We received a number of useful comments from Stefan Berthold, Simone Fischer-Hübner, Stefan Lindskog, Philipp Winter, and the reviewers of NordSec 2012. This work has been funded by a Google research award on "Usable Privacy and Transparency Tools".

References

[1] The Legion of the Bouncy Castle, http://bouncycastle.org/, (accessed June 5, 2012)

[2] Commission proposes a comprehensive reform of the data protection rules (January 2012), http://ec.europa.eu/justice/newsroom/data-protection/news/120125_en.htm (accessed April 24, 2012)

[3] Directive 95/46/EC of the European Parliament and of the Council of 24, on the protection of individuals with regard to the processing of personal data and on the free movement of such data (23111995) (October 1995)

[4] Bellare, M., Boldyreva, A., Desai, A., Pointcheval, D.: Key-Privacy in Public-Key Encryption. In: Boyd, C. (ed.) ASIACRYPT 2001. LNCS, vol. 2248, pp. 203–211. Springer, Heidelberg (2001)

[5] Bellare, M., Desai, A., Pointcheval, D., Rogaway, P.: Relations among Notions of Security for Public-Key Encryption Schemes. In: Krawczyk, H. (ed.) CRYPTO 1998. LNCS, vol. 1462, pp. 26–45. Springer, Heidelberg (1998)

[6] Bichsel, P., Camenisch, J., Preiss, F.-S.: A comprehensive framework enabling data-minimizing authentication. In: Proceedings of the 7th ACM Workshop on Digital Identity Management, DIM 2011, pp. 13–22. ACM Press, New York (2011), http://doi.acm.org/10.1145/2046642.2046647

[7] Byun, J.W., Rhee, H.S., Park, H.-A., Lee, D.-H.: Off-Line Keyword Guessing Attacks on Recent Keyword Search Schemes over Encrypted Data. In: Jonker, W., Petković, M. (eds.) SDM 2006. LNCS, vol. 4165, pp. 75–83. Springer, Heidelberg (2006)

[8] Camenisch, J., Van Herreweghen, E.: Design and implementation of the *idemix* anonymous credential system. In: Atluri, V. (ed.) ACM Conference on Computer and Communications Security, pp. 21–30. ACM (2002)

[9] Camenisch, J., Leenes, R., Sommer, D. (eds.): PRIME – Privacy and Identity Management for Europe. LNCS, vol. 6545. Springer, Berlin (2011)

[10] Camenisch, J.L., Lysyanskaya, A.: An Efficient System for Non-transferable Anonymous Credentials with Optional Anonymity Revocation. In: Pfitzmann, B. (ed.) EUROCRYPT 2001. LNCS, vol. 2045, pp. 93–118. Springer, Heidelberg (2001)

[11] Camenisch, J., Lysyanskaya, A.: Signature Schemes and Anonymous Credentials from Bilinear Maps. In: Franklin, M. (ed.) CRYPTO 2004. LNCS, vol. 3152, pp. 56–72. Springer, Heidelberg (2004)

[12] Chang, F., Dean, J., Ghemawat, S., Hsieh, W.C., Wallach, D.A., Burrows, M., Chandra, T., Fikes, A., Gruber, R.E.: Bigtable: a distributed storage system for structured data. In: Proceedings of the 7th USENIX Symposium on Operating Systems Design and Implementation, OSDI 2006, vol. 7, pp. 15–15. USENIX Association, Berkeley (2006)

[13] Crosby, S.A., Wallach, D.S.: Efficient data structures for tamper-evident logging. In: USENIX Security Symposium, pp. 317–334. USENIX Association (2009)

[14] Crosby, S.A.: Efficient tamper-evident data structures for untrusted servers. Ph.D. thesis, Houston, TX, USA (2010), aAI3421155

[15] Danezis, G., Clayton, R.: Introducing traffic analysis. In: Attacks, Defences and Public Policy Issues. CRC Press (2007)

[16] EUR-Lex - Access to European Union law (2012), http://eur-lex.europa.eu/LexUriServ/LexUriServ.do?uri=CELEX: 32006L0024:EN:NOT (accessed May 14, 2012)

[17] Fischer-Hübner, S., Hedbom, H., Wästlund, E.: Trust and assurance hci. In: Camenisch, J., Fischer-Hübner, S., Rannenberg, K. (eds.) Privacy and Identity Management for Life, pp. 245–260. Springer, Heidelberg (2011)

[18] Harnik, D., Pinkas, B., Shulman-Peleg, A.: Side channels in cloud services: Deduplication in cloud storage. IEEE Security & Privacy 8(6), 40–47 (2010)

[19] IBM Research – Zurich: Specification of the identity mixer cryptographic library – version 2.3.4 (2012), https://prime.inf.tu-dresden.de/idemix/

[20] Kamara, S., Lauter, K.: Cryptographic Cloud Storage. In: Sion, R., Curtmola, R., Dietrich, S., Kiayias, A., Miret, J.M., Sako, K., Sebé, F. (eds.) RLCPS, WECSR, and WLC 2010. LNCS, vol. 6054, pp. 136–149. Springer, Heidelberg (2010)

[21] Kamara, S., Papamanthou, C., Roeder, T.: CS2: A semantic cryptographic cloud storage system. Tech. Rep. MSR-TR-2011-58, Microsoft Technical Report (May 2011), http://research.microsoft.com/apps/pubs/?id=148632

[22] Pfitzmann, A., Hansen, M.: A terminology for talking about privacy by data minimization: Anonymyity, unlinkability, undetectability, unobservability, pseudonymity, and identity management (August 2010)

[23] Popa, R.A., Lorch, J.R., Molnar, D., Wang, H.J., Zhuang, L.: Enabling security in cloud storage slas with cloudproof. In: Proceedings of the 2011 USENIX Conference on USENIX Annual Technical Conference, USENIXATC 2011, pp. 31–31. USENIX Association, Berkeley (2011)

[24] PrimeLife WP4.2: End User Transparency Tools: UI Prototypes. In: Wästlund, E., Fischer-Hübner, S. (eds.) PrimeLife Deliverable D4.2.2. PrimeLife (June 2010), http://www.PrimeLife.eu/results/documents

[25] Pulls, T. (More) Side Channels in Cloud Storage. In: Camenisch, J., Crispo, B., Fischer-Hübner, S., Leenes, R., Russello, G. (eds.) Privacy and Identity 2011. IFIP AICT, vol. 375, pp. 102–115. Springer, Heidelberg (2012)

[26] Shen, E., Shi, E., Waters, B.: Predicate Privacy in Encryption Systems. In: Reingold, O. (ed.) TCC 2009. LNCS, vol. 5444, pp. 457–473. Springer, Heidelberg (2009)

[27] Slamanig, D.: Efficient Schemes for Anonymous Yet Authorized and Bounded Use of Cloud Resources. In: Miri, A., Vaudenay, S. (eds.) SAC 2011. LNCS, vol. 7118, pp. 73–91. Springer, Heidelberg (2012)

[28] Soghoian, C.: Caught in the cloud: Privacy, encryption, and government back doors in the Web 2.0 era. Journal on Telecommunications and High Technology Law 8(2), 359–424 (2010)

[29] Sommer, D., Mont, M.C., Pearson, S.: Prime architecture v3 (July 2008), https://www.prime-project.eu/

Author Index

Adolphi, Benjamin 17

Blom, Arjan 1
Brune, Philipp 73

Clark, Jason W. 199
Clarke, Dave 121

de Koning Gans, Gerhard 1
de Ruiter, Joeri 1
Duan, Huiying 215

Fritsch, Lothar 169

Groner, Ramona 73

Hallberg, Jonas 47
Hansen, René Rydhof 31
Helkala, Kirsi 153

Jensen, Torben 31
John, Wolfgang 184

Langweg, Hanno 17

Massacci, Fabio 89
Mellstrand, Per 137
Milushev, Dimiter 121

Nikiforakis, Nick 105
Noorman, Job 105

Olesen, Mads Chr. 31
Olovsson, Tomas 184

Paci, Federica 89
Pedersen, Heine 31
Piessens, Frank 105
Poll, Erik 1
Proctor, Tony 61
Pulls, Tobias 231

Rajabi Nasab, Mazdak 184

Sangchoolie, Behrooz 184
Sommestad, Teodor 47
Ståhl, Björn 137
Svendsen, Nils Kalstad 153

Thorsheim, Per 153

Verdult, Roel 1

Wiehe, Anders 153

Zibuschka, Jan 169
Zirn, Cäcilia 215